DESIGNING AND CREATING A MEDITERRANEAN GARDEN

DESIGNING AND CREATING A MEDITERRANEAN GARDEN

FREDA COX

THE CROWOOD PRESS

First published in 2005 by
The Crowood Press Ltd
Ramsbury, Marlborough
Wiltshire SN8 2HR

www.crowood.com

British Library Cataloguing-in-Publication Data
A catalogue record for this book is available from the British Library.

ISBN 1 86126 782 7

For Sean, with love.

Designed and typeset by Focus Publishing, 11a St Botolph's Road,
Sevenoaks, Kent TN13 3AJ

Printed and bound in Malaysia by Times Offset (M) Sdn Bhd

Contents

Preface and Acknowledgements   7

Foreword by Roy Lancaster   9

1   Can Mediterranean Gardens Really Work?   11

2   Water-wise Gardens   25

3   Creating a Mediterranean Garden   39

4   Making Plans   53

5   Dealing with Lawns   67

6   Patios, Terraces and Outdoor Living   81

7   Hardscaping and Decorative Effects   97

8   Getting it Right   117

9   Mediterranean Gardens in Cool Countries   129

10 Classical Italian and French Country Style   147

11 Spain, Greece and Other Mediterranean Climate Regions   169

12 The Bare Necessities: Maintenance and Garden Care   193

Plants for Mediterranean and Dry Gardens   207

Gardens Reference   229

Further Reading   235

Index   236

Preface and Acknowledgements

Last autumn I was lost. I'm good at getting lost! Late for an appointment, I sped down ever narrowing lanes, rocketing past a large notice, whose big black letters proclaimed 'Pick Your Own Sunflowers & Olives'. I couldn't believe my eyes. Skidding to a halt I quickly reversed. But that is exactly what it said. No time to investigate, I was far too late, and on I charged. We are constantly warned about Global Warming, but I certainly had not realized we grew 'Pick Your Own' crops of olives in this country. This really would be something for the book!

The following weekend I went back. Passing the 'Pick Your Own Sunflowers & Olives' sign, I drove up a long track into a yard. Huge crates of apples stood everywhere, mountains of enormous, orange pumpkins waited to be carved into faces for Halloween, and sure enough, great buckets of yellow sunflowers stood all around. No sign of olives though. I would have to ask. Suddenly I spied another large notice, but this time the 'O' of olive had a miniscule gap on the right, turning it into a 'C'. Closer inspection showed the notice actually invited 'Pick Your Own Sunflowers at Clives! I bought a large pumpkin and left – and yes, the first notice also had an indiscernible gap on the right of the 'O', which I had failed to spot. I consoled myself with the thought that it was an understandable mistake, what with rushing and bad eyesight. But who knows, one day perhaps? Olive trees do fruit in Britain. I am not completely mad.

In researching this book I visited gardens across the UK, from Cornwall to northernmost Scotland, and have been amazed at the tremendous variety of tender, Mediterranean climate region plants growing in the most inhospitable areas. A pomegranate tree flowering profusely in Dundee for instance.

For centuries we have happily grown hundreds of Mediterranean plants in the UK. Where would our gardens be without them? Increasing numbers of 'tender' species are readily available and we are ever more aware of environmental issues, including the urgent need to conserve water. Over the last few years, many gardeners have developed stunning dry and gravel gardens filled with great drifts of conservation-conscious, drought tolerant species, emulating Mediterranean regions. These gardens are attractive, exciting, full of colour and form year round, are easily maintained, and they do not require constant watering.

This book is about developing ideas, incorporating elements from Mediterranean countries and using plants that at one time, we would never have considered could possibly grow in cooler climates, away from that hot Mediterranean sunshine.

As I write storms batter the house, here on a Shropshire hillside. Wind has blown frenziedly for days. Rain lashes the glass. Last, deep-pink Lavatera flowers have been torn free and blown away, together with final petals of winter scorched roses. One could not imagine more un-Mediterranean like weather. But, at the end of January, we have still only had a brief, light sprinkling of snow and few frosts. In Mallorca heavy falls of snow have blanketed gardens and countryside.

Predictions of Global Warming forecast changing weather patterns, and we venture into unknown territory. An expected rise of only 2-3°C by the end of this century will see us growing ever increasing numbers of tender Mediterranean plants. Last year, for the first time ever, English Nature recommended growing Mediterranean species in our gardens. We recently experienced the warmest decade on record, the hottest recorded UK temperature, and the heaviest ever rainfall...

And as I write I know outside, braving the elements, tiny snowdrops are forcing through solid earth, first starry crocus are opening, cyclamen coum unfurling pink blossoms beneath the trees, almonds and hellebores are blooming, rosemary and box showing flower buds. All plants originating in countries far warmer than ours, introduced by intrepid plant hunters generations ago, and accepted now as commonplace in our gardens. But that was simply the beginning.

We can use not only Mediterranean plants, but ideas as well, to create exciting, rewarding and ecologically friendly gardens, which are labour saving, and full of beautiful plants we never dreamed we could grow. So sit back and borrow yet another idea, that enviable siesta, as we relax and enjoy our new Mediterranean gardens.

OPPOSITE: Paeonia cambessedesii, *endemic to the Balearic Islands, happily adapted to cooler climates. This specimen was photographed at Kiftsgate Court, Gloucestershire.*

Preface and Acknowledgements

Many people helped create this book, not least custodians of gardens who gave me free reign to take and use photographs. There is a reference section at the end so I hope you too will visit these gardens.

In particular I must thank Louise Allen, Curator, The University of Oxford Botanic Garden; R and L Arbuthnot, Stone House Cottage Garden; Rosie Atkins, Chelsea Physic Garden; David and Pat Austin, David Roberts and Michael Marriott, David Austin Roses; Chris Byrd, Snowshill Lavender; Chris Beardsley, Worthing Borough Council, Highdown; James and Sharon Bishop, Long Cross Victorian Gardens; J. G. and A. Chambers, Kiftsgate Court; Beth Chatto, Beth Chatto Gardens; Hector Christy, Tapeley Park; Richard Compton, Newby Hall; Jonathan Denby, Morecombe Bay; Simon Dorrell and David Wheeler, Bryan's Ground; Robert Dudley-Cooke, Lamorran House; Clive Elliott and Jennifer Roberts, Angel Gardens; Gordon Fenn and Raymond Treasure, Stockton Bury; Waltraud Fröhlich, Mallorca; Rupert and Alexandra Galliers-Pratt, Mawley Hall; Hampton Court Gardens, Herefordshire; Lance and Jane Hattatt; David and Kathleen Hodges, Brook Cottage; Trustees of the Hoghton Tower Preservation Trust; Alasdair Hood, Curator, University of Dundee Botanic Garden; John and Jenny Jefferis, London; D. and V. Keeble, Stansfield; Hugh and Sue Kennedy, Shropshire; Chris Lacey and The National Trust; Frank and Marjorie Lawley, Herterton House; Leeds Castle; Val McCluskie, Devon; Museum of Garden History; Peter and Sylvia Phillips, The Hundred House; Terry and Anne Pullen, Ludlow; The Royal Horticultural Society, Harlow Carr, Hyde Hall and Rosemoor; The Sutherland Trust, Dunrobin Castle; R. A. Price, Bolfracks Garden; Mark Robson, Bide-a-Wee Cottage; Katherine Swift, The Dower House, Morville Hall; Ann Trevor-Jones, Preen Manor; Ann Turner, The National Herb Centre; Carol Valentine and Isabelle Green, California; Lee and Pamela Wheeler, Jessamine Cottage; Bill White Nurseries; Susie White, Chesters Walled Garden.

Thank you to friends for photographs of gardens I was unable to reach. Ursula Brunner, Val Corbet, Marianne Falk, David Fenwick, Jennie Gay, Heidi Gildemeister, Sue Graham, Gill Guest, Trevor Nottle, Sue Pendleton, David and Sandra Tate, and Lars Vestergard.

A special 'Thank you' to all my friends in The Mediterranean Garden Society for invaluable help and support, including Andrew and Marianne Beith, Lindsay Blyth, George and Marilyn Brumder, Isabel Carvajal, John and Pamela Connell, Barbara Diamantides, Derrick Donnison Morgan, Yve Dyson, Carmen Fraile, Duncan and Sue Graham, Katherine Greenberg, Peter and Signe Groos, Carolyn Hanbury, Caroline Harbouri, Joan Head, Marjorie Holmes, Renata Hurst, Tim Longville, Allan Lover, Diana Mavroleon, Michael and Sharon Michieli, Joanna Millar, Fleur Pavlidis, Kimberly Peters, Vivien Psaropoulou, John and Jay Rendall, Carol Smith and John Garner, Charles and Jenny Smith, John and Jill Stallworthy, Elsbeth Stoiber, Ron and Annabel Swann, Nancy Swearengen, Gordon and Elizabeth Todd, and Juliet Walker. A sincere and special thank you to Sally Razelou, Sparoza, for her wonderful work, invaluable knowledge, and loving friendship.

Other thanks go to: Andrewjohn and Eleni Stephenson Clarke and Robin Williams for the plan of Borde Hill Garden; Elizabeth Donald, Mark Steward and Collins Bartholomew Ltd. for the Mediterranean Climate Region map; Ursula Yelin, Gartenwerke, Switzerland; Mr and Mrs Kochel, Germany, and Julia Morrell, Ludlow, for offering help; Brent Elliott, Elizabeth Koper, Charlotte Brooks and staff of The Royal Horticultural Society Lindley Library; The Royal Horticultural Society for allowing me to take and use numerous photographs of their wonderful gardens; The National Trust for allowing me to use garden photographs; Janet Uttley and Ian Bull, RHS garden Hyde Hall; Charles Quest-Ritson for advice and information; Alison Rutherford, The Hedera Project.

To friends and family who gave encouragement while I only had time for the book! Kathleen Allanson, John and Joy Barker, Daphne Brown, Clare Chapman, Pat Cordingly, Michael Derrett, Sandra Humphries and family; Joseph Donlan, Irene Furneval, Barbara Handy, Mike and Sandra Hawthorne and family, Chris Haycox, Bernard Jones, Margaret Jones, Arthur and Pat Lacey, Bob and Ros Mathews, Shaunah Murrell, Irene Preece, Clive and Veronica Rawlins, Rosemary Rawlins, Claude Reed, Ian, Pauline and Phillipa Tomson, Linda Walker, Penny Westgate and Pamela Varey.

Last but certainly not least, my family, who bore the traumas of writing with me: Sean Cox, Lorna and Chris Hawthorne, John, Elaine, Matthew, Christopher and Rebekah Norton, Kathleen Norton and Dominic Marsden, Mark Norton, Leslie, Marita and James Rawlins, Camilla and Peter Stewart. With a very special thank you to Camilla for her hard work and support in checking and correcting the manuscript.

For plant identification I relied mainly on The Royal Horticultural Society Index of Garden Plants by Mark Griffiths (Macmillan ISBN 0-333-59149-6), The Royal Horticultural Society Gardeners' Encyclopaedia of Plants and Flowers, editor-in-chief Christopher Brickell, (Dorling Kindersley, ISBN 0-86318-386-7), and the Pan Garden Plants Series by Roger Phillips and Martyn Rix. Any mistakes, however, are entirely my own.

Finally a sincere and heartfelt 'Thank you' to Roy Cheek for botanical editing, and to Roy Lancaster, who both gave their time, expertise and support so freely.

January 2005

Foreword by Roy Lancaster

As a self confessed and long time lover of cool temperate plants, especially those of mountain and woodland, you might well question my motives if not my qualifications in writing a foreword to a book extolling the virtues of Mediterranean plants and gardens. The fact that my garden in Hampshire is well stocked with rhododendrons, camellias, ferns, trilliums, podophyllums, hostas and a 101 other denizens of cool moist soils if not shade should be further proof of my unsuitability for the request made to me by Freda Cox. And yet, my tastes in plants are notoriously catholic and as far as my own gardening is concerned, ever since I began to find the cultivation of Asiatic primulas and meconopsis increasingly difficult due to warmer summers and milder winters, I have cheerfully resigned myself to growing more of those plants recommended in this book.

The more I think of it, the more I realize that Mediterranean plants have played an increasingly important role in my gardening education and have been a major factor in my travels. As well as the Mediterranean Basin itself, I have visited all the world's major Mediterranean Climate regions including S. Africa, S.E. Australia, C. Chile and S. W. United States in search of plants many of which I have grown or still grow in my garden. My first introduction to Mediterranean plants was probably in a seafront public garden at Grange-over-Sands on the northern fringe of Morecambe Bay where Jersualem sage, rosemary and at least one Cistus caught my roving eye.

We grew quite a few Mediterranean plants in Moss Bank Park, Bolton where I began my gardening career in the early 1950's and I encountered many more ten years later when a student gardener at the Cambridge University Botanic Garden. I still remember the famous limestone rock garden there with its doline and plants such as *Pancratium illyricum* and *Iberis gibraltarica*, together with other sun worshippers.

Eighteen years working for Hillier and Sons Nursery, including 10 years as Curator of the famous Hillier Arboretum, finally brought home to me the realization that Mediterranean and other sun seeking plants form a substantial slice of our garden flora and have been so for a very long time, all of which brings me back to my own garden and the purpose of this book. My small front garden is on Bagshot Sand which must be the nearest equivalent in England to the Gobi Desert. Here I grow a wide selection of plants tolerant of low moisture levels most of which thrive though any new planting here is best done in autumn to make use of winter rain. Halimiocistus, Cistus, *Mathiola maderensis*, *Allium schubertii*, *Chamaerops humilis*, *Eryngium bourgatii* are but a few examples.

Behind the house on the south side I maintain some of my favourite sun seekers including dieramas, watsonias, Fremontodendron, grevilleas, *Lavatera maritima*, *Abelia floribunda* and a magnificent *Erythrina crista-galli* that behaves as an herbaceous perennial and flowers like a dream. So, far from eschewing Mediterranean plants, I could not live without them providing as they do some of the most attractive foliage and most colourful flowering effects of my gardening year. I have found most of them easy to grow whilst the cultivation of a few have provided the sort of challenge no true gardener can resist. As the author so passionately yet patiently reminds us, our climate is becoming increasingly warm, and if we are to be of any help to future generations of gardeners, let alone ourselves, then we should be planting and experimenting with those plants most likely to cope.

Freda Cox's suggestions and advice encourage us to be more inventive and adventurous both in the way we garden and in our choice of plants. One thing for sure, there are thousands of plants out there waiting to be discovered by those gardeners whose horizons have, up till now, been fashioned if not limited by cool climate gardening. As the author points out, water is and always has been a precious gift of nature too often neglected or abused. Gardeners of the new millennium are going to have to learn to respect and use it more wisely if they are to stay in business and I can think of no better book than this to point the way.

1 Can Mediterranean Gardens Really Work?

Creating Mediterranean gardens in cooler climates seems a contradiction in terms, especially when using Mediterranean plants. But countless plants originating in Mediterranean regions have grown successfully in Britain for many hundreds of years, adapting so well they have become an integral part of our gardens and countryside. It is hard to believe these plants have not always grown here.

We imagine such 'tender' plants, used to growing beneath hot Mediterranean sunshine, will perish during our winter months. But past history tells us this is not the case. Temperatures in parts of the Mediterranean can drop to below freezing, with frost and snow. During recent years winter temperatures in Athens, for instance, have fallen well below those experienced in Britain. Many Mediterranean regions have suffered heavy snowfalls, while in the UK we have escaped relatively lightly. Mediterranean gardeners are just as frustrated when choice specimens are lost to frost during the winter months. It is not only colder countries that suffer Arctic conditions!

There is one major difference between Mediterranean gardens and those in more northerly latitudes. Whereas we expect our gardens to be full of colour all summer and dormant during winter, in the Mediterranean the seasons are reversed. Summer is the dormant period with plants remaining below ground during the hottest part of the year. As summer ends and cooler autumn months arrive, welcome rainfall soaks the sun-scorched earth, bringing plants to life again. Gardens and countryside are filled with colour through autumn, winter and spring.

OPPOSITE: *Topiary hedges shelter tender plants at Herterton House Gardens, Northumberland.*

RIGHT: Cyclamen hederifolium. *Cyclamen quickly adapted to the cooler climate and have naturalized beautifully in many gardens throughout the British Isles.*

Many Mediterranean plants adapt successfully to cooler climates with the added bonus that most are drought tolerant. If we do get a dry summer, and dry summers are on the increase, these plants survive happily, with the minimum of attention and water.

What About the Romans?

So when did the first Mediterranean plants arrive in our country and how? Since man has travelled, plants have travelled too, initially to provide food or prized for their healing properties, and only later for interest and beauty alone. This process has been aided by exploration and conquest.

During the Neolithic period, from about 4000BC to

Papaver rhoeas. *Neolithic settlers are credited with introducing poppies into Britain. They are now common 'weeds' in gardens and countryside, where their vivid red colouring never fails to attract attention.*

roughly 1700BC. Mediterranean settlers arrived in Britain, bringing their agricultural experience and the first Mediterranean plants. Common poppy, *Papaver rhoeas*, for instance, came with their seed corn. We have long considered this handsome plant a pernicious weed of cornfields, but in ancient times it was thought corn only grew well with its companion poppy. In the Bronze Age (about 1800–600BC) Good King Henry, *Chenopodium bonus-henricus*, was introduced as a crop plant from southern Europe.

Early visitors to our shores undoubtedly brought plants and seeds with them and there was a steady stream of travellers, traders and invaders. But it is the Romans who have been credited with introducing vast numbers of Mediterranean plants into Britain. The quantity of plants they are supposed to have brought with them, however, has become a matter of debate. Did they or didn't they?

The answer is that they undoubtedly did bring many plants from their Mediterranean homeland, probably beginning with the Roman invasion of 'southern Brittania' in 55BC. The problem is that without accurate historical records it is impossible to know exactly which plants they brought and when, although the first plants would almost certainly have been for food or medicine.

Narcissus bulbs were regularly carried by Roman warriors for their therapeutic properties. Galen (AD130–200), a Greek surgeon and physician to Emperor Marcus Aurelius, is recorded as using the juice of the bulbs to 'glue together great wounds, cuts and gashes'. Surely they would have brought narcissus

bulbs with them. They might also have been responsible for introducing the dreaded stinging nettle, but was it really because the British climate was so cold it necessitated them flagellating themselves with stinging leaves to keep warm?

The Romans certainly used alexanders, *Smyrnium olustratum*, as both vegetable and tonic and the plant later became a favourite of monastic gardens. Lavender, *Lavandula × intermedia*, native to western Mediterranean regions, was reputedly used for perfuming bath water, flavouring food, and for its mild sedative and tonic properties. However, there appears to be no hard evidence to suggest Romans used lavender at all, let alone introduced it into Britain, and the first records of lavender in this country date from the early 13th century.

Snake's head fritillary, *Fritillaria meleagris*, was thought to be a Roman introduction, although research shows it was possibly introduced or reintroduced during the 16th century. Geoffrey Grigson in *The Englishman's Flora* suggests fritillaries escaped into the wild from Tudor and Jacobean gardens. Lilies too were very popular; *Lilium martagon* grew in Tudor gardens, while *L. candidum* was said to have been brought back by the Crusaders.

Normans, arriving in the eleventh century, introduced the clove pink, *Dianthus caryophyllus*. One of the first plants to be hybridized, its deep, clove-like fragrance was much esteemed by the Tudors. By the seventeenth century more than 50 varieties were recorded in England and many old varieties are still in cultivation. *D. caryophyllus* was the main ancestor of clove-scented pinks and carnations.

Other Mediterranean introductions included pot marigold, *Calendula officinalis*, introduced in the Middle Ages and also called Mary's gold, in honour of the Virgin Mary. Used as a bitter spice, marigold flavoured and coloured food, while medicinally it treated stings, pestilence, ulcers, varicose veins, measles, chilblains and warts. Cornflower, *Centaurea cyanus*, became a common cornfield weed before elimination by modern herbicides. Farmers called it 'Hurt-sickle', as Gerard wrote, 'because it hindreth and annoyeth the reapers by dulling and turning the edges of their sicles [sic] in reaping of corn'.

Garden iris, *Iris germanica*, was indispensable. Roots were pleasantly perfumed and made good ink. Leaves were used like rushes for patching roofs, were woven into matting and strewn on floors. Medicinally, iris treated headaches, fevers, chills, coughs, colds, ague, loose teeth and the bite of adders. In Tudor times small shreds of iris root fragranced linen.

Campanula, including *Campanula rapunculus*, were grown for their edible tubers. Wallflowers, *Erysimum cheiri*, arrived from southern Greece and the Aegean. Even our wild roses originated in Mediterranean regions, developing from crosses of *Rosa gallica*, *R. × damascena* and *R. arvensis*, with *R. gallica* introduced into Britain during Roman times. The list is endless.

As people travelled further, so did plants and, subsequently, garden ideas. Important country houses developed Italian and French style gardens, seeking authentic plants to embellish them. Plant collecting became the vogue of the day.

ABOVE LEFT and ABOVE: Fritillaria meleagris *and lavender. Were they Roman introductions or not? We will probably never know. Fritillary, like cyclamen, adapted well to Britain and naturalized beautifully. Gerard called them 'Checkered Daffodill'. It is hard to imagine an English garden without lavender and many specialist growers colour the countryside with huge lavender fields, as here at Snowshill Lavender in Worcestershire.*

BELOW: Lilium martagon. *Huge swaths of L. martagon naturalized at Benthall Hall, Shropshire. (The National Trust)*

  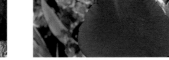

Marigolds, iris and wallflower, all Mediterranean introductions.

The First Gardens

Around 35,000BC archaeological sites show man derived food from plants, gathered from the countryside rather than cultivated. Eventually a few plants were collected around dwellings purely for convenience, and by 15,000BC there is evidence of effective cultivation. Plants with leaves or roots that could be used for food were planted close to the house, and having herbs to hand was far more expedient that scouring the countryside hedgerows to find them in an emergency. Perhaps later a tiny scatter of attractive blooms might be included purely for aesthetic reasons. In earliest times, however, the majority of plants would have served useful purposes only.

Around 8,000BC cereals and legumes were cultivated by Neolithic peoples in the Near and Middle East. These reached Greece by 6000BC, continuing to spread through Europe and arriving in Britain between 4000 and 2000BC.

Ancient Egyptians used irrigation techniques on their land around 3500BC, and development of gardens followed. Paintings in Egyptian tombs show walled gardens with fruit trees and fish pools, and by 1500BC private gardens were cultivated for relaxation and privacy. These were filled with flowers, trees, vines, pavilions and pools. In Ancient Greece private gardens were considered unnecessarily extravagant, but public gardens were created and great Greek writers began recording plant names. In the first century AD Dioscorides described 600 plants and their medicinal uses in *De materia medica*. This remained the standard medicinal and botanical work for the next 1,500 years.

Romans too developed gardens and by the second century BC thriving farms and market gardens existed, as well as stylish, decorative, pleasure gardens. In Persia, during the sixth century BC, Cyrus the Great encouraged the development of extremely sophisticated gardens. These ideas were taken over after the forces of Islam invaded Persia in AD637, and then to Spain, when they invaded that country in AD711. Gardens developed Moorish influences in the west and Mughal and Indian influences in the east. Greek texts were translated into Arabic and later into Latin, and extensive lists of medicinal plants began circulating through the new medical schools spreading across Europe.

By the late eleventh century increasingly sophisticated gardens were developing in Britain. Henry I constructed gardens to complement his castle at Windsor. Henry III built gardens at Clarendon, Kempton, Guildford, Gloucester, Winchester and Nottingham. Other monarchs, wealthy aristocrats and merchants followed suit and the importance of the pleasure garden spread across the country.

Monastic Herb and Physic Gardens

The earliest written records of medicinal plants in Egypt date back to the Ebers Papyrus in the sixteenth century BC, although this was itself a compilation of earlier works. Records are found in Mesopotamia (Iraq) from 3000BC and numerous treatises on medicinal plants and herbs followed in successive generations. Hippocrates (460–377BC), the 'Father of Medicine', set guidelines for the preparation of medicinal herbs. He also wrote a treatise on medicinal plants including

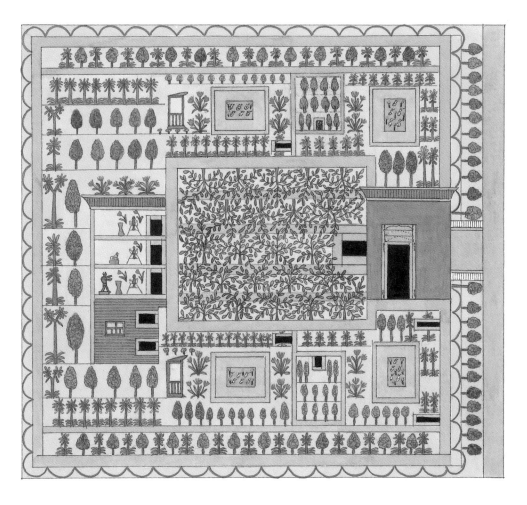

This drawing of a garden at Thebes shows the intricacies of an Ancient Egyptian garden with its tree-lined water canal, formal pools, avenues and central area shaded by plants.

Borage, Borago officinalis; *fennel,* Foeniculum vulgare; *and rosemary,* Rosemarinus officinalis, *were all important plants in monastic herb and physic gardens.*

thyme, mint, marjoram, coriander and saffron. Many of the 400 remedies recommended are still used today.

Charlemagne (AD742–814) encouraged larger, more organized cultivation of herbs including fennel, flax and fenugreek to supplement ancient but smaller, physic gardens. In his *Capitularo de villis*, or 'Decree concerning towns' , he detailed plants to be grown throughout his empire, with seventy three herbs including caper spurge, clary, iris, houseleek, lily, mallow, poppy, rose, rosemary, rue, sage and tansy, together with sixteen fruit and nut trees.

During the Dark Ages, cultivation of herbs continued in European monasteries. As people became more informed, knowledge and use of these plants spread. The first botanical garden was created at the University of Pisa, Italy, in 1543.

Monks had extensive medical knowledge and cultivated large areas around monasteries to grow herbs and medicinal plants, including narcotics such as hemlock, henbane, mandrake and opium poppy for the infir-

This tiny walled garden is surrounded by climbing roses and beds of scented herbs, creating a sheltered, perfumed haven.

mary and treating the sick. Food and salad crops, called 'potage plants', were also grown, not only for the monks, but to feed passing travellers, lay people and the poor as well. Vines were planted for wine production, orchards for fruit, and gardens for quiet contemplation and study. Monastic contributions to horticulture cannot be emphasized enough, and include the production of careful records and illustrations of plants in manuscripts.

Medieval times saw three main types of garden. Monasteries, cultivating medicinal and food plants; cottagers growing food and healing plants on a smaller scale, and the wealthy who paid to have vast pleasure and leisure gardens planted.

Although our climate was too cold for many Mediterranean plants, large numbers were successfully carried northwards from early botanic and medicinal gardens in eleventh-century Spain, finding their way into northern Europe and Britain.

Monastic physic and herb gardens eagerly sought new additions, building up principal collections of both medicinal and culinary plants – plants that are remarkably unchanged to this day. These included fennel, *Foeniculum vulgare*, which the Romans named *Foeniculum* from the Latin, *foenum*, meaning hay, possibly because the plant smelt like hay; caraway, *Carum carvi*, seeds were used for flavouring, its roots as a vegetable, and it relieved indigestion; parsley, *Petroselinum crispum*, was a medicinal, sacred and culinary plant, employed for garnishes and flavouring, with roots, leaves and fruits all used medicinally for various disorders, including healing wounds, stimulating the appetite and alleviating bladder and kidney problems. Borage, *Borago officinalis*, with anti-inflammatory properties, was a mild diuretic and treated bronchitis, colds and rheumatism. Young leaves, rich in vitamin C, were used in salads, while the beautiful blue flowers, which attracted bees, decorated food and wine. Thyme, *Thymus vulgaris*, our most popular culinary herb, treated respiratory and gastro-intestinal problems; coriander, *Coriandrum sativum*, used for more than 3,000 years as a culinary and medicinal herb, was beneficial as a digestive tonic and sedative, with its roots used as a vegetable.

Rosemary, *Rosmarinus officinalis*, known as a wonder herb, had culinary, medicinal, ornamental and perfumery properties and was introduced into Britain during the fourteenth century. It was difficult to grow in Britain. About 1380 Henry Daniel wrote a treatise espousing its virtues and cultivation. This was probably the first treatise dedicated to a Mediterranean plant written in England and it began a wild passion for the herb. Daniel grew 252 herbs in his garden, including a rare novelty, the wallflower.

Peony, *Paeonia mascula*, was found in an Augustinian priory on the island of Steep Holme, off the north Somerset coast, and had been introduced originally from the Mediterranean. Peony seeds warded off evil spirits and medicinally treated muscle spasms, kidney stones, gout and asthma.

Monasteries probably founded the first nurseries within their grounds and records show a big demand for vegetables, fruit and flowers from Westminster Abbey. A 1275 account also shows that Westminster Abbey purchased peony roots and lily bulbs at the price of 1s a quart for lilies, and 2s for peonies.

Saffron crocus, *Crocus sativus*, was prized by Arabs for its culinary, medicinal, disinfectant and colouring properties. It was introduced to Europe through the Moorish Empire in Spain, and its use travelled to Britain via Germany and the Low Countries. Arabs strictly forbade the export of the bulbs, but eventually some were said to have been smuggled out of the country in an English pilgrim's hollow walking stick. The bulbs grew well, initiating an important trade in the Essex village that became known as Saffron Walden.

By the sixteenth century botanists and herbalists were regularly growing large numbers of plants, many imported from Mediterranean regions. Early gardens were often enclosed with hedged or walled sections, and perfumed plants, eagerly sought, added the further facet of fragrance to practical usage and visual beauty.

An early watercolour of Ranunculus.

Sixteenth Century Onwards

Sixteen- and seventeenth-century Britain saw many new introductions from Mediterranean regions. These soon became established favourites, though obviously in their wild forms rather than the sophisticated hybrids of later years. These included *Anemone*, *Cistus*, *Colchicum*, *Crocus*, *Cyclamen*, *Helianthemum*, *Iris*, *Narcissus*, *Ranunculus*, *Scilla* and, of course, the notorious tulips.

Plants from the Americas appeared in Britain from the seventeenth century, and by the early nineteenth century there was widespread importation of plants from around the world, including other Mediterranean climate regions such as Australia, South Africa and Chile. Initially these 'tender' plants were kept in conservatories, until it was realized many would grow outside without protection.

At this time we see the introduction of such plants as *Acacia*, *Agapanthus*, *Amarylis*, *Amelanchier*, *Arbutus*, *Banksia*, *Buddleja*, *Crinum*, *Crocosmia*, *Eschscholzia*, *Freesia*, *Gazania*, *Gladiolus*, *Grevillea*, *Kniphofia*, *Nemesia*, *Nerine*, *Oenothera*, *Pelargonium*, *Phlox*, *Tradescantia*, *Tropaeolum*, *Yucca*, *Zantedeschia* and various South African succulents.

Some plants, however, arrived by mistake. Ivy-leaved toadflax, *Cymbalaria muralis*, for example, came as stowaway seed in packaging used to protect imported Italian sculptures. The dreaded ground elder, *Aegopodium podagraria*, was initially introduced as a vegetable and also for the treatment of gout. Now it threads its way inexorably through our borders!

Early Plant Hunters

Mediterranean countries benefited hugely from the spice trade, and new spices, herbs and plants flooded into Mediterranean areas and through Europe to reach Britain. The era of the great plant hunters had begun,

The tiny, ivy-leaved toadflax, Cymbalaria muralis, *arrived as stowaway seed in packaging around imported Italian sculptures.*

and expeditions set off across the world. Wealthy patrons funded ever more extravagant missions, and plant hunters risked life and limb to be first to bring back rare and beautiful plants and seeds to Britain.

Joseph Pitton Tournefort (1656–1708) introduced Mediterranean plants. Francis Masson (1741–1805) and William Rollisson (c. 1765–1842) travelled to South Africa and the Mediterranean. John Tradescant the Younger (1608–1662), Sir Joseph Banks (1743–1820) and Douglas David (1799–1834) scoured North America, while William Lobb (1809–1864) visited Chile and California, amongst other places. These are a mere handful of the many, now famous, plant hunters who vied to bring back specimens for their patrons and for the new nurseries springing up around the country.

The first botanic garden in Britain was the Oxford Physic Garden, established in 1621. By 1656 Tradescant's botanical garden at Lambeth in London included more than 1600 named plants in cultivation. The Chelsea Physic Garden was founded in 1673 by the Apothecaries' Society, and William Kent's garden designs from 1730 were to be developed after 1759 into what was to become the Royal Botanic Gardens at Kew.

Highdown is set amongst the rolling South Downs, between Worthing and Angmering, on the south coast of England. In 1909 Sir Frederick Stern began creating a garden on this chalky, exposed, coastal hillside, which regularly suffered drought conditions. He introduced many Mediterranean species including those brought back from Greece by the plant hunter E.K. Balls. Sir Frederick and Lady Stern bequeathed Highdown to Worthing Borough Council, which now maintains the garden to an extremely high standard.

Books and Manuscripts

Although plant lists and treatises in various countries dated back many centuries, the first gardening books were printed in England around the late sixteenth century. Earlier manuscript examples in Britain included Master John Gardener's *Feat of Gardening* (c. 1440). John Gerard's 1597 herbal, *The Herball or Generall Historie of Plants*, contained 1,360 pages and gives an excellent indication of plants available at that time. *Achillea*, *Allium* and *Verbascum* were some Mediterranean introductions that he grew. In 1652 the English physician Nicholas Culpepper produced his *Complete Herbal*. John Evelyn, the English diarist, travelled extensively in France, Italy and other Mediterranean regions, and also wrote books on gardening.

From here on interest in plants and gardens increased rapidly, leading to numerous books being published on various aspects of the subject, including works by John Parkinson (1567–1650), Sir Thomas Hanmer (1612–1678), John Rea (c. 1620–1677), Joseph Pitton Tournefort, Robert Sweet (1782–1835) and Jane Wells Webb (1807–1858).

The first garden magazines were published and

ABOVE: *An illustration of cyclamen taken from John Parkinson's* Paradisus Terrestris *(London, 1629), the first illustrated English book on garden flowers. Parkinson grew and described 10 different forms of cyclamen and more than 100 varieties of tulips. (Reproduced by kind permission of The Royal Horticultural Society Lindley Library)*

RIGHT: *Title-page from John Sibthorp's* Flora Graeca, *iv (London, 1823). (Reproduced by kind permission of The Royal Horticultural Society Lindley Library)*

A well-established Mediterranean garden in Cumbria includes many species from Mediterranean climate regions in specially prepared, free-draining beds dug in with gravel to a depth of 45cm. Phoenix canariensis; Cordyline australis; and Chusan palms, Trachycarpus fortunei, thrive throughout the garden, as do herbs and numerous rare, delicate and unusual plants. (Photograph courtesy of David and Sandra Tate)

Florists' Societies prospered. These specialized in collecting, developing and showing plants that became known as Florists' Flowers, including auricula, carnation and pinks, hyacinth, polyanthus, ranunculus and tulips. Florists' clubs were established in London by 1679 and were later superseded by horticultural societies. In the late eighteenth century John Sibthorp, an Oxford botanist, decided to try to identify the plants that Dioscorides had included in his treatise during the first century AD, resulting in the *Flora Graeca*, which was published between 1806 and 1840.

From humble beginnings, gardening and plant collecting became major passions. Hundreds of books are now written every year and gardening magazines abound. Nurseries and garden centres appear on almost every corner, stocking vast selections of plants from around the world, including hundreds from Mediterranean regions, while specialist nurseries supply the rare and unusual. Horticultural societies and flower shows fan the flame, exhibiting exotic creations that we too can all own, however small our patch.

This book mainly concentrates on plants originating in Mediterranean climate regions, but plant hunters explored and brought back plants from all regions of the world including China, Japan, the Himalayas and India. Many of these plants are now commonplace in our gardens.

A secluded corner filled with tender plants, Stockton Bury Garden.

The New Mediterranean Garden

From gardens developed in Mediterranean regions, and the first few plants collected from Mediterranean fields and hillsides, a massive, multi-million pound industry has developed. We are still discovering further aspects of Mediterranean gardens that we can borrow, and Mediterranean plants and gardens are having a new impact in Britain.

With present day emphasis on climate change and ever increasing awareness of global issues, including the need to conserve the precious commodity of water, many British gardeners are turning towards the experience of their Mediterranean counterparts who have long coped with problems of extended drought and too little water for their plants and gardens.

Over recent years Britain has regularly suffered drought conditions, water shortages, hosepipe bans and escalating water charges. We can gain from the valuable experience of our Mediterranean cousins, employing their water-wise techniques, using a selection of drought tolerant plants and careful plant groupings to enhance our own gardens. Above all we can learn how use of water. a valuable and increasingly expensive commodity, can be drastically reduced.

Gardeners in cooler climates are rediscovering Mediterranean plants and techniques to build beautiful gardens that are lush and full of colour, but require little water and even less maintenance, giving us the opportunity to relax and enjoy our gardens rather than constantly having to work in them. We thus continue to benefit from those early days when the first plants gathered from Mediterranean meadows and mountains found their way into Britain.

Crown vetch, Coronilla varia, *grows well in British gardens.*

Glowing red peony seeds at the University of Dundee Botanic Garden.

Warning

Sadly, increasing numbers of species are gathered to extinction in their native habitats. Many are now protected and it is illegal to remove numerous plants from their natural habitats.

It is of paramount importance to remember that plants should *never* be collected from the wild, however tempting it may be to dig up a small root or bulb for our own gardens when on a Mediterranean holiday.

When buying plants *always* check they are from sustainable sources and refuse those that might have been collected from the wild. None of us wishes to perpet-

uate the problem and endanger even more of our planet's ever decreasing species. Certain countries grow plants on a commercial basis, providing local employment, as well as protecting the country's natural habitats. This trade should be encouraged. With such wonderful plants at our fingertips in nurseries and garden centres, there is certainly no longer any need to collect plants from the wild.

Early Plant Introductions from Mediterranean Climate Regions

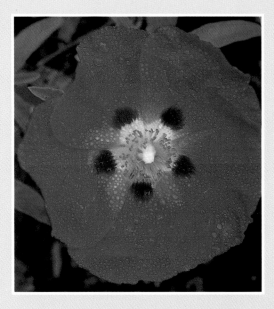

Cistus. *Dry hillsides of Southern Europe, Turkey, North Africa and Canary Islands.*

Crocosmia. *South African grasslands.*

Agapanthus. *South African coasts and grassland.*

Colchicum. *Hillsides of North Africa, Asia, India, China and Europe.*

Eschscholzia. *Annuals from Western North America.*

Oenothera. *North America mainly.*

Kniphofia. *Mountainous areas of Southern and Tropical Africa.*

Phlox. *North America mainly.*

Pelargonium. *South African deserts and mountains.*

Tulipa. *Hot dry areas, Middle East, Asia and temperate Europe.*

23

2 Water-wise Gardens

The Mediterranean Environment

We imagine the Mediterranean as a paradise with eternally blue skies and hot sunshine – a place for holidays when we wish to escape the ravages of the British winter or to laze on sun-kissed beaches and bake ourselves brown. Perhaps, if we are lucky, it is a place to have a second home and garden – a gleaming white villa smothered with magenta bougainvillea, surrounded by acres of vines, citrus, olives, almond and fig trees. We are bitterly disappointed if the weather is less than the eternal summer we expect.

Mediterranean regions are those countries bordering the sea of that name. However, other parts of the world are also classed as having 'Mediterranean' type climate zones, generally those areas between 30 and 40 degrees latitude in the southern hemisphere and 30 and 45 degrees latitude in the northern hemisphere: south western Australia, parts of New Zealand, the Cape Province of South Africa, central and southern coastal California and central Chile.

In general, Mediterranean type climates are composed of very hot, dry summers, with temperatures regularly rising to around 30°C or even to 40°C. Winters are mild to cool, averaging between 5°C and 10°C. There is little, if any, rain in summer, most rainfall occurring between autumn and spring. This varies from light, scattered showers to torrential storms lasting for days. Drought, however, can still occur during winter.

Winter temperatures drop below freezing in some

areas, and snow is not unknown, even in the Mediterranean. Gardens and plants suffer damage and plants are lost to frost, although frosts are rare in coastal regions. Temperatures in mountainous areas are generally several degrees lower than those in coastal regions. Strong, drying winds also feature in this type of climate.

Many Mediterranean climate zones are distinguished by coastal plains, often backed by protecting mountains that create a unique environment. Air humidity is low in summer, but can also be low during winter months. Long hours of scorching sunshine, and the highest light intensity on earth, create problems for plant growth in the Mediterranean. Plants solved this problem by becoming dormant throughout the summer months, springing back into life with the cooler temperatures and first rains of autumn.

Historically, much of the Mediterranean region was covered by woodland, which has been destroyed over the centuries. Without its protecting cover, fertile soil slowly eroded away. Ground now tends to be free-

OPPOSITE: Spindle berries, Euonymus, *originated in Japan but adapted well to dry gardens, where their brilliantly coloured fruits and foliage brighten late summer and autumn.*

RIGHT: Vivid magenta coloured Bougainvillea is so reminiscent of Mediterranean holidays and hot sunshine.

25

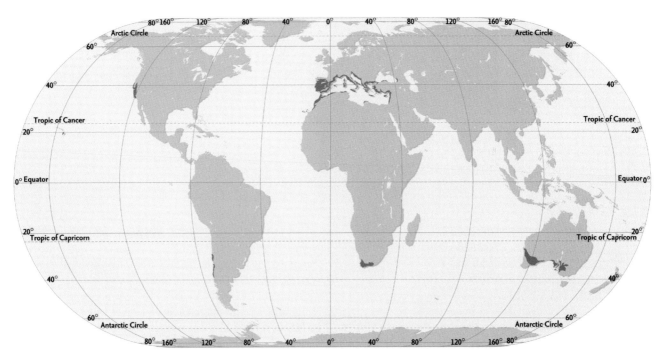

A map of the Mediterranean climate regions of the world. (Reproduced by kind permission of Collins Bartholomew Ltd)

Native to New Zealand, Cordylines thrive throughout Britain. This tree happily survives in Scotland at the University of Dundee Botanic Garden.

draining but dry, lacking in humus and organic matter, while many areas have been denuded to bare rock.

With the hot climate, poor ground, drought, light intensity and often limited rainfall, Mediterranean plants have to be tough to survive.

We consider our British climate to be exceedingly wet, but for many years Britain has regularly experienced drought conditions in summer. Instead of the expected downpours, we receive inadequate rainfall, resulting in the inevitable hose pipe bans; reservoirs and rivers are reported as dangerously low and costs of water escalate. When it does rain it is generally insufficient to restock our dwindling supplies fully. There is an urgent need for water conservation.

By looking to Mediterranean regions, we can learn and benefit from the long experience of these countries, where water has always been at a premium.

Mediterranean Gardens in Britain

There is a misconception that tender plants and 'Mediterranean' gardens are confined to sheltered parts of the British coastline such as Cornwall or the west coast of Scotland, bathed by the Gulf Stream. This is not true and 'Mediterranean' gardens extend from London to Wales, the Yorkshire Moors, Pennines,

Northumberland and even the less hospitable areas of Scotland. They are not sparsely planted areas of concrete slabs or gravel with a few phormium spikes or potted plants to relieve the monotony. They are as lush and full of colour as any traditional 'English' garden. Tender trees such as citrus, pomegranate and olive grow across the country.

One of the main advantages of using Mediterranean plants in our gardens is that they are labour saving and conservation friendly, something we badly need to consider as we continue depleting our planet's natural resources, including the precious commodity of water. Of course plants are lost during an exceptionally cold winter or prolonged hard frost, but we must remember this also happens in Mediterranean regions, and even our hardiest natives can succumb to severe frost.

Many drought tolerant plants adapt well to cooler climates, requiring less maintenance and little, if any, water once established. Good soil and drainage are important for nearly all plants and, given these, many Mediterranean plants, including tender species, thrive happily in northerly latitudes. An added winter bonus is that many drought tolerants supply year-round colour and interest, even when not in flower.

Transpiration and Storage Techniques

Plants take in water through their roots and lose excess moisture through stomata (minute openings in the leaves) in a process called 'transpiration'. This helps plants maintain an even temperature. When they do not have enough water they wilt and eventually die. Sometimes they lose water faster than they can take it in through their roots, and this can result in die-back.

Mediterranean plants have evolved highly sophisticated techniques for minimizing transpiration and storing water.

Minute hairs or 'felting' in plants such as *Salvia*, *Stachys* and *Phlomis* stop sunlight penetrating to the plant, reducing evaporation. Grey and silver leaves, such as *Eucalyptus* and *Lavandula* species, reflect sunlight and heat, cooling leaves and limiting water loss. Thick or glossy leaves like *Ceanothus* or *Camellia* create shade. Small or needle-like leaves such as *Erica*, *Genista* and *Rosmarinus* minimize leaf surface area. Plants that are densely covered in hairs effectively trap moisture present in the air, directing it down their stems to the roots, making good use of moisture-laden, foggy atmospheres, particularly in coastal regions, even though it does not rain.

Bulbs, corms, tubers and rhizomes, such as *Crinum*, *Cyclamen*, *Narcissus*, *Crocus*, *Iris*, *Lilium* and *Tulipa*, have evolved swollen storage units, enabling them to lie dormant for long periods through Mediterranean summers. Cacti and succulents such as *Agave*, *Euphorbia*, *Yucca*, *Sempervivum* and *Sedum* store water in their stems, leaves and roots. Many have reduced surface areas with minimal stomata, which stay closed during daytime, so reducing water loss, whereas other plant families' stomata remain open during the day, allowing photosynthesis to take place. Some plants fold their leaves at night and others channel water down leaves, to roots. Variously coloured evergreens are invaluable in the Mediterranean for year-round interest, particularly when other plants are dormant.

Palms and other tender species thrive in this Mediterranean garden in Cumbria, in the north of England. (Photo courtesy of David and Sandra Tate)

What is Water-wise Gardening?

The urgent need for water conservation cannot be stressed enough. In their natural state the Mediterranean countryside and gardens lie dormant throughout summer. Sadly, in an attempt to impose our own ideas on nature, and with no thought of water conservation, Mediterranean gardeners have created gardens that require watering to excess.

Paradoxically, while we are planning 'Mediterranean gardens' in our cooler climes, Mediterranean gardeners have long held the 'English' garden as their ideal. Lord Brougham built the first 'English' garden above Cannes, southern France, in 1824. But it has always been a struggle to maintain such green perfection. Plants that could not survive such heat without constant and massive quantities of water have become the norm. Decadent and inconsiderate use of water comes at a price, both financial and ecological. When will common sense prevail? With the increasingly urgent need for water conservation, it is imperative we resolve these problems.

New villas and developments in Mediterranean countries still want their green lawns with lushly stocked and over-watered borders. Rather than wait for trees and shrubs to develop and grow naturally, enormous specimens are transplanted at astronomical expense, then heavily watered over long periods to get them established. Sadly many of these fine specimens die anyway. Smaller trees may take longer to mature, but they transplant better, establish more quickly and do not require such massive amounts of water.

The cry is heard for 'instant gardens', but at what cost? Thousands of gallons of precious water are poured onto the earth each day in an attempt to keep a lush lawn green, or to persuade plants to grow that would never normally survive in such conditions. With increasing demands for plants, new nurseries and garden centres are opening in the region – almost as many as in the UK! With more of the wrong type of plants available, the demand for more water to keep them alive increases. The pressure this puts on each country's natural reserves is enormous and unsustainable.

Almonds, for instance, are 'dry' trees requiring no irrigation to produce their crops, but acres of almond trees are being ripped out and replaced with citrus orchards, which require large amounts of water. Golf courses cover immense swathes of land. And what keeps them green? Massive supplies of water! This depletes the level of ground water and, as more and more water is pumped from the earth, levels continue

This Greek hillside is smothered with colourful, drought tolerant plants, which happily survive with little or no water.

This garden on Mallorca is planted with drought tolerant species, providing lush vegetation and colour throughout the hottest summer, with little or no water. (Photos courtesy of Heidi Gildemeister)

to drop, aggravating an already difficult and dangerous dilemma.

Many gardeners, even in cooler countries, invest huge amounts of money in intricate irrigation systems and state of the art technology to make sure every last inch of garden gets its constant supply of water, whether required or not. How sad, when you only have to look at a natural, Mediterranean hillside to see the wonderful variety of plants that survive without man's interference. But no, people want 'green' gardens where green gardens would not normally grow.

In the Mediterranean climate zone of California people are inordinately proud of their unlimited supplies of water (at present) and pour it onto gardens in vast quantities, not bothering when water continually runs to waste. This cannot and will not last, and serious attempts towards water conservation should be made before it is too late, before water shortages begin to bite and the Californian countryside becomes a desert wasteland.

This is *not* what water-wise gardening is about, wherever we live in the world. Water-wise gardening is gardening with nature and not against it, taking into account our planet's natural resources and not depleting nature's assets.

Mediterranean gardeners have abundant lists of native plants, created by nature to resist the ravages of the climate. Gardens can be planted with whole ranges of colourful vegetation, and an extensive variety of evergreens, that happily survive hot summers with minimal water. But we gardeners must always have more, and struggle to attain the unattainable.

Following Mediterranean water-wise guidelines means thoughtful planning and planting while using dwindling water resources conscientiously and efficiently. This can be achieved by following a few simple guidelines.

The Ten Rules of Water-wise Gardening

- Reassess your garden to see how improved planting can minimize water consumption and simplify maintenance.
- Slowly reorganize the garden, placing plants that need least water furthest from the house, those requiring regular water closer, for ease of management.
- Replace labour intensive annuals and bedding plants with drought tolerant perennials that happily survive for years, saving time, money, effort and water.
- When buying new plants choose those requiring little or no water once established, then group according to their water requirements.
- Introduce new plants in autumn so they establish using winter rain, before the following summer.
- Use organically based approaches to cultivation with emphasis on composting and mulching to conserve nutrients and water in the soil and limit evaporation.
- When watering *is* required, limit to morning or evening, never in full sun when water evaporates away.
- Overwatering damages plants, discouraging roots from penetrating deep into the earth to find their own water supply, making plants shallow rooting and susceptible to wind damage.
- Site suitable containers to collect valuable rainwater.
- Recycle household 'grey' water and use household water thoughtfully and efficiently. Make every drop count and make sure water does not run to waste.

This small lawn area requires constant attention and is difficult to mow.

The same garden, but the lawn has been replaced by stone slabs, enhancing the appearance, making for simpler maintenance and reducing the need for water. (Photos courtesy of Marianne Falk)

First Steps

We can begin making changes immediately with simple and effective modifications to revolutionize our gardens, requiring less work and less water.

Lawns

Lawns soak up water like blotting paper. Think about eliminating lawns completely, or at least decreasing their size, substituting paving, gravel, ground cover, lawn-substitute plants or other surfaces. This immediately reduces large percentages of water overuse, as well as hours spent with mowing machines. Softened by groups of plants these areas become attractive and virtually maintenance-free zones.

Beds

Create new beds or extend existing beds into lawn-filling spaces with drought tolerant plants. Begin grouping plants to accommodate their water-wise needs.

Pathways

Grass pathways are slippery when wet and dried up in summer. Replace with stone, gravel or 'stepping stones' set into low growing thymes or chamomile, which are good to look at and have a heavenly perfume when scented plants are lightly crushed underfoot. Introduce new pathways or widen existing paths.

ABOVE: *Grass pathways become a quagmire after rain, making walking difficult and damaging grass.*

RIGHT: *A brick path curves attractively through lawn at Preen Manor in Shropshire, reducing lawn area and creating a good surface for walking, whatever the weather.*

BELOW RIGHT: *Stepping stones, here at a garden in Ludlow, Shropshire, may also be laid to create an all-weather surface.*

BELOW: *Plants happily seed into this gravel path, which replaces lawn at Chesters Walled Garden in Northumberland.*

Important Essentials

Soil

Soil condition is important for all plants. Many Mediterranean areas have sparse soil over impenetrable rock, so to plant your garden you may first need to make a hole with a pick-axe! Plants hang on tenaciously, but soil quality can be improved and this in itself helps water retention. Light soils drain moisture away quickly while heavy clay soils hold excessive amounts of water. Both conditions are extremely damaging to plants, but both can be enhanced with composts and mulches. Improving soil quality and drainage is essential for successful plant growth.

Compost

Compost is a 'must', home-made wherever possible. Compost bins fit the smallest corner of any garden, quickly repaying the initial expense of purchase. Some local councils supply composting bins at reduced rates to encourage use. Collect leaf mould, green waste, household scraps and vegetable peelings, farmyard, stable or chicken manure for composting. Applying compost once a year dramatically improves soil quality.

It helps water retention, encourages earthworms and provides valuable nutrients, resulting in better growth and healthier plants, which in turn are stronger and need less water.

Mulching

Mulching protects soil from drying winds and hot sunlight, thereby reducing water loss and keeping roots cool and moist. Mulches also inhibit weed growth, meaning more water available for the plants you had intended growing.

Good mulches allow roots to breathe while conserving and retaining moisture. There are wide varieties of materials available.

Plant Groupings

All plants require water until they are established. After this, however, Mediterranean plants survive on little or no water.

Grouping plants according to their water needs also drastically reduces the use of water. Site plants that need little water furthest from the house and those requiring more regular water nearer the house. If groups of plants with different water requirements are mixed together, water is simply wasted on plants that have no need of it.

In this Greek hillside garden, plants hang on tenaciously in a few centimetres of soil over rock.

Plants and pots requiring regular watering are sited near to the house for ease of maintenance, Preen Manor, Shropshire.

Plants requiring little or no water are positioned further from the house, as here at Jessamine Cottage, Shropshire.

Annuals and bedding plants require excessive watering to get them established. As time does not generally allow these short-lived plants to create deep rooting systems, they require constant water throughout summer to keep them alive. Within a few weeks of planting, they are dug out again and thrown away. Think of the time, effort and money saved if drought tolerant perennials are used instead.

Global Warming

Today there is constant discussion about Global Warming and the 'Greenhouse Effect'. It is predicted this will dramatically change our climate, although scientists do not always agree on exactly how Global Warming will affect us or when.

Sunlight enters the earth's atmosphere through a mixture of gases. The earth's surface absorbs the sunlight's energy, reflecting it back into the atmosphere. Some energy escapes into space but much remains trapped by these greenhouse gases, causing the world to heat up. This is a natural occurrence, essential for life on earth, for without it the earth would be too cold for habitation.

Since the onset of the Industrial Revolution the use of fossil fuels has grown dramatically, leading in turn to an increase in greenhouse gases being released into the atmosphere. Carbon emissions are the main culprit and there is unequivocal evidence to show their dramatic and continuing rise in this period. Scientific research shows the earth's atmosphere is definitely warming, although this effect is not uniform and some areas of the planet have actually cooled.

Temperatures are predicted to rise between 1 and 4°C by the end of this century. With an increase of only 2–3°C, Mediterranean plants and vines would

This dry bank at the National Herb Centre in Oxfordshire is full of colour from drought tolerant, Mediterranean species.

A rose-covered archway at Preen Manor, Shropshire, creates shade and protection, conserving moisture at plants' roots.

become the norm in present-day, cooler countries. Warmer temperatures will see further melting of glaciers and ice caps, leading to higher sea levels and more flooding. There will be increased levels of winter rainfall, often torrential, accompanied by extreme storms. In the short term we could expect violent swings in climatic extremes. Warmer temperatures will exacerbate drought conditions. Other hazards include increased risk of fire, which will further release methane gasses, trapping ever increasing quantities in the lower atmosphere. We can expect additional nasty surprises as weather systems move into unknown territory. These changes will inevitably have an effect on humanity, animals and plants.

Government scientists agree that Global Warming is a far greater threat to the world than global terrorism. Despite all these predictions and fears, it seems little is being done to halt the situation. It is not too late to reverse the detrimental effect of these greenhouse

gasses, but we need to do this now and not at some stage in the long distant future, or it really will be too late.

By becoming more aware of our environment many of these problems could be alleviated, but everyone needs to take action and behave responsibly towards the planet – *now*.

In May 2004, for the first time ever, English Nature, the Government's conservation advisory body, urged people to plant non-native species rather than traditional native plants. They recommend that, by creating Mediterranean style areas in the garden, we will be able to provide continuing food supplies for native birds, butterflies and insects as the climate warms and certain species are lost. Records show species of Mediterranean fish and sea creatures are moving closer to our shores, while increasing numbers of Mediterranean butterflies and insects are being reported in southern Britain as our native species begin to move northwards.

Action Plan

- We must take Global Warming seriously and look at how each of us can help alleviate the problems.
- Begin planting Mediterranean species to help conserve water, time and effort.
- Unless building a new garden from scratch, it is obviously impractical to replace everything in one go. But look at the garden carefully and draw up an action plan for the future:
- Take a dispassionate view of lawns. Are they needed? What could be used instead?
- Gradually rearrange beds and begin grouping plants for their water-wise needs – those requiring most water, just a little, or none.
- List plants you need to acquire and collect a few at a time.
- Introduce trees and shrubs, arches and pergolas for climbing plants. These create areas of shade, helping protect plants from hot sun and drying winds, as well as conserving moisture.
- Plant deep-rooting species that find their own sources of water.
- Start putting these ideas into practice now to provide a sound basis on which to begin building your new 'Mediterranean' garden.

ABOVE: Echium pininana *has been described as 'the equivalent of a multi-storey restaurant for bees'. Long Cross Victorian Gardens, Cornwall.*

LEFT AND BELOW: A paved corner of the Mediterranean garden at Leeds Castle, Kent (left). Gravel replaces lawn in this tiny London garden.

Water Conservation Adaptations of Plants

Camellia. *Thick and glossy leaves create shade.*

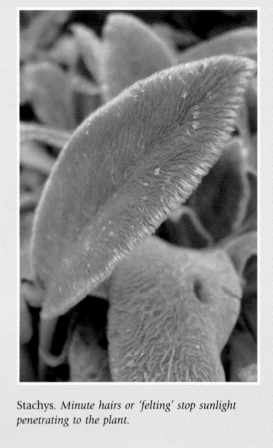

Stachys. *Minute hairs or 'felting' stop sunlight penetrating to the plant.*

Echeveria. *Succulents store water in stems, leaves and roots.*

Tamarind. *Folded leaves minimize transpiration.*

Rosemary. Small or needle-like leaves minimize leaf surface area.

Lavender. Silver and grey leaves reflect away sunlight and heat.

Iris, cyclamen *and* narcissus. *Bulbs, corms, tubers and rhizomes store water, enabling them to lie dormant for long periods.*

Fascicularia. *Narrow, channelled leaves direct water down to roots.*

3 Creating a Mediterranean Garden

First Thoughts

What do you want to achieve in your Mediterranean garden? Will it reflect romantic memories of sun-soaked holidays, or be purely, but beautifully, utilitarian – a garden that is both water and labour saving? The chances are it will combine both elements.

Films, photographs or visits to Mediterranean countries all conjure up images that we hold in our minds. What is it about the countryside that you remember most? What are the predominant colours? Yes, Mediterranean countries have that wonderful blue sky for most of the summer and the bluest of deep blue seas. Occasionally we can replicate that in cooler climates, but not all the time. What colours dominate the landscape? Great banks of golden yellow mimosa, *Acacia dealbata*, are spectacular along Riviera coasts in the early spring. In Greece ancient ruins predominate, and hillsides are a riot of wild flowers, liberally scattered with scarlet anemone, *Anemone coronaria*, cream and gold crown daisy, *Chrysanthemum coronarium*, minute purple iris, *Iris cretensis*, violet grape hyacinth, *Muscari commutatum*, pink and red tulips, *Tulipa saxatilis* and *T. orphanidea*, and a million other delicate and fantastic blooms in a myriad of colours.

Italian gardens are more formal affairs: slim green cypress trees, *Cupressus sempervirens* 'Stricta' clipped box, *Buxus sempervirens*; bay, *Laurus nobilis*; twining strands of white jasmine, *Jasminum officinale*; and wisteria,

Wisteria sinensis. The baked ochre landscapes of southern Spain have acres of pale pink-blossomed almond trees, *Prunus dulcis*, big bushes of pink and scarlet pelargoniums, *Pelargonium zonale*, citrus orchards splashed with ripe golden lemons, and glowing oranges set amidst deep green leaves and sweetly scented white blossoms. And all of these countries have that indefinable Mediterranean perfume that catches the senses, an exquisite and subtle blend of citrus blossom, fragrant herbs, lavender, lilies, myrtle, roses and pine blended with baked earth and hot sunshine.

Think about what Mediterranean countries mean to you, and your mind will soon begin to focus on exactly which images you consider most important. Do you crave the decorative, Moorish influenced tiles and buildings of Spain, for instance, or simply the colours of the hard baked, red earth? The gleaming marble columns, whitewashed houses and terracotta tiles of Greece or the grey granite rocks and dark green pines of Italy? Formal gardens or informal?

Spend time thinking about and planning your garden. How you would like it to look and what you want to achieve in it. Consider using curves and circles rather than planning everything around basic rectangular shapes. Keep a notebook to record your thoughts and preferences, a few photographs and illustrations, details of plants you would especially want to include, or features you specifically like. Soon a picture will begin to form, the first seed of your new garden, the beginning of how *your* Mediterranean garden will look.

Next look at the garden you already have and imagine how your ideas will fit in with the existing plan. Perhaps you are creating a completely new garden and have a blank canvas to work with. If your garden

OPPOSITE: *Romantic arches of roses – and runner beans. Unusual but effective planting combinations at Preen Manor, Shropshire.*

ABOVE: *Alcea rosea growing on the shore in Greece reminds us of the vivid colours of plants, sea and sky.*

LEFT: *Italian gardens are generally more formal affairs with carefully clipped trees and hedges but few flowers, as here at the Villa Gamberaia, with its elegant water parterre.*

BELOW LEFT: *Gleaming columns against a deep blue sky.*

BELOW: *Brilliant scarlet anemones on a Greek hillside.*

A sun-scorched Greek hillside of dry scrub and rocks, with ancient stone buildings.

Moorish influences in a Spanish square. (Photo courtesy of Sue Pendleton)

is already well established, however, it is not practical to dig everything out and start again from scratch. How can existing features be worked into your Mediterranean theme? Do you have space to build up large collections of Mediterranean plants, or only a tiny courtyard for pots and tubs? Do you want to concentrate on drought tolerant plants that are easy to maintain, or do you want your garden to look like a replica corner of some Mediterranean country, transported into Britain? There are so many things to consider, so perhaps a few guidelines might help.

Colour

When we think of Mediterranean countries, we think of sun-bleached colours or bright, vivid hues. Blue sky, golden sunshine, red earth, dark green pines, brilliantly coloured flowers, gleaming white buildings, brightly patterned tiles and mosaics, sun-faded paintwork. Things somehow seem that bit larger than life and look wonderful beneath the hot Mediterranean sunshine. However, careful consideration is needed before transplanting these into the British landscape. Coloured

Hard-baked red earth and ancient olive trees in Spain.

A tiny courtyard garden in Shropshire, crammed with Mediterranean plants.

Brilliantly coloured flowers in the garden at Sparoza, Greece.

The free-draining, open stone in this scree garden at Stansfield, Oxfordshire, suits drought tolerant, Mediterranean species to perfection.

paints and finishes are fashionable in today's garden designs, but paint will fade and peel and requires constant maintenance, and will it fit in with your surroundings anyway? Unless you feel like being very outrageous and daring, use colour in moderation, especially to begin with.

Texture

How can we recreate the Mediterranean theme in our own gardens? Do we favour smooth walls, slabs and tiles reminiscent of some French or Italian villa or a more rugged, boulder-strewn landscape resembling a Greek hillside? Areas of gravel, shingle, pebbles and scree, suggesting a sea shore or dry river bed? Cobbled pathways and rough textured, whitewashed walls simulating a corner of a Spanish village? Smooth areas of desert-like sand? 'Hardscaping' in the garden forms a framework and background for the multi-textured plants and other features that will bring it to life. Terracing, walls, pathways, paving, patios, pergolas and arches all add character and create a backdrop for the plants. Each of these in turn can be broken down into various design elements.

Style

Is the garden to be an elegantly terraced and formal affair with low, clipped hedges, stylized water canals and fountains, columns and statuary, or something more informal? What about raised banks set with rocks and boulders, wilder, more naturalistic areas, romantic pergolas and arbours? Perhaps you feel something even more dramatic would be better, or maybe you

A formal water canal in the garden of Preen Manor, Shropshire.

prefer a tranquil, understated garden with simple charm? Whatever you decide to do, you have to live with and feel happy with the result, although a garden is, of course, always evolving and changing.

Climate

Between 1150 and 1300 Europe passed through a period of comparative warmth. Vineyards became practical and popular to cultivate, as were more exotic plants. Gardens became an extension to the house and

This Mediterranean style terrace at Chesters Walled Garden, Northumberland, invites relaxation.

were used for eating, drinking and relaxation. As temperatures lowered again, after 1300, the use of gardens and outdoor pursuits diminished. Now scientists predict Global Warming will see an increase in temperatures and people are beginning to think about Mediterranean plants and gardens in cooler climates, not merely as fashionable, but as an economic reality.

Plants

Plants can be brightly coloured and exuberant or can have more restrained shades and textures. They can behave themselves and always look neat and tidy, be carefully clipped into shapes with clean, severe lines, or they can be wildly rampant, tumbling over walls and pathways, a riot of mixed colours in every shape and size. Plants themselves can form architectural features in the garden.

We might be thinking of planting 'Mediterranean' plants in our gardens but, paradoxically, many Mediterranean plants actually originated outside those countries. We all borrow from one another. Almonds, olives and figs were brought to Mediterranean regions in ancient times but it is now difficult to imagine those hot landscapes without them. The great bushes of deep red and shocking pink *pelargonium* originated in South Africa, but once introduced into Mediterranean countries they adapted happily to their new environment. Many plants introduced into Britain from Mediterranean countries are now accepted as part of our heritage: to name but a few, these include campanula, hellebores, hollyhock, iris, lavender, love-in-a-mist, marigold, peony, poppy, rosemary, sweet pea and verbascum.

Most Mediterranean plants are drought tolerant of necessity, and this in turn means they are labour saving and require little, if any, water once established.

Existing Features

If you are starting a completely new garden from bare earth you can more or less do anything you choose. However, most people move into, or already have, an established garden and are not in a position to change

Originally from the West Indies, Central and North America, sword-like leaves and pendant, goblet-shaped flowers of yuccas are now firmly established favourites in both Mediterranean countries and Britain.

This wisteria-smothered summerhouse at Stone House Cottage Gardens, Worcestershire, is reminiscent of the Mediterranean and makes a warm, sheltered retreat in springtime.

RIGHT: *Wide selections of hardscaping materials are available from architectural salvage yards.*

everything at once – or might not want to anyway. Take a good hard look at the garden you have and decide which features you need to retain. Do you want the lawn or would it be better to replace it with some other suitable surface: decking, slabs or gravel, for instance? Are the paths practical, can they be widened to lessen the lawn area, or can new paths be incorporated into the design? Do you already have terraces, or a sloping site that would benefit from terracing? Do you want more or fewer beds and plants than already exist in your garden? Trees are generally immovable objects, difficult to take out and a long time in growing. If you have established trees can you incorporate them into your new design or will they have to be felled? What about greenhouses, sheds or summerhouses? Can these be resited to offer a more pleasing aspect?

Consider all of these things carefully rather than rushing in and demolishing everything in one fell swoop. It could be that you have some features that, with a little careful thought and planning, will enhance your garden and fit well in your new design. You might come to regret having moved too hastily. Change takes time and is probably better for it.

New Materials

There is an ever increasing supply of new materials coming onto the market. Most larger garden centres stock a wide range of paving materials in various colours, shapes and sizes, bricks and blocks for build-ing walls, differently sized pebbles or gravel, again in a range of colours, for patios and pathways, and decking in assorted woods and textures. They also supply wood preservative paints in natural or coloured finishes, archways, obelisks, pergolas, frames and trel-lising, starting with the flimsiest of plastic coated tubing, which will blow down in the first gale, to great solid structures that will last for many, many years. Builders' merchants are another source of supply. Architectural salvage yards sell a range of brilliant mate-rials to suit every pocket: reclaimed weathered tiles and bricks for paths and edging, pieces of carved stone for ornament, marble, slate, railway sleepers, statuary, mirrors, metal grilles and iron railings, pots, tubs and chimney pots.

Furniture

Most large stores sell metal, wood and plastic garden furniture, starting at very reasonable prices. Much of this furniture has a distinctly Mediterranean feel. In this area, as in many others, you get what you pay for. Try to buy the best garden furniture you can afford, and make sure it is well maintained. This not only prolongs its life but also encourages relaxation and comfort. It is far more appealing to sit outside on a well-cared for wooden bench, padded with a colourful cushion, than it is to take your coffee to a discoloured, cracked, plastic chair and table the birds have decorated, or that bears the stains of past barbecues! Gaily patterned

A vine-covered arbour at RHS garden Rosemoor, Devon.

umbrellas definitely add a Mediterranean twist, as do awnings and canopies. An endless range of seating is available including luxurious, reclining chairs – after all, you will occasionally want to sit down and enjoy your handiwork. Do not forget that all important Mediterranean siesta!

Decorative features

Many forms of decoration can be used in the garden that are not only practical, but can be used to enhance and delude.

Arbours – generally plant-covered structures, shading a comfortable seat for relaxation – are always romantic features. They can be built from various materials or created by training bushes or hedges into the required shape.

Arches can be used in various ways to divide areas, as an entrance, at the beginning of a path or for framing a view. They can be plain or decorative, built from stone, brick, wood, metal or hedging, and can be adorned with plants.

This simple, wooden, rose-covered arch encourages exploration of the garden beyond.

Pergolas, such as the one at RHS garden Hyde Hall, Essex, make striking features, creating shade and support for plants, but make sure they are strong enough to support the weight of plants and are high enough to walk beneath when plants clothe the whole structure.

Pergolas provide necessary shade in hot countries but are striking features in cooler climates, forming attractively covered walkways. Built from stone, brick, wood or metal, their construction must be substantial enough to support plants.

Pots and containers enhance even the smallest garden or balcony. They come in all shapes and sizes from a simple, stone trough, or terracotta pot, up to huge urns, classical garden vases, hanging baskets, barrels and wooden tubs. You can limit your choice to a few carefully sited decorative pots of special plants or fill every available corner with containers that overflow abundantly. But remember, pots need constant water and attention.

Raised beds are not only attractive and practical in a Mediterranean garden, they are ideal since they allow good drainage for drought tolerant plants and show plants off to their advantage. Walls can be constructed from concrete or stone blocks, dry-stone walling or bricks. Wood is another alternative, but it is not as long lasting as stone and will eventually decay. Railway sleepers make good, solid, retaining walls that last for years.

Terracotta pots overflow with plants at RHS garden Rosemoor, Devon.

Strong stone retaining walls support raised beds.

Railway sleepers have been used to make low retaining walls at Stone House Cottage Garden, Worcestershire.

ABOVE: *Decorative trellises divide two areas and create support for plants at RHS garden Rosemoor, Devon.*

ABOVE: *A simple, classical urn looks stunning in this Shropshire garden.*

BELOW: *Steps edged with railway sleepers at RHS garden Hyde Hall, Essex.*

BELOW: *Natural stone creates solid steps that fit well into this informal garden at Bolfracks, Tayside.*

Screens and trellises of numerous forms, divide or conceal, and can be smothered with climbing plants.

Sculpture and garden ornaments add points of interest and are a purely personal choice. You could consider incorporating some of the following: a simple block of smooth stone; traditional or modern stone, wood or metal sculptures; a Grecian urn; modern containers; a sundial; a wall plaque or a bird table – anything to enhance the design of the garden.

Steps and paths can be built from a variety of materials and are decorative as well as functional.

Topiary creates sculptured shapes from living trees and shrubs.

Trompe-l'oeil – the decorative use of a painted scene or other materials to create an illusion of something that is not really there – can artfully provoke the imagination to wander beyond the confines of the garden.

Walls and fences form boundaries or divisions adding privacy and protection. Construct from stone, bricks, wood, fencing panels or hedging plants. South or west facing walls of a house provide invaluable warmth and protection for tender species of shrubs or climbing plants.

Water features add a further dimension to the garden. The cooling sight and sound of water was one of the first elements to be introduced into gardens in hot countries. Pools can be formed from butyl liners, pre-cast shapes or concrete. A winding stream fits well in an informal garden while a more stylized water canal suits a formal design. Fountains come in a wide range of sizes and designs from massive, classical structures to tiny jets of water bubbling out between stones.

Planning

Gardens are very personal things and it is only by exploring ideas and using the imagination that we are able to build a more complete picture of how we would like our own patch to look. You may prefer to employ a specialist designer, but quite often you know in your mind exactly what you hope to achieve and are disappointed when a highly paid professional cannot realize your dream.

It is worth doing some basic groundwork by gathering together ideas, looking at other gardens, consulting books and magazines, making notes and

Clipped topiary shapes abound at Herterton House Garden, Northumberland.

ABOVE LEFT: *This imposing brick wall at the National Trust Garden, Dudmaston, Shropshire, adds privacy and protection for plants.*

ABOVE: *A simple, elegant fountain and stylized water canal at the Lance Hattat Design Garden, Herefordshire.*

LEFT: *A formal, Italianate courtyard garden with straight lines and neatly parterred shapes.*

A more relaxed, informal garden with curving borders and rampant, colourful plants.

seeking advice, before you actually begin to dig over the land and choose the plants. This will give you a sound framework, but will also furnish you with ideas you may never have considered in order to make your garden individual and personal. Planning your garden opens up a whole new spectrum of interest, and is so much more satisfying than reproducing a design directly from a book or having a landscape architect devise the garden for you.

When choosing plants, it is so tempting to rush off to the nearest garden centre and load a trolley with everything that happens to be in bloom at that time, only to discover a few weeks later that the garden is devoid of interest and colour and there is nothing to follow on. Planning is therefore of paramount importance, especially in the early stages.

Drawing and Design

You do not have to be an expert to design your own garden. A little knowledge certainly helps, but most gardeners have a basic understanding of garden techniques and favour plants and designs that they like and feel comfortable with. Some of the greatest garden designers formulated their first ideas on the back of an old envelope!

There are hundreds of books and magazines crammed with ideas of what to do, how to do it and where to start. Arm yourself with the notebook in which you have recorded your initial thoughts, get some sheets of paper, a ruler, pencil and compass and you are ready to move on to the next stage.

4 Making Plans

You are creating a 'Mediterranean' garden and your notebook is full of inspired ideas. So where do you start?

Stage 1: Before You Begin

The first step is to make a plan, including the various features you want to retain, marking in manhole covers and other immovable objects. Ideally this should be to scale to provide an overall view of how the garden will fit together. Keep plans simple, unless you're training to become a fully fledged landscape architect! Graph paper makes a good basis for plans, and the squares make calculating measurements simpler. A good scale to work on is 2cm to 1 metre for a small garden or 1:100 for larger gardens.

Remember that some features in the garden, such as garden sheds, summerhouses and fences, are vertical. Take into account any shade they might cast. Mark the house on your plan, showing the positions of doors and windows. Gardens are viewed from many different angles, so sight lines from kitchen or living room windows are important

Other significant considerations must be taken into account before you begin. A garden can be low maintenance, requiring minimum attention, meaning that your design will lean towards hardscaped areas, easily managed beds, perhaps one or two trees and shrubs and strategically placed pots. Alternatively, gardens can be more labour intensive by including beds that require regular maintenance, a wide selection of plants, trees, shrubs and climbers, pergolas, arbours and water features – solar powered, if we are to be energy conscious.

Colour is always important. Gardens can be burgeoning with every colour of the rainbow, they can concentrate on simple, restrained plantings in soothing tones of green, or they can have colour themed beds.

Drainage is a major consideration when growing Mediterranean plants, while soil type dictates to a large extent which plants will grow. Soil testing kits are cheap, effective and easily obtained.

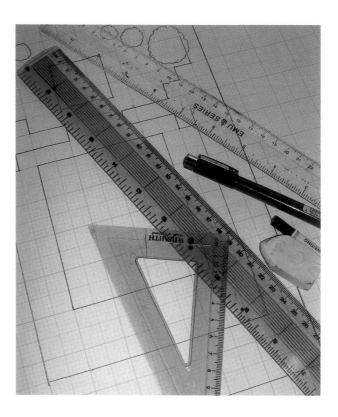

OPPOSITE: *Cool colours and architectural shapes of drought tolerant plants in Beth Chatto's Dry Garden in Essex, south-east England.*

RIGHT: *Graph paper makes a good base for plans. When the garden has been surveyed and measurements transferred onto paper, you can begin to work out the new design.*

A well-designed, easily cared for small garden, with stone-slabbed path, gravel and drought tolerant plants for year-round interest.

Stockton Bury Gardens, Herefordshire, are kept immaculately and require a high degree of maintenance with neatly mown and edged lawns, and well-stocked, weed-free borders of herbaceous plants, shrubs and trees.

RHS garden Hyde Hall, Essex, has a series of colour-themed borders. This 'hot' border radiates warmth with its strong, glowing reds and oranges. There is also a cool, blue border; white, silver and greys, and a sunshine yellow border.

Decide where the compost heap and washing line will go – preferably not in full view of the sitting room! Views are important, so make sure that as plants mature they do not obscure attractive outlooks from the garden. Certain features can enhance a view, particularly if there is something in the distance you wish to emphasize and use as a sight line from your garden. Include seating areas for relaxation and dinner parties.

Check and mark due north and other compass points on the plan. This indicates the direction the plot faces and how light and shade will move around the garden with the sun's progress. Note which areas will get most sun and therefore be warmer, and which areas will lie mostly in cooler shade. The position of the house also casts a shadow as the sun moves round. You are aiming to grow Mediterranean plants and most of these prefer sunshine, so shady areas will affect the planting.

View the site from different angles. Look out from the main windows of the house and from upstairs. Similarly look back at the house from the end of the garden and see how unsightly drain pipes and undesirable features can be camouflaged, or whether the house creates sheltered, warm corners, offering protection for particularly tender species. Sitting in the garden also gives a different perspective to when standing.

A garden is always full of light and shade. High walls and other tall features cast shadows, so it is important to check how light moves around the garden with the sun's progress.

Stage 2: Drawing a Plan

Perhaps you are already confident and have experience with garden design. In this case you can prepare to use a range of geometric equipment to help: compasses to calculate angles, set square, protractor and slide rule. Plans, however, can become extremely complicated and it is far better to keep lines as simple as possible. The more complex the equipment, the more difficult the plan! Simple plans suffice, particularly when just beginning.

Lay the graph paper onto a flat surface. A piece of smooth board is ideal, since you need to walk round the garden as you measure and mark your plan. Fix paper with drawing pins, tape or clips to eliminate the irritation of it flapping around as you work.

Using a tape measure, and having someone else to help here is definitely a bonus, measure the total area of the plot, from front to back and side to side. If you find it simpler, pace out the site instead. As a rough guideline, one pace measures approximately 1 metre. With ruler and pencil plot the outline onto the graph paper, counting the squares. Using pencil in these early stages makes later adjustments simpler. Mark in the house, boundaries and accesses.

Next include things that must be retained, such as existing trees, paths, hedges, walls, fences, gates, manhole covers, drains – anything that is a permanent fixture. Measure carefully and keep to scale. Mark trees with a circle to show their spread, rather than with just a dot.

When the outline plan is finished – and it could take several attempts before you are completely satisfied – go over the pencil lines with a ruler and waterproof drawing pen. When dry, carefully rub out pencil marks and tidy up the design. It is worth taking a little extra care at this stage as it makes things far simpler later.

This outline plan forms the basis for your continuing design. It is now a good idea to take a number of photocopies of the plan. This means that when you begin to fill in the small details, and are constantly revising and correcting in the early stages, you will not end up with a rubbed-out mess, which is not only demoralizing, but also difficult to work with. Alternatively use tracing paper over the basic design and continue the next stage of the plan on that, marking in changes and new features.

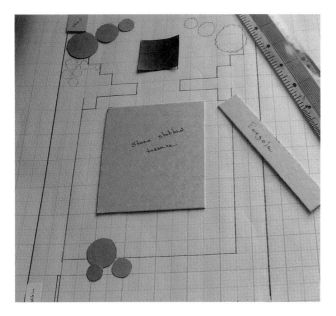

Movable cut-outs give you the freedom to change things around on your plan until you are satisfied with the final result.

Stage 3: Down to Detail

First mark in places for functional items such as dustbins, compost heap and washing line, before adding any new features you wish to include. If you prefer, cut shapes from paper first, and move them around on the plan until you are satisfied they are in exactly the right position before drawing them in. It takes time, and probably numerous attempts, before you are completely satisfied with the final design. It makes a good project for winter months, when little can be undertaken outside, and thinking of new ideas and inspiring Mediterranean plants and sunshine will ease away the winter blues.

The shape of your garden dictates the finished design, whether it be rectangular, triangular, long and narrow, short and wide, sloping or flat. Some shapes are more challenging than others, but with careful consideration and planning you should be able to come up with a suitable plan.

Privacy is important, especially in towns, so consider whether you prefer hedges, fences or walls. Will the garden be used solely by adults or will children need consideration? What about household pets? Also think about areas of the garden that catch the wind or where wind gets funnelled down alleyways. All are important issues to be considered when working on your design.

Before you begin designing front gardens, check there are no local restrictions on what you are able to do. Take practicalities such as car parking into account. Even large areas of tarmac can be treated in an interesting way to relieve the monotony.

Keep ideas flexible, anticipating the future as well as designing for the present. Gardens continually evolve and you may wish to extend beds later to accommodate more plants. A children's play area, for instance, could be redesigned for a different function in later years.

The National Trust Garden at Hidcote, Gloucestershire, is carefully designed so that the circular lawn expands the width of the garden with its hedges and paths, but the eye is still drawn to the distance.

Careful planning in this tiny London garden creates the illusion that the space is far larger than it actually is. It has interesting collections of Mediterranean plants, a tiny patio area, steps, gravel, pergola and garden shed.

The large expanse of tarmac driveway at Stockton Bury Garden, Herefordshire, is carefully designed so that a 'pathway' of cobbles cuts across at an angle to the house.

This stone terrace at Herterton House, Northumberland, is more appropriate to a drought tolerant garden, rather than a large expanse of lawn.

Stage 4: Order of Importance

With your basic plan clearly drawn to scale you can begin incorporating the different areas and features you want to include. Experiment with various ideas, either on tracing paper placed over the original plan, or on one of the photocopies.

You still should not rush out and buy plants though, as they are the very last things to go onto the plan and into the garden! As you begin to draw in the detail, consider the following points.

Open Spaces

These are the first areas to design. Bearing in mind water-wise gardening considerations, decide whether you need lawn or prefer to substitute a terrace or patio. Gravel is excellent and Mediterranean plants in particular happily grow in gravel. Children need open areas in which to play, and seating is also important.

Square- or rectangular-shaped areas work better with formal designs. Hard, straight edges can be softened with plants as they grow and merge together. Oval

An informal path of concrete and brick at The Hundred House, Shropshire.

shapes, circles and flowing lines enhance informal designs.

Open areas can be covered with paving, decking, gravel, shingle, pebbles, or lawn substitute plants such as chamomile. Plant grass only if you absolutely must.

Paths

Decide whether to keep existing paths or create new ones. Paths can be formal or informal, giving access to different areas of the garden, but not necessarily in a direct line. Paths to utility areas such as compost heap or dustbins, however, should be direct, otherwise people take short cuts! Paths should be wide enough to allow easy access and all-weather surfaces are more practical.

Terraces

Varying levels add interest in the garden, and terraces make sloping sites simpler to manage. Terraces fit

Well-designed terraced beds with strong retaining walls on the sloping hillside at Angel Gardens, Shropshire.

well with the Mediterranean theme, but need strong retaining walls and probably interconnecting steps or paths.

Seating

Seating is essential. There is no point in doing all this hard work if you are unable to relax and enjoy it occasionally. It is desirable to provide somewhere to unwind on a balmy summer evening, or a sheltered corner for a coffee with the first spring sunshine. There is plenty of comfortable garden furniture available, but you could also consider stone or wooden benches set into low clipped box, or mould a hedge around the bench. Sweetly scented plants such as chamomile and thyme, planted along the bench top, give a wonderful fragrance when lightly crushed as you sit. These are simply constructed from a 'box' framework of wood, filled with firm compost, before planting 'cushions' of scented plants on top. Locating perfumed plants near seating areas is a good idea.

Dining

Whereas you rarely used to see gaily-set tables outside town restaurants, we have become far more continental in our attitude to eating out of doors over recent years. Somewhere to eat *al fresco* in the garden is a must, however small. If the area is paved, feet need not get soaked after rain. Again, scented plants can enhance an evening dining experience. Think of jasmines and brugmansia: Lady of the night, *Cestrum nocturnum*, and *Trachelospermum jasminoides*. You will need a little shade for leisurely lunches on hot summer afternoons, so include a vine or rose-draped arbour.

Unfortunate Necessities

Certain things must fit into your garden but be hidden rather than seen, such as the compost heap, dustbin etc. Look at methods of screening, such as shrubs, trellis, walls and climbing plants.

Limiting Choice

Be restrained rather than over-enthusiastic when choosing materials. Two or three varieties create unity and harmony, while proliferations of unrelated materials become confusing and fussy.

This simple stone bench, circled with vanilla scented wisteria, looks out from a sheltered corner across the garden at Stockton Bury, Herefordshire.

A quiet retreat set around with greenery at the Museum of Garden History, London.

Small Gardens

Here, good design is essential. Will your garden have low maintenance paving with a few specimen plants, or be high maintenance, overflowing with an abundance of colour and greenery? First consider your needs and design accordingly. Climbers trail up and across, clothing a mini arbour, adding height as well as shade. Using paving or gravel is particularly effective in small areas, where colourful plants can be set in narrow borders, or pots. Relaxation is important so find room for a simple table and chair at least, or incorporate a seat into a raised wall. A space can be found for a chair even in basement corners or tiny balconies, and it can be surrounded by vibrantly coloured and perfumed plants. A specimen tree in a pot also adds height. Twine climbers over rails or wall, and construct a trellis for a truly Mediterranean vine canopy!

Existing Gardens

As previously stated, it is impractical to dig everything out of an existing garden and begin again. Not only is it an incredible waste of time, effort and money but the destruction of plants in the process is unnecessary. Make a plan and work gradually through your garden changing things as it becomes practical to do so, introducing drought tolerant plants where and when you are able. Be flexible, adapting ideas as the garden evolves and changes, working with your garden rather than against it. Gardens and gardening should be pleasurable experiences, despite the hard work. The overall object is to achieve unity, even though the whole might be divided into different shapes, styles and elements. Aim for a harmonious balance, and do not be tempted

A secluded corner for a romantic meal on this small, gravel terrace surrounded by climbing plants, shrubs and pots of perfumed lilies. Preen Manor, Shropshire.

59

A tiny arbour at The Hundred House, Shropshire, complete with benches and table surrounded by perfumed, twining plants.

A truly Mediterranean vine canopy!

Local materials fit harmoniously into the landscape in this mellow courtyard garden at Brook Cottage, Oxfordshire.

to crowd in too many individual features as this will make the garden disjointed and fussy.

Expense is also a major consideration. Costs escalate alarmingly, especially when undertaking major renovations. However, it is always worth trying to purchase the best-quality materials as these generally last longer.

Hardscaping

Choosing materials is a matter of personal preference. Local materials generally fit better into the landscape than stone brought from hundreds of miles away, although this can work with careful consideration. Too many strong colours and finishes detract from planted areas, making gardens less pleasing on the eye. Yes, there are bright colours in the Mediterranean, but the light is stronger and hot sunshine soon mellows strong colours to an acceptable level.

Constantly review your original plan as you work, undertaking inevitable fine-tuning. Consider each new feature from the house as well as garden, and viewing from an upstairs window gives a further perspective. Mark each addition to scale on your plan, including open areas, patios, terraces, paths, walls, arches, pergolas and anything else you choose to incorporate.

Marking Out

When you are satisfied with the design, progress to marking out the main structures onto the actual ground. Small pegs or canes linked with string work well. A long hosepipe is effective as it can be simply moved or curved to obtain exactly the right angle. Coloured sand is another option. Careful measurement is essential to make sure the ground plan conforms to your original design. However, at this stage you may also feel certain adjustments are necessary. Mark alterations onto the original plan.

Stage 5: Finally the Plants

As the drawing evolves so excitement mounts and finally you can at last think about the all-important plants. Marking these in colour on your black and

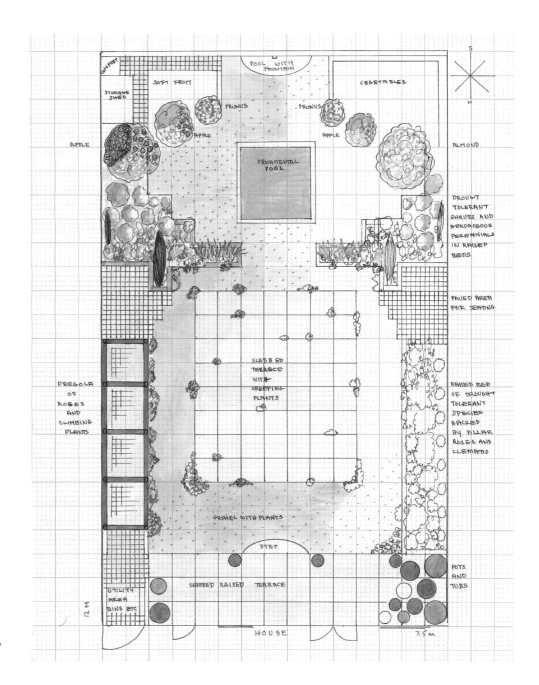

Adding plant suggestions and colour to your basic black and white plan really brings it to life.

white plan really brings the design to life. Use canes as markers when transferring plant positions to the garden.

Trees

Trees come first, mainly because they are the largest things you will plant and the slowest to mature. Mark their positions on the plan with a circle, allowing for their eventual height and spread. Will they obscure an important view or limit light when they are fully grown? Will falling leaves create problems? Deciduous trees lose their leaves during winter, leaving skeletal branches to frame distant views, but too many bare branches are a constant reminder of our cooler climate. Consider using evergreens and conifers, which give year-round colour and interest as well as privacy in town gardens, for example the very Mediterranean Italian cypress, *Cupressus sempervirens* 'Stricta'. Trees are tremendous value, many giving wonderful foliage, spring blossom and fantastic autumn colour with leaves, fruit and berries. You could use mountain ash, *Sorbus aucuparia*, whitebeam, *Sorbus aria*, or Judas tree, *Cercis siliquastrum*. Trees that can also be planted in pots or clipped into shapes as in many Mediterranean gardens include box, *Buxus sempervirens*, holly, *Ilex aquifolium*, and yew, *Taxus baccata*.

Shrubs

Shrubs are next, forming intermediate layers between taller trees and lower growing plants. Overwhelming arrays of Mediterranean shrubs are available in garden centres and it comes down to a matter of personal preference. Shrubs can also include low growing hedges, a parterre framework of clipped box or bay or a mixture of shrubs and herbaceous plants in borders.

Climbers

Walls and fences supply perfect support for endless choices of climbers, from roses to vines, jasmines and more tender species that like south-facing walls, where they receive some protection during winter. Climbers will grow up through trees or twine around arbours, arches, pergolas or statuary.

Bulbs, Corms, Rhizomes etc.

There are extensive ranges of bulbs, corms and rhizomatous plants from Mediterranean climate regions for every position in the garden. Agapanthus, anemone, crinum, cyclamen, iris, lily, narcissus, tulip – the list is endless.

Borders

Suitable drought tolerant plants for beds and borders, which will flower and add interest throughout the year, come in all shapes and sizes. They vary from a few centimetres high up to 3 metres or more. Certain plants complement more restrained styles in formal beds, while others enhance a natural look, tumbling out of borders and across pathways and patios.

Beautifully clipped shrubs line the drive at Preen Manor, Shropshire.

Cistus, native to Southern Europe, North Africa and the Canary Islands, are a 'must' in the drought tolerant garden and are good shrubs for coastal areas. The exquisite flowers of Cistus × purpureus are carried over a long period, although individual flowers last only a single day. Stone House Cottage Garden, Worcestershire.

Pots and containers edge the steps at Mawley Hall, Shropshire.

ABOVE AND BELOW: *Leeds Castle, Kent. Borders of Mediterranean climate region species have colour, shape and texture throughout the year.*

Pots and Containers

Many Mediterranean plants and bulbs adapt admirably to containers. This also means that very tender species can be grown that would not otherwise survive outdoors during winter, and pots can be simply brought inside for protection.

Water-wise Gardening

Throughout the planning, particularly when choosing and placing the plants, bear in mind the water-wise gardening rules outlined in chapter 2. Group plants in order of their water requirements, those needing little or no water furthest from the house and those requiring more water closer to water sources. Pots require constant watering during summer, so make sure they are near a water supply for ease of maintenance.

And do not forget to include space on your plan for that all-important rainwater butt, to collect valuable water run-off from roof and guttering.

Some Plants for Mediterranean Gardens

Cercis *species have delicate, pea-like flowers in spring, followed by light green or dark red leaves and good autumn colour. Stockton Bury Garden, Herefordshire.*

Vivid orange-red flowers of Embothrium coccineum, *Chilean firebush, glow in the late spring sunshine.*

Pittosporum tenuifolium *'Purpureum', native to New Zealand, thrives at RHS garden Rosemoor, Devon.*

Phlomis fruticosa, *native to Mediterranean regions, is another shrub that has happily adapted to our cooler climate.*

Wisteria sinensis *may have originated in China, but has made itself at home both in Mediterranean regions and cooler climates. Twining anticlockwise, it can grow up to 40m, and an established plant is spectacular in spring with its long racemes of perfumed, pale mauve flowers.*

Lilium 'Harmony' is spectacular in summer, with its glowing orange flowers spotted with maroon.

Anemone blanda, *Windflower, with their delicate blue flowers in spring, are native to the eastern Mediterranean, Albania, Greece and Lebanon and are easily grown in light shade or full sun, naturalizing happily. There are also white- and pink-flowered forms.*

Paeonia 'Auguste Dessert' is a semi-double with masses of fragrant, carmine flowers and lighter, silvery margins to the petals.

Jasminum grandiflorum, *or Spanish jasmine, was cultivated by the Moors in Spain; a scrambling, evergreen shrub with deliciously perfumed, white flowers, it trails over walls or climbs arbours.*

Lonicera periclymenum, *common honeysuckle, is native from Ireland to North Africa. A deciduous climber with highly fragrant, purple-tinged, tubular flowers, it is ideal for pergolas or arbours.*

5 Dealing with Lawns

Eliminating, reducing or retaining a lawn will probably be the most important decision in your new garden design.

We love lawns and are prepared to put much time and effort into achieving and maintaining that smooth, velvet green sward. We worry when grass browns in summer, or becomes a quagmire in winter. Lawns require constant mowing, weeding, fertilizing, raking, aerating and treatment of pests, diseases, moss, clover and dandelions in order to keep them in tip-top condition. And then there is the problem of what to do with the grass cuttings when only a limited number go on the compost heap, or can be used as mulch?

After holidays you frequently return to a hayfield and have trouble mowing long grass. The mower jams and you have trouble disposing of grass cuttings. What a relief when winter arrives and the grass does not need cutting. But even then there are problems. Rain makes lawns impossible to walk on, shoes get soaked. In mild winters grass continues growing, but is too wet to mow, creating further problems for spring.

Are we mad? Is working to maintain all this grass really necessary? You may find it difficult to imagine not having a lawn because they are such integral parts of most gardens. At the turn of the twentieth century, when 'English' gardens became the vogue in Mediterranean countries, the first essential was a good, emerald lawn, heavily watered and fertilized to keep it

green throughout boiling Mediterranean summers. Then labour was cheap and conservation was not an issue. Now Mediterranean gardeners have a greater awareness of the impact this excessive demand for water has on the environment. Instead they substitute grasses with coarser textures, which stay green without constant irrigation, and can be used in hot countries. In some parts of America two types of grass are sown. One is brown during summer and green in winter, the other stays green in summer and dies off in winter.

OPPOSITE: Mellow brick courtyard and an abundance of Mediterranean plants at Chesters Walled Garden, Northumberland.

RIGHT, TOP: The lawns at Hoghton Tower, Lancashire, are well maintained, but require constant maintenance and water to keep them looking at their best in hot summers.

RIGHT, BOTTOM: In late summer, after months of baking sun and no rain, the drought tolerant grass in this water-wise garden in Mallorca is still green without additional water.

Unusual designs are created with the two grasses. As water becomes more expensive and conservation issues increasingly desperate, we must accept that lawns cannot be so heavily watered. They *will* go brown in hot, dry weather.

Lawns are so time- and water-consuming that anything we do to lessen that burden is important. The simplest solution is to hardscape lawned areas. However, you may decide you simply cannot manage without some lawn, and in larger gardens it is not practical to replace all grass with other materials. The aesthetic feel of the garden as well as the needs of children and pets must also be taken into consideration.

If you decide you must have some lawn, there are ways of simplifying maintenance. Raising mower blades slightly leaves grass a little longer, retaining more moisture at the roots, helping lawns stay greener in summer. Newer grasses are being developed that are harder wearing and slower growing. Good ground preparation also helps when laying a lawn. Drainage is important and a well-balanced mixture of grit and organic material beneath the lawn helps improve soil, provides better drainage and retains more moisture. Consider varieties of rye grass, or good mixes containing stronger fescue grasses. Tougher than standard lawn mixtures stay green for longer with less water. Rubber matting laid beneath lawns allows grass to grow through for heavier duty surfaces receiving constant use, such as car parking or children's play areas.

Acaena microphylla.

Lawn Substitutes

If you decide to remove your lawn, there are many suitable and attractive alternatives worth considering, although lawn substitute plants generally need to be low growing and uniform. Certain plants supply the 'green' aspect, without using vast quantities of water to maintain that colour. Some are purely decorative ground covers such as sedums and succulents, others such as chamomile and thyme happily stand some traffic and give off wonderful fragrances when lightly crushed. None are as tough as grass, and all require some maintenance, but they are attractive and eye catching. Paths or 'stepping stones' facilitate access and minimize wear. Certain nurseries now supply lawn substitute plants by the square metre. Grown in special, flat trays, plants root together, resembling carpet tiles, and are laid in the same way.

Most of the following plants work well in smaller areas. If initial costs are daunting, suitable supplies can be raised from seed, or by purchasing a few stock plants to use for cuttings or layering, and planting the following year. Ground should be well prepared, well drained and weed free. Placing plants closely together quickly forms a dense covering and reduces weeding. In the same way grass suffers damage from pests or diseases, so too can grass substitutes, but damaged areas can quickly be replaced with new cuttings.

Acaena

A. caesiiglauca, 5cm. Evergreen, hairy, blue-green leaflets and clusters of tiny flowers with brownish bracts, developing into red coloured burs. *A. microphylla*, 4cm. Glossy grey-green, bronze tinged leaflets, with globose red bracts.

Artemisia

A. schmidtiana 'Nana', 8cm. Fern-like silver-green foliage and minute, yellow, daisy-like flowers in summer. Trim lightly in spring and dress with gravel or sharp grit in winter. Well-drained, sandy or peaty soil.

Chamomile

Chamaemelum nobile, 10cm. Used for centuries as popular lawn and path substitutes, but can be invasive. Feathery, green, aromatic foliage, and daisy-like white

Chamaemelum nobile *'Treneague'*, grown in trays to be laid as lawn substitute at Bill White Nurseries, Worcestershire.

Trifolium repens, *white clover.*

Cotoneaster *'Skogholm' syn. C. 'Skogsholmen'.*

flowers in summer. Trim lightly as required. Chamomile lawns are reasonably hard wearing, with the added benefit of scent. Non-flowering, creeping varieties such as *C. nobile* **'Treneague'** form lush, pale green carpets without flowers. Hardy perennials, chamomile prefers sun and poor soil with good drainage. Grow from seed, although cuttings or off-shoots create better lawns. Set 23cm apart, plants spread forming a thick mat that can be lightly mown.

Clover

Most gardeners eradicate clover, especially from lawns, but white clover, *Trifolium repens*, makes a good grass substitute with its three-lobed leaves and white flowers. It is relatively tough, as anyone who has tried weeding out clover will testify! Stays green in summer, and needs light trimming. *T. repens* **'Purpurascens'**, 8–12cm. Bronze-green foliage edged brilliant green.

Cotoneaster

C. **'Skogholm'** syn C. 'Skogsholmen'. 60cm. Spreading, low-growing, evergreen shrub with small, glossy, dark green leaves and tiny white flowers in summer, followed by sparse, red fruits. Sunny, well-drained sites. Propagate from cuttings.

Cotula

Again classed as a lawn weed but grows thick and fast to produce creeping stems with fern-like foliage and small yellow flowers in summer. Species include *C. coronopifolia*, *C. dioica*, with yellow flowers; *C. lineariloba*, and *C. squalida* (*Leptinella squalida*), forming flat, bronze-green carpets with purple flowers. Plant 10–15cm apart in good, gritty loam and full sun. Can become invasive unless checked.

Hedera

Low growing ivies produce good ground cover in shades from light to dark green, also variegated with cream, silver or gold. Most prefer alkaline soil and grow in dry shade and sun. Clip as necessary. *H. helix* **ssp. helix** is native to the Mediterranean. **'Nigra'** has dark leaves, **'Nigra Aurea'** dappled yellow. For small areas

Hedera helix *'Glacier'.*

69

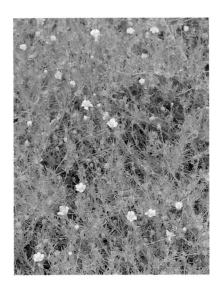

Pearlwort, Sagina subulata, *grown in trays to be laid as lawn substitute at Bill White Nurseries, Worcestershire.*

Sedum obtusatum.

Mind Your Own Business, Corsican Curse, Soleirolia soleirolii.

try **'Buttercup'**, yellow in good light, and an Italian ivy, H.'Oro di Bogliasco', or **'Goldheart'**. *H. algeriensis* **'Gloire de Marengo'**, silver, cream and green, is increasingly offered for outdoor use forming good cover. *H. hibernica* comes in many forms and requires sun and acidic soils, as well as tolerating both drier and wetter conditions than common ivy. **Madeira ivy**, *H. maderensis*, forms tough, dense layers of yellowish green. **Moroccan ivy**, *H. maroccana*, requires sun to stop it becoming rampant, but grows on poor ground.

Heterocentron elegans

5cm. Creeping evergreen perennial with dark purple flowers in summer and autumn. Can be frost tender and requires well-drained soil and sun.

Raoulia

R. australis, 1cm. Mat-forming perennial with tiny, grey leaves and yellow flowers in summer. *R. tenuicaulis*, silver leaves; *R. hookeri* slightly taller. Well-drained, peaty soil and sun or semi-shade.

Sagina

S. subulata, 2–10cm. Good cover with white flowers in summer. Gritty loam and full sun, but dislikes very dry conditions.

Sempervivum and Succulents

Grow into dense mats, especially over small areas, but are purely decorative and cannot be walked on. A range of colours from green, grey and bronze. *Sedum obtusatum*, small yellow flowers and tiny, fat leaves that turn red in summer. Dislikes too much moisture. *S. lydium*, 5cm. Narrow, red-tinged, fleshy leaves and clusters of small white flowers in summer. Most *sempervivum* spread into good-sized, low-growing clumps, in a range of shapes and colours. Main rosettes die after flowering but produce numerous offsets, which are easily propagated. *S. tectorum*, common houseleek, 10–15cm. Vigorous evergreen perennial, leaves often flushed deep red. Clusters of purple-red flowers in summer, up to 30cm. *S. arachnoideum*, cobweb houseleek, 5–12cm. Mat-forming perennial, red-tinted, fleshy leaves smothered in 'cobwebs' of fine white hairs. Rose-coloured flowers in summer.

Soleirolia soleirolii

Mind Your Own Business, **Corsican Curse**. This spreading, evergreen perennial with minute leaves can become invasive.

Teucrium pyrenaicum

Low-growing perennial with rounded, notched leaves and tiny purple-tinged, white or yellow flowers.

Thymus Species

The second most popular contender for lawns and paths, after chamomile. Prostrate thymes have fragrance, and white, pink, mauve or purple flowers in summer. Create jewel-like carpets by arranging groups of five to six plants of one type, for contrasting texture and colours. For lawns and paths use creeping, mat-forming species such as *T. pulegioides*; *T. herba-barona*, pink/purple flowers and caraway scent; *T. praecox arcticus*, syn *T. druce*, or *T. pseudolanuginosus*, syn *T. languinosus*, woolly thyme, 2–5cm. Thyme also spreads between paving or in gravel. *T.* × *citriodorus* 'Bertram Anderson', golden foliage throughout winter. There are also silver and variegated forms. Well-drained, dry, sunny positions and alkaline soil. Plant 20cm apart and trim lightly after flowering. Plants eventually become woody but are easily replaced from cuttings.

Verbena

V. peruviana syn *V. chamaedrioides*, *V. chamaedrifolia*, 8cm. Prostrate perennials with tiny, scarlet flowers in summer and autumn. Like poor, dry soil, but can be frost tender.

Vinca

V. minor. 20cm. Long, spreading, evergreen shoots with lanceolate to ovate leaves and blue, purple or white flowers. *V. major*. 30cm.

Edible 'Lawns'

Ground cover plants, generally slightly taller than grass, but setting mower blades only 2cm higher, and regular cutting, produces large crops of nutritious, edible leaves. Plants can also be left to grow and flower in summer, before trimming again. **Yarrow**, *Achillea millefolium*; **bugle**, *Ajuga reptans*; alliums including *A. oleraceum* and *A. vineale*. **Common daisy**, *Bellis perennis*, continues flowering however hard it is cut. Various species of plantago including *P. lanceolata*, *P. major* and *P. media*; **self heal**, *Prunella vulgaris*, continues producing small, purple flowers if not cut too short; **sheep's sorrel**, *Rumex acetosa*.

Thymus *species, grown in trays to be laid as lawn substitute by Bill White Nurseries, Worcestershire.*

Teucrium pyrenaicum.

Greater periwinkle, Vinca major.

Reducing Lawns

Lawns can be reduced by enlarging present beds, creating new beds, or replacing sections of grass with paths and patios.

Existing Beds

Enlarge existing beds into lawn areas, filling spaces with drought tolerant, Mediterranean species, grouped to their water-wise requirements.

Island Beds

Make new beds or form island beds in the lawn. If island beds are viewed mainly from the front, place low plants at the near edge, taller plants towards the back. If viewed from all angles, lower plants follow the outer contours, with larger plants in the centre. Island beds can also be planted with low-growing species such as thymes, or other creeping plants, and top-dressed with gravel. Strategically placed rocks add interest. Beds can also be raised, allowing the opportunity to include good drainage material, which is highly advantageous to Mediterranean plants. Walls can be from a few

This Mallorcan garden has eliminated all lawn and substituted numerous island beds surrounded by gravel.

Lawn area has been greatly reduced, resulting in an attractively laid out garden, simply by cutting a series of square beds into the grass and planting with drought tolerant species. Chesters Walled Garden, Northumberland.

centimetres up to waist height, depending on space, plants and preference. Dry-stone walls, brick, wooden kerbing and railway sleepers all make good, solid boundaries for raised beds. A sundial, statue or elegant pot overflowing with plants also adds interest.

Chequer Board

Design beds in chequer board style, filling each square with one type of low-growing perennial, or pave alternate squares. This also works well with circular, semi-circular or fan shapes. Parallel rows of small beds across the lawn form an avenue, with a vase, statue, specimen tree or shrub at the far end to draw the eye. Fill beds with low-growing perennials, a single *Cupressus* species, clipped or topiary trees, standard roses or one species of shrub. When creating smaller, individual beds in grass, make sure there is enough space for mowers to pass easily between.

Changing Shapes

Turn square lawns into round lawns, filling resulting corners with Mediterranean plants, or create borders completely surrounding the lawn. Circular shapes can be further emphasized with low, clipped box hedges.

Going Wild

Certain areas of grass can be naturalized and cut only two or three times each year. Longer grass holds moisture in the ground and wild flowers can be established, creating havens for wild life.

Parterres and Knot Gardens

Parterres and knot gardens are very similar – and very different! Knot gardens became fashionable in the six-teenth century, parterres in the late sixteenth century and the early eighteenth, with a revival in Victorian and Edwardian eras. Both types derived inspiration from needlework designs. Hedges in knot gardens rise where they cross, indicating crossing threads, while parterre hedges are uniform in height. Both are built on level ground, but knot gardens are smaller and traditionally use gravel or coloured earth to set off woven hedges.

Reducing the lawn; variations on a theme

(i) The original garden was very basic, a square of grass with borders on three sides.

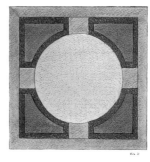

(ii) In the new design lawn has been cut back to a circle, edged with brick paths and low box hedges. Beds can be planted with roses, drought tolerant perennials or herbs. As well as dramatically reducing lawn area the garden is immediately more interesting. Eliminating lawn completely is by far the best option.

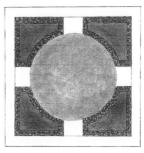

(iii) Lawn is replaced with gravel and paved areas are stone.

(iv) Simple outlines of trimmed box set into gravel make for even easier maintenance.

LEFT: *Here, part of the lawn is left to naturalize and filled with a colourful mixture of wild flowers, forming an attractive foil to the neatly mown areas of grass.*

BELOW: *Neat box hedges surround beds of roses in this sunken parterre garden at Mawley Hall, Shropshire.*

A simple knot of heart-shaped box set with flowers at the Hundred House, Shropshire.

Parterres are generally larger and more grand, with planted beds of perennials, roses or herbs between hedges. Both are symmetrical, with square boundaries and geometric patterns. Both are best viewed from above, originally the important rooms on the first floor. Designs use low, clipped, evergreens 'woven' together. Good, easy maintenance combinations include box or yew with clipped cotton lavender, *Santolina chamaecyparissus*, or dwarf varieties of lavender.

These make effective, exciting and interesting replacements for lawns. Anything from a simple heart shape of low, clipped box, enclosing gravel or a specimen tree, up to large, intricate designs of intertwining hedges and beds. Hedges generally require clipping twice a year, not nearly as often as lawns require mowing!

Lawn Preparation

If you simply *must* have lawn, initial preparation is important. After all, grass is a plant like any other and requires the same attention. South-facing sites dry out quickly in summer and grass turns brown faster. Too

much tree shade makes lawns patchy, while autumn leaves require regular removal.

Grasses are shallow rooting and good drainage is essential. Solid, wet clay soils may even need drainage pipes below ground so water does not stagnate around the roots. Sloping sites make mowing difficult, while level sites simplify maintenance.

The New Lawn

When planning new lawns, dig and level the area. Calculate levels by knocking pegs in across the site, until the tops are even when checked with a spirit level.

With heavy ground, or bad conditions, topsoil might need replacing completely. Medium soils benefit from additions of leaf mould or compost, while light soils are improved by digging in well-rotted farmyard manure. Incorporating coarser materials such as ash or fine gravel aids drainage.

After preparation, let ground settle for at least a week, then correct irregularities and remove new weeds. Tread and firm light soils. Rake to a fine tilth, clearing stones and other debris, until you have a firm, flat, even surface.

Sowing Seed

Seed is best sown in autumn, preferably September, or in spring, around early April. Soil should be damp but not wet enough to clump or be muddy. Spread seed thickly to achieve good growth, especially if birds are watching! Specialist seed spreaders give even distribution, or divide areas into squares with string, sowing measured amounts of seed in each square. Mixing seed with fine soil also makes distribution simpler. Standing on a plank ensures feet do not make indents in the soil. Lightly rake seed into the ground and, if not too wet, firm gently with a garden roller. Water if necessary and remove perennial weeds as they appear. Expect growth in ten to fourteen days and trim lightly at around 10cm, with mower blades set fairly high.

Turf

Turf gives instant lawns, but at far higher cost to seeding. Ground preparation as above. Autumn is best for laying as turves can dry out in spring without careful watering. Choose good quality turf, of coarser, harder wearing, meadow grass that requires less water than finer grasses. Turves measure approximately 1 metre by 30cm. They should be damp, of even depth, and are best laid across a lawn, rather than up and down. Set them like bricks, joins corresponding to the centre of neighbouring turves. Remove noticeable weeds as you go. Gently beat down with the back of a spade, ensuring turves lie firm against the ground. Dress and brush

finely sifted soil into the joins with a broom. Remove surplus soil and lightly roll the area. Do not allow turves to dry out; water if necessary, but do not over-water. Roll occasionally, and mow when growth commences.

Maintenance

Grass comes into active growth during spring and summer, so undertake maintenance work during autumn and winter. Rake and remove debris from lawns. Aerate with a garden fork or aerating roller to improve drainage. Dress with appropriate fertilizer, mixed with sharp sand to facilitate application. On acid ground with considerable growths of moss, apply powdered lime or chalk in early winter. Spreading finely sifted compost is also beneficial.

Mowing

Mowers are expensive to buy and maintain. They break down when you need them most, require costly repairs and also need storing. The more lawn you have, the more time mowing takes.

Consider a modern robot mower, more affordable now than when first on the market. Stored in small, low 'sheds', once programmed they are left to their own devices, emerging on a regular basis to cut the grass. Perimeter wires stop mowers savaging borders and shrubs.

Turf is laid in the same manner as bricks with joins corresponding to the centre of neighbouring turves. A guide line keeps work straight and a plank enables the turf to be set without heavy indents of footprints.

Invest in a good mower, ensure it is regularly serviced, and set blades at the correct height according to season and length of grass. Ride-on mowers are beneficial for large areas of grass. Motor-powered mowers are suitable for medium sized gardens; rotary mowers cope with short and long grass; small areas can be controlled with hand or small electric machines. Mowers that float on a cushion of air are useful for sloping sites, but leave untidy grass cuttings and can be dangerous. Trim lawn edges with long-handled edging sheers, or use a motorized version if you have miles!

Grass Paths

Grass pathways are best eliminated from gardens. They are wet and slippery in winter, dried up and brown in summer. Heavy-duty walkways soon become denuded and look unsightly. Grass paths require the same maintenance regimes as lawns, albeit on a smaller scale. If paths are not wide enough for mowers further problems are created. Paths bordered with plants are difficult to cut, damaging plants in the process. Grass paths also need regular edging.

Replacing lawns and grass paths with something requiring less or very little maintenance is definitely the preferred option in our Mediterranean garden.

An attractively designed path at Leeds Castle, Kent, will accommodate large numbers of visitors whatever the weather.

Maturing plants can reduce the width of paths, while wet or dry weather both create adverse wear.

This crazy paving path at Tapeley Park, Devon, requires little maintenance and keeps feet dry.

Knot Gardens and Parterres

Knot gardens and parterres are created in an endless range of designs from a simple heart shape of low clipped box to a large and intricate design filled with patterns of colourful flowers.

Lyme Park, Cheshire, (The National Trust). A magnificent and extravagant parterre of box and ivy hedges inset with brilliantly coloured bedding plants.

Chesters Walled Garden, Northumberland. An intricate design of low, weaving hedges set amidst gravel.

Jessamine Cottage, Shropshire. A newly created parterre of box set with drought tolerant plants.

RHS garden Rosemoor, Devon. Neat and pleasing, clipped herbs and hedges.

Mawley Hall, Shropshire. This knot garden exhibits the traditional rise as the hedges cross.

The Hundred House, Shropshire. An attractive looking quartered design of box hedges filled with colourful Helichrysum bracteatum.

Preen Manor, Shropshire. A small circular and quartered design of box and ivy filled with culinary herbs.

University of Oxford Botanic Garden. A large parterre filled with roses and shaded by trees.

The Hundred House, Shropshire. A simple chequer board design enclosing herbs.

Italian Garden, Shropshire. A knot of woven box hedges filled with herbs.

6 Patios, Terraces and Outdoor Living

When deciding to remove lawns from our gardens the question arises about what to use instead? Having discussed substitute plants we now consider hardscaping alternatives.

Patios

Patios are perfect for replacing some or all of a lawn, as well as being useful additions to the garden. A 'patio', from the Spanish meaning 'interior courtyard', provides a relaxing area offering shade from intense sun. In cooler countries patios are popular in summer and on milder days of the year.

This book is not a builder's guide, or brick by brick account of building techniques. 'Do It Yourself' manuals abound, fully detailing all the technical information you require. Ideas and suggestions here simply serve as examples of styles, materials and outline methods of construction when creating hardscaped areas in the garden.

Design

Try to move away from the stereotype of a small, square, paved area abutting the back of the house, even though patios near the house are convenient. Consider round, semicircular or hexagonal shapes. The hard lines of square or rectangular shapes can be alleviated

OPPOSITE: *The Italianate garden at Mawley Hall, Shropshire. The inset plantings in the terrace floor and onlooking statues lend the garden a classic Mediterranean feel.*

RIGHT: *Ideas for patio shapes other than the stereotyped square: (i) Circle or semicircle; (ii) Circle and square (perhaps adding interest to an existing square patio); (iii) Oval; (iv) Triangular; (v) Octagonal; (vi) Curving.*

by removing occasional slabs, thereby creating an irregular border. Plants can be grown in the spaces. Boring outlines can be disguised by building low retaining walls, and growing plants along the tops if space is provided for compost.

Drawing accurately measured, detailed plans helps avoid possibly expensive mistakes and facilitates estimates of costs and materials. Dimensions should relate to the size of materials being used, i.e. bricks or slabs, to avoid constantly cutting materials to fit. Decide

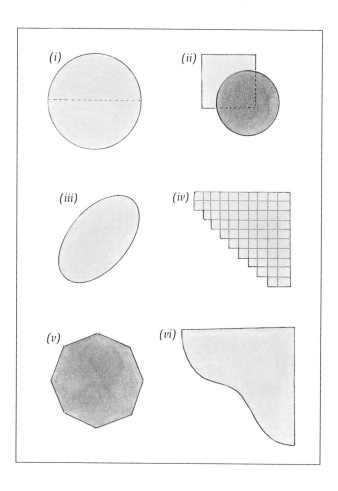

'Patio', from the Spanish meaning 'an interior courtyard'. (Photo courtesy of Sue Pendleton)

where pergola supports and planting areas will go, marking these on the plan. Check you will not mistakenly excavate drains, service pipes or electricity cables, and that tree roots will not become a problem, undermining foundations.

Will the patio be in full sun or shade? South-facing patios are preferable, but, if impossible, build the patio to catch morning or evening sunlight. Check views and see whether privacy from neighbours is an issue, or whether nearby buildings cast shadows when the patio is most likely to be used. Moving the patio a metre or two to either side might easily solve the problem.

Consider screening for privacy or protection from chilling breezes. Screens can be of stone, brick, decorative open blocks, glass bricks, fencing or trellising, all of which accommodate climbing plants. Shrubs also make good screens if space allows. Arbours, pergolas or simple arches add valuable shade as well as privacy, especially when draped with climbing plants, roses or vines. Whitewashed walls, terracotta tiles and colourful awnings add that Mediterranean feel, while awnings provide shelter in mildly inclement weather.

Terraces and patios become extensions to the interior living space, used for dining, barbecues, relaxation, entertaining or even work. They can be level with surrounding areas, raised or sunk below ground.

An interestingly shaped patio in a garden in Ludlow, Shropshire.

Plan where pergola supports will fit before building the patio. Jessamine Cottage, Shropshire.

No problem with the view from this patio overlooking beautiful countryside to distant hills. Angel Gardens, Shropshire.

The mellow brick wall at the back of this patio provides privacy and protection as well as support for plants. Wisteria peeps through a tiny 'window' making an attractive feature. Stone House Cottage Garden, Worcestershire.

Seating is important on the patio, providing somewhere to sit and relax with a drink. Leeds Castle, Kent.

Six Paving Finishes

Natural pebbles.

Brick and tile.

Simple brick design.

Cut stone slabs.

Brick and stone.

Natural stone.

Decide the dimensions in relation to the rest of the garden. Mark outlines with pegs and string to see how the patio will fit in with its surroundings. Check the site over a few days to ensure it suits your requirements. Is it correctly positioned? Does the patio feel too large or too small? Is it too shady or windy?

Check you will not contravene local planning regulations. What surface material will you use? Should it be stone paving, bricks, gravel, wood? Or perhaps combinations of no more than three different materials – more begins to look muddled. For an ultra-modern approach incorporate stainless-steel or copper sheeting. Bearing Mediterranean themes in mind, consider coloured ceramic tiles, whitewashed walls and vines.

Garden centres and builders' merchants carry stocks of hardscaping materials and timber, though prices vary considerably and it is worth shopping around. Also investigate what is on offer at local architectural salvage merchants.

Mark circular shapes by attaching an appropriate length of string to a peg knocked firmly into the centre of the area. Attach a metal skewer to the loose end and, keeping the string taut, walk round in a circle, scribing the shape directly onto the ground, or mark with sand or spray paint. Flexible hosepipes are useful for divining curves. Check from upstairs to see how shapes look from above.

Decking adds strong directional lines. Jessamine Cottage, Shropshire.

Paving

Slabs provide one of the simplest and fastest methods of creating patios in various shapes, sizes, colours and materials. They can be pre-cut natural stone, such as granite, slate, limestone or sandstone, reconstituted stone in various shades and finishes, cast concrete, or pre-moulded designs of brick or cobble, which look effective and save labour. Shaped slabs fit together to form circular designs. Break the monotony of large areas of paving by incorporating other materials such as natural stone, bricks, cobbles or wood, or leave spaces for plants. Plan mosaic effects with patterns of coloured slabs or tiles in freestyle or geometric designs. Ideas are endless. Seek further inspiration from suppliers' catalogues, gardens, books or magazines.

Timber Decking

Decking is popular and fashionable. Use pressure-treated timber, maintained with regular applications of wood preservative. Various styles of panels or strips are available that add strong, directional lines to the garden. Ridged surfaces help prevent slipping. Timber can be left natural or painted. Special paints made for boat decks provide non-slip surfaces. Whatever the finish or colour, make sure it harmonizes with, and complements, the rest of your design, garden and plants.

Timber decking requires a free flow of air, so needs raising above ground level for air to circulate beneath. It is good for defining two or three different levels, securing decking on firm, strong, wooden battens, brick or concrete piers. These, and any retaining walls, must be of solid construction, with firm foundations. The final decking surface should be smooth and splinter free. Use rust-proof nails or screws that will not stain the timber.

Railway sleepers create simple but sturdy patios when properly laid on level foundations. They are also excellent for edging raised beds and supporting terraces. They can exude oily substances, however, so weathered sleepers are preferable and care should be taken with clothing.

Care also needs to be taken if decking or wooden

Timber decking requires a free flow of air. Here the gap has been disguised with large stones, which also allow air to circulate. Angel Gardens, Shropshire.

Old, weathered railway sleepers make simple, substantial and natural looking supports for wooden decking. Jessamine Cottage, Shropshire.

surfaces become slippery when wet. A build up of algae can be unsightly, but it is easily removed with a stiff brush and appropriate fungicide.

Small Gardens

In small gardens the whole area can be replaced with paving, gravel or decking. Plants thrive in gravel or they can be set between stones to creep across in a natural fashion. Where planting areas are limited, groups of pots and containers are attractive and practical alternatives. As a general rule, keep designs clean and simple in small gardens, sticking to between one and three different materials to achieve an uncluttered and harmonious effect. Smaller slabs, set into simple designs, look better than overpowering larger slabs. Intricate designs also appear too fussy in small gardens.

Construction

Consider the above points and check the patio fulfils your requirements. Make sure it is large enough for your needs and sufficient to accommodate chairs and table. Minor adjustments are easily made now. Decide

Plants happily creep between paving that provides them with a cool root run. National Herb Centre, Oxfordshire.

on materials and check they will dry out quickly after rain and will not dazzle in sunlight. Be wary of bright colours: although these fade with age, they can detract from the plants.

Raised Patios

Differing heights add further dimensions to the garden. Patios built on sloping sites necessitate either levelling the area or building up on one side. They must have good, firm foundations to avoid subsidence, which could leave stones and tiles dangerously loose. Retaining walls must be properly constructed and strong enough to last for years. The floor area is raised to the required height with hardcore, topped with sand, firmed into place and finished with slabs. If patios are against the house they must slope away at a slight angle, so rainwater runs off freely and does not seep back into foundations or walls. If necessary, insert a drain into the patio with slabs sloping gently towards it. Drainage is important to avoid pools of water. Water can be angled in the direction of surrounding plants. Constructions against the house must also be at least 15cm below damp-proof courses to avoid problems.

Depending on the finished height, raised patios will require steps and retaining walls or rails for safety, up to around waist height. Walls can become decorative features by having a cavity, filled with good drainage material and topped with compost for plants. Set a seat into the wall, or top with trellising or pillars to support plants

Building patios is not as simple as it might first appear. Are you sufficiently accomplished and knowledgeable to undertake the work or will you need help? Is the overall price within your budget? Make sure the site is accessible and you do not need to hire a

giant crane, at astronomical cost, to get materials into position!

Having decided on a design, mark out the shape and remove good top soil for use in other areas of the garden. For patios finishing at ground level, excavate to a depth of 20–25cm, level the site and spread 15cm of hard core, firming well. Finish with an even layer of sand, and firm into place, filling any gaps. Slabs can be set directly onto the sand, with fine gravel brushed between joints afterwards.

For longer lasting and weed-free finishes, cement or mortar slabs in place to a depth that ensures they are flush with the surrounding area when finished. Accurate distances between slabs are achieved with spacers, which are removed later. Two or three days after laying, infill spaces between slabs with mortar and a small trowel, finishing slightly below the slab's surface for a sharp effect. Wipe away stray mortar before it dries and mars the finished appearance.

A patio constructed on two levels to accommodate a sloping site. Raised patios need solid retaining walls and foundations. Angel Gardens, Shropshire.

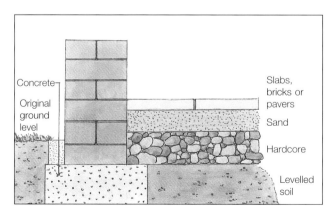

Cross-section showing the basic foundations for a patio with retaining wall.

A tiny sunken patio of natural stone at Stockton Bury Gardens, Herefordshire.

Sunken Patios and Gardens

Sunken gardens or patios are romantic and again help reduce lawn area. You can trail plants down walls or allow them to creep through paving. A small pool or fountain is a picturesque addition.

Such areas require perfect drainage to stop them becoming pools during wet weather. Excavate and build strong retaining walls of brick, stone or railway sleepers: steps are also necessary. When using slabs or stone, leave a narrow border around the perimeter and fill with gravel to aid drainage. In heavy clay areas it may be necessary to install a drain beneath the surface to remove surplus water. A defunct swimming pool also makes an excellent foundation for a sunken garden.

Existing Patios

If your garden already has a well-laid, but boring, patio, minor modifications can create a tremendous difference to its appearance. New slabs can surface a concrete patio, while removing occasional existing slabs interrupts the monotony of a standardized surface. Fill spaces with decorative patterns of tiles, bricks, cobbles, creeping plants, taller plants or a small tree. Extend the patio area using contrasting materials. Build low, retaining walls or beds. Add a small circular or square, central raised bed, or install a water feature or fountain. Group attractive and colourful pots and containers, overflowing with brightly coloured plants, or add a sculpture, Cretan terracotta pot or old olive jar.

An attractive finish to this patio area with tiny central pond filled with Zantedeschia at RHS garden Rosemoor, Devon.

Stones and Gravel

These make attractive and harmonious surfaces, although too small or too deep an aggregate makes walking difficult. Excavate and add a layer of hardcore with low, firmly set, retaining boundaries to stop gravel moving untidily into surrounding areas. A minimum level for gravel should be 8cm, although this can benefit from being up to 15–20cm if you intend growing plants.

Arbours, Arches and Pergolas

However much you love the sun, patios benefit from some shade. Decorative arches, arbours or pergolas are ideal. Smother with perfumed, climbing plants, which scent the evening air when you sit down for a relaxing meal. These attractive structures provide shade and shelter, while also helping the ground retain moisture to benefit plants, an important factor in water-wise gardens.

Arbours create romantic, protected and private areas for sitting out. They are simply constructed from wood, metal or trellis panels, and twined with plants. Incorporate a comfortable seat for relaxation.

Arches can be made from timber, trellis, metal or a combination of materials. Countless ready-made designs are available, costing from a few pounds up to many hundreds, depending on budget. Again, the better the quality, the more durable the product. Arches can be a simple span or more decorative constructions, but will need firm anchoring so they do not fall over.

Pergolas are constructed to the required length and height from timber posts, cemented into the ground, and held together with crossbeams. The more substantial the structure, the longer it will last. Mediterranean pergolas often have brick supporting pillars. Other materials such as iron can be used, while ready-made construction packs are available to purchase. Pergolas form shady walks beneath their plant-entwined spans.

Before building any tall structures in the garden always check where shadows will fall to make sure sunny areas are not suddenly plunged into permanent shade. When calculating the height, also remember that internal heights will decrease as plants mature and clothe the structure.

Nothing is more romantic than sweetly perfumed roses tumbling over arbours or pergolas. Numerous other climbing plants are also ideal. Achieve balance

Plants happily grow and seed in gravel.

Honeysuckle and roses twine this tiny arbour at Stone House Cottage Garden, Worcestershire.

ABOVE: *At Preen Manor, Shropshire, arches have been treated in a number of interesting ways: (LEFT) Beautifully trained apple trees; (RIGHT) Roses and runner beans.*

LEFT: *An intricate, trellis pergola, twined with roses, honeysuckle and jasmine, also shelters tender plants at its feet. Bodnant Gardens, Clwyd. (The National Trust)*

between evergreen and deciduous plants, for colour and interest, even in winter. More unusual choices include laburnums and trees that can be trained into shape, fruit trees, or even the humble runner bean, which forms a colourful canopy as well as bounteous harvest. Grape vines create the ultimate Mediterranean ideal. Who could resist sitting outside on a late summer's evening and reaching up to cut a bunch of luscious grapes?

Finishing Touches

Surrounding the patio with perfumed plants fills the air with wonderful fragrance. In addition to climbing plants, you could try some pots of lilies, *Brugmansia*, herbs and lavender. Scented plants creep between paving and give additional perfume when lightly crushed underfoot. You could train a peach or

Plants for Arbours, Arches and Pergolas

Clematis cirrhosa. Evergreen, with bell-shaped, greenish-white flowers in winter and spring. *C. flammula*. Semi-evergreen with masses of small, single, almond-scented, white flowers in summer and early autumn.

Decumaria barbara, **climbing hydrangea**. Generally evergreen with corymbs of sweetly scented white flowers in late spring and early summer.

Hedera colchica, **Persian ivy**. Fully hardy evergreen with heart-shaped, dark-green leaves. **'Dentata'**, larger, lighter leaves. **'Dentata Variegata'** brightens up a dark corner with creamy-yellow leaves.

Humulus lupulus **'Aurea'**, **golden hop**. Lobed, golden-yellow leaves and pale green flowers in summer.

Ipomoea purpurea, **morning glory**. Treat as annual. Heart-shaped leaves and brilliant blue, purple or reddish, trumpet-shaped flowers.

Jasminum officinale, **summer jasmine**. Pinnate leaves and clusters of sweetly scented white flowers.

Lonicera etrusca. Generally evergreen with large clusters of creamy yellow flowers in summer. Can take several years to bloom.

Rosa **'Madame Alfred Carrière'**. Light green leaves and strongly perfumed, large, white double flowers. **'Climbing Etoile de Holland'**, perfumed crimson flowers. **'Blush Noisette'**, clusters of small, clove-scented, semi-double, lilac-pink flowers. **'Paul's Lemon Pillar'**, strongly fragrant, large, creamy yellow flowers, tinged with green. **'Albertine'**, salmon buds opening to fragrant, copper-pink, semi-double flowers. **'Paul's Himalayan Musk'**, hanging

Humulus lupulus 'Aureus', *golden hop*.

sprays of strongly fragrant, small, blush-pink flowers. **'Rambling Rector'**, small, perfumed, creamy white, semi-double flowers. *R. banksiae lutea*, small, semi-double, deep yellow flowers. **'The Garland'**, small, perfumed, creamy salmon flowers.

Vitis vinifera **'Brant'**. Strong growing vine producing sweet, edible black grapes with good autumn colour.

Wisteria sinensis, **wisteria**. Light green leaflets and long racemes of perfumed, blue-violet flowers in spring. **'Alba'**, white flowers. **'Black Dragon'**, dark purple, semi-double.

Rosa *'Madame Alfred Carrière'*.

Wisteria sinensis.

nectarine against a wall; fig trees grow well but require restricted planting areas otherwise they become rampant and grow leaves at the expense of fruit. Even a tub or two of tomato plants or peppers makes a bright, useful and edible addition.

Furniture

Mediterranean gardens call for relaxing siestas on comfortable furniture – long low loungers, sun beds, hammocks, or deeply padded seating. Enhance the theme with brightly coloured cushions, table cloths, umbrellas or canopies. Provide a small table for wine glasses and 'tapas', and a larger table for dining. Items that stay outside must be weather- and rustproof. Treat timber furniture with preservative each autumn, to prolong life and keep it looking attractive. Plastic can be wiped down, but deteriorates outdoors, particularly in winter.

Decorative Extravaganza

Further decorative features in the garden, apart from the design and plants, are purely a matter of personal

LEFT: Tender plants are protected on this enclosed patio at Brook Cottage, Oxfordshire.

BELOW LEFT: Wonderfully perfumed lilies greet the visitor at the front door of Stockton Bury Gardens, Herefordshire.

BELOW: Decking patio surrounded by Mediterranean plants at Angel Gardens, Shropshire.

While away a summer afternoon playing chess on this giant board patio at Preen Manor, Shropshire.

choice, but there are numerous items that can be used to great effect to draw or deceive the eye and create illusions of space.

TROMPE-L'OEIL

Cheer up a plain wall by adding a 'view'. Paint a simple, three-dimensional, *trompe-l'oeil* mural of a garden or scene to expand horizons artificially: a country scene painted onto a wall and enclosed by a 'window frame'; a half-open door or gate onto a garden view; a *trompe-l'oeil* archway, niche, garden vase or grotto. If you do not trust your artistic talents, a suitably waterproofed, mounted and enlarged photograph acts just as well.

TRELLISES

Trellises have long been used to great effect to construct receding perspectives, thereby creating illusions of space. Similarly, grouping large plants at the front and smaller plants with like foliage behind gives the appearance of distance.

MIRRORS

Mirrors create ongoing reflections, making vistas appear larger than they actually are. Set into a doorframe for instance, it implies that the garden continues on through the door. Mirrors require air

This diminutive Devon yard has a simple but effective trompe-l'oeil *scene of an open door leading onto a Mediterranean hillside. The shuttered window promises delights as yet unexplored. One imagines the brilliant burst of heat and light that will flood into the tiny yard if the shutters are suddenly thrown open to reveal a distant landscape.*

circulation behind them, so mount on battens fixed firmly to the wall and give the back of the mirror two coats of 'Unibond' to prevent moisture and damp penetration.

Inspiring Designs for Patios

Stone slabs at RHS garden Hyde Hall, Essex.

Old quarry tiles at Stone House Cottage Garden, Worcestershire.

An intriguing design of bricks and contrasting gravels at Preen Manor, Shropshire.

A stunning dragon design on the tiled floor at Preen Manor, Shropshire.

A quiet corner to relax at Newby Hall, North Yorkshire.

A patio of paving slabs at Leeds Castle, Kent.

Mixed materials for this circular patio at RHS garden Rosemoor, Devon.

A simple summerhouse and stone patio at Stockton Bury Gardens, Herefordshire.

This summerhouse at Angel Gardens, Shropshire has an attractive decking patio hanging over the lake.

This raised corner patio at Hoghton Tower, Lancashire, is enclosed by brick walls and archways for shelter and privacy.

7 Hardscaping and Decorative Effects

Paths

Grass paths should be eliminated from gardens wherever possible, in the same way as lawns. They are slippery in winter and dry out in summer. Functional paths are preferable in water-wise gardens, providing all-weather surfaces, cool root runs for plants, and minimizing water evaporation.

Paths add shape and form, giving access to different areas, but do not necessarily have to form a direct line. Although most have utilitarian purposes, they become attractive and decorative features in their own right. Straight paths fit well with formal schemes, while winding paths create a more relaxed, informal feel. Paths open up vistas, or wind out of sight, encouraging exploration. Paths draw the eye along, so site a focal point such as a bench, statue or tree that provides a visual pause when the eye alights on it. If slightly hidden, these retain an element of surprise when they suddenly appear as you round a corner. However, do not include too many different 'features' or the eye gets distracted rather than drawn.

In general, paths should be wide enough for two people to walk along side by side, or to get a wheelbarrow or mower down. As plants fall over paths, their accessibility is narrowed, so bear this in mind when deciding the width of the path. Above all, paths must be safe and convenient.

As well as helping reduce the lawn area, mowing is simplified when hard paths are placed between flower borders and lawn, also protecting overhanging plants from damage. If the path is fractionally lower than the lawn, mowers cut across, eliminating the need for edge trimming. Paths can meander across the lawn, or be set as 'stepping stones' into the grass.

OPPOSITE AND RIGHT: Paths can be formal or informal, as these brick paths show at RHS garden Rosemoor, Devon.

Check whether existing paths in the garden will fit with your new design or whether you need to create new paths. Some paths will, of necessity, get more wear than others, so choose materials accordingly. Heavy-duty paths and drives require proper excavation and solid foundations for durability and safety. Guard against cracking, rocking or protruding slabs and stones that might cause a hazard. Excavate, level and roll the area firm, removing material that might make finished surfaces uneven. Lay hardcore and top with sand before applying the appropriate finish.

The long borders at Stockton Bury Gardens, Herefordshire, are edged with a slabbed path, protecting plants from the mower.

Stepping stones meander through the lawn at Preen Manor, Shropshire, ensuring feet keep dry after rain.

Paving Materials

Endless supplies of paving materials are available, and materials can be mixed to create different textures and add interest: bricks or tiles with cobbles; concrete paving slabs, too utilitarian on their own, look effective mixed with cobbles or bricks; round slabs act as 'stepping stones' through chippings; railway sleepers can be bedded into gravel. Add firmly fixed, decorative edgings of bricks, tiles, slates or wooden

battens, checking heights with a spirit level. Plan detailed designs on paper and work out types and quantities of materials required.

Aggregates

Gravel, shingle and pebbles make excellent informal paths. Loose materials need excavating to a depth of at least 15cm and require retaining edges to stop them

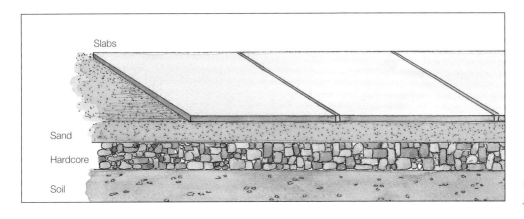

Cross-section showing foundations for a basic path.

spreading into surrounding areas. Battens held in place with wooden pegs are ideal.

Paving Slabs

Ordinary flagstones look dull and uninspiring, but are cheap. They give a better finish when mixed with other materials. Numerous shapes, styles and colours of paving stones are available in both natural stone and pre-cast slabs, suitable for every design. Check colours fit the overall scheme and, unless the garden is very large, keep a continuity of colour, style and materials. Slabs can be set into sand, mortar or concrete and have joints cemented to stop weeds. Leave occasional spaces if you want to introduce plants.

Crazy Paving

Crazy paving is cheaper still, but the broken paving slab variety can be unattractive. Alternative forms of broken, natural, or man-made slabs are also available. Set stones into concrete on good foundations, leaving spaces for plants if necessary. Clearly define path edges and set these stones first. For a safe path, ensure paving

is level by inserting height markers along the edges of the path and checking intervening stones with a straight edge, resting on top of the markers.

Pavers and Setts

These come in a range of colours, shapes and sizes, made from concrete, clay or reconstituted stone and can be laid in a variety of patterns. Interlocking pavers do not require mortar. Set top and side boundaries first, with concrete or mortar where necessary, checking height with a spirit level. Fill intervening areas with a 5cm layer of sharp sand, level and firm. Take small sections, roughly 1.5–2m across, and lay pavers into chosen designs. Make sure they sit securely together and against the boundary. Firm with a wooden batten and club hammer. Finally brush sand between the joints and firm again. Setts are excellent for smaller areas and simple to lay into curved designs.

Bricks

Bricks can create all manner of patterns and can also be mixed with other materials to form attractive and

Large stone chippings.

Cut stone slabs.

Crazy paving at Tapeley Park, Devon.

Stone sets create interest in an otherwise bare expanse of concrete at RHS garden Rosemoor, Devon.

A good, all weather surface on this shingle path between long herbaceous borders at Dunrobin Castle, Sutherland.

hard-wearing surfaces. Weathered bricks are preferable, but must be in good condition and frost durable. Achieve continuity by using the same bricks for paving and walls. Make sure cross-joints are not continuous, whatever the pattern.

Tiles

Old and modern tiles come in attractive shades, while glazed, coloured tiles add a very Mediterranean feel. Tiles must be frost and waterproof. Whole areas can be tiled or tiles can be included with other materials for decorative effects. To lay, take small sections at a time and set in concrete, sealing with suitable adhesive when dry.

Concrete

Although this looks uncompromising, it provides long-lasting surfaces that can be softened with plants. A minimum excavated depth of 25cm is required, with a base of hardcore, topped with a concrete mixture of one part cement, two parts sand and four parts small aggregate, mixed well together. Fix boards to act as moulds before pouring the mixture. Ridged or patterned effects can be drawn into the path before the mixture sets firm, or the path can be brushed just before it sets, to reveal some of the aggregate.

Pebbles and Cobbles

Many interesting and highly intricate designs can be created with pebble mosaics, another Mediterranean technique. Use stones of contrasting tones and sizes,

Old tiles can be set flat or on end, as here at RHS garden Hyde Hall, Essex.

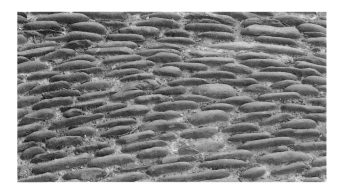

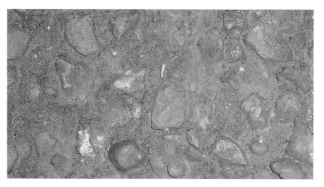

This concrete path has been brushed back before completely set to reveal the aggregate.

Cobbles and pebbles can be set naturally (TOP), or woven into intricate designs like this one at Brook Cottage, Oxfordshire (BOTTOM).

laid flat or on end. Children enjoy creating their own designs, but some supervision is probably advisable! Plan designs on paper first.

Wood

Wooden surfaces provide natural finishes for informal gardens. Cut logs set into the ground, wooden decking, or railway sleepers can be used with other materials. Even when treated, wood perishes more quickly than stone, and can become slippery when wet.

Railway sleepers form a substantial path, but wood can become slippery when wet.

101

Bark looks particularly attractive in a woodland setting, as here at the Beth Chatto Gardens, Essex.

Mixed materials at Stockton Bury Gardens, Herefordshire.

Bark

Mulching bark also supplies good surfaces for paths, especially in natural gardens. It makes useful ground cover for children's play areas, is soft to walk on, but needs replacing regularly, probably only lasting for one, or at most, two seasons.

Sand and Shale

These form good, level paths, but small particles can stick to shoes, especially when the path is wet.

Sand and shale make serviceable paths, but they can be a problem when wet.

Mixed Materials

Achieve interesting effects by mixing two or three materials together. Large square or circular slabs can act as 'stepping stones' through pea gravel; chequered effects can be obtained by using slabs as retaining edges for gravel in alternate squares; gravel and cobbles mix well, easily adapting to curves; open patterns of setts can form boundaries for infilling with small stones.

Weed Control

Weeds can be a problem unless materials are set into cement and joints firmly sealed. Weeds are easily removed from gravel. Hand weeding is time consuming but necessary, unless you resort to chemical weedkillers. Moss build-up can be cleared with a stiff brush or proprietary moss remover. Make sure weedkillers cannot drift into surrounding areas, and keep separate and clearly marked cans or sprays for weedkillers alone.

Plants

Plants look extremely attractive and natural, spreading amongst paving, softening large expanses of stonework and hard edges, while stones keep roots cool and limit evaporation. Add occasional taller plants for interest.

ABOVE AND BELOW: *Create numerous interesting effects with mixed materials.*

ABOVE: *A woodland path at RHS garden Hyde Hall, Essex.*

BELOW: *Plants grow happily through paving, Mawley Hall, Shropshire.*

A Collection of Paths

Stone slabs at Preen Manor, Shropshire.

Bricks in a Shropshire garden.

Lavender path at a garden in Ludlow, Shropshire.

Reconstituted stone slabs in a Shropshire garden.

A simple cobble pattern at Tapeley Park, Devon.

An intricate pebble mosaic in Instow, Devon.

A rock path in Shropshire.

Stone slabs set into grass at Long Cross Gardens, Cornwall.

An aggregate path at Angel Gardens, Shropshire.

Pebble mixture in Shropshire.

Plants for Paving

Erigeron karvinskianus.

Erigeron alpinus. 25cm. Clump-forming perennial with hairy, oval leaves and yellow-centred, mauve flowers in summer.

Erigeron karvinskianus. 10–15cm. Spreading perennial with lance-shaped leaves and small, daisy-like flowers fading from white to deep pink, in summer and autumn.

Helianthemum 'Ben Ledi'. 23cm. Compact evergreen shrub with narrow leaves and bright rose-coloured flowers in summer. *H.* 'Ben Phada'. 23cm. Grey-green leaves and yellow flowers with orange centres.

Iberis saxatilis. 15cm. Evergreen, dark green leaves and clusters of tiny white flowers in summer.

Morisia monanthos syn. *M. hypogaea*. 2.5cm. Low-growing perennial with leathery, dark-green leaves and deep yellow flowers in early summer.

Saponaria × *oliviana*. 8cm. Sprawling perennial with narrow grey-green leaves and single, pale pink flowers in summer.

Thymus serpyllum. Dwarf spreading thyme with grey-green foliage and numerous tiny pink flowers. Many cultivars.

Arabis alpina **subs.** *caucasica* (syn. *A. caucasica*). 15cm. Evergreen perennial with grey-green leaves and white flowers in early summer.

Aubrieta deltoidea '**Argenteo-variegata**'. 5cm. Evergreen trailing perennial with cream and green variegated leaves and pink flowers in spring.

Campanula carpatica. 15cm. Perennial with oval, toothed leaves and bell-shaped blue, purple or white flowers in summer and autumn.

Helianthemum 'Ben Ledi'.

Saponaria × oliviana.

Steps

Wherever levels are raised or lowered, steps or ramps are necessary if slopes are more than gentle inclines. On small gradients, one or two steps might suffice throughout the whole garden. However, on steeply sloping sites, terraces and steps form major parts of the structure. Make sure steps are not so steep they become dangerous.

Steps can be purely functional or highly decorative, straight, semicircular, curved, square, rectangular, wide, narrow, steep or shallow. They can be left in their natural state, painted or set with decorative patterns in bricks or pebbles. Construction follows the same rules as the preparation and construction of paths and patios, and steps must be securely keyed in to abutting walls. Treads should be wide enough to stand on easily, and risers should not be too steep or too shallow.

Simple steps are achieved by piling blocks of wood or stone on top of one another. Railway sleepers, used full length or suitably cut to size, stack beautifully and can be immovably fixed with wooden pegs, knocked firmly into the ground. Bricks must be weatherproof and measurements calculated carefully, so bricks do not require constant cutting to fit.

Whatever your design or materials, steps must be safe, firm, and non-slippery – you may need to add a hand rail if necessary.

Wide steps can be flanked with arrangements of pot plants, or have occasional plants inserted between the risers. Small, single trees in pots, statues or garden vases can fit on either side, top and bottom, providing they do not overcrowd the appearance.

Stone and slate steps at RHS garden Rosemoor, Devon.

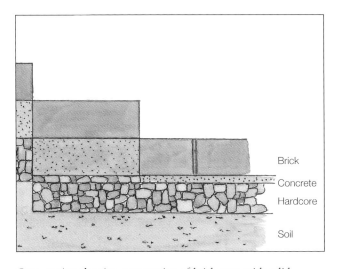

Cross-section showing construction of brick steps with solid foundations.

Brick
Concrete
Hardcore
Soil

Well-designed brick steps at Preen Manor, Shropshire.

Ideas for Steps

Semicircular bricks.

Well-angled paving slabs and stone at Stockton Bury Garden, Herefordshire.

Mixed materials at Preen Manor, Shropshire.

Wood and gravel at Leeds Castle, Kent.

Brick steps with plants, Shropshire.

Steps with pots of Mediterranean plants at the Beth Chatto Gardens, Essex.

Woodland steps with wooden risers at Bide-a-Wee Cottage, Northumberland.

Tiles in Gloucester.

Wood and gravel at RHS garden Rosemoor, Devon.

Slate and cobbles, Cornwall.

109

Terraces

Gardening on steeply sloping sites is difficult and challenging, especially when torrential rains constantly wash soil and nutrients down the slope. Thousands of years ago Mediterranean countries developed terracing techniques to manage such difficult areas. Each terrace was manually dug into virgin hillside, moving rocks to build up retaining walls. Those days are long gone and now serious terracing is usually undertaken with mechanical equipment that shifts as much earth in an hour as it would have taken to move in a day before. Good topsoil can be saved on one side for refilling terraces later.

Plan exactly where each terrace will be, then divide the site into 'steps', working down the slope. The width of each terrace is determined by the gradient. Very steep sites require narrower terraces, while gentle gradients can have wider, shallower sections.

Each terrace must have strong retaining walls of stone, brick, wood or railway sleepers, although, as always, ensure materials are in keeping. It is of paramount importance that retaining walls are strong enough to support the weight of the material held inside them. Walls require solid foundations and should slope slightly inwards. Drainage pipes, inserted periodically along the base of each section, allow excess water to seep away. Ideally walls should be around 1–1.25m high. At this height dry-stone walling is sufficient to support the weight of the soil. With practice, this form of construction produces satisfying results. Anything higher and stones must be mortared together. After terraces are excavated and walls built, add a layer of drainage material before refilling with topsoil and compost. On heavy clay, work fine gravel into topsoil for good drainage.

Terraces provide level beds and also offer plants extra protection. Parallel paths between terraces give excellent views of the beds, while trailing plants tumble over walls and grow from crevices.

An occasional seat can be incorporated into the terrace wall and finished along the top with stone, wood, or creeping plants such as thyme or chamomile for a soft, scented place to rest. Steps running between terraces can also be softened by plants. Again safety is important, so consider fitting handrails. Steps need not lead straight down the site, they can zig-zag sideways against each terrace, leading to the path below.

Where gradients are not too steep, sections can be divided with sloping banks. Traditionally these would be lawn, although mowing sloping banks can be time consuming, difficult and dangerous. Ground cover plants that require little maintenance are better options. *Hypericum, Helianthemum, Cotoneaster* and horizontal Junipers are all well suited to the water-wise garden.

Drainage

One benefit northerly climes have over Mediterranean regions, as far as plants are concerned, is reasonably regular rain. We sometimes go for weeks without but, inevitably, before long the rain returns. Water-wise gardens, with drought tolerant Mediterranean plants, flourish without regular or additional water, but suffer

Ancient terracing on a Mediterranean hillside.

when rain is held at plant roots for long periods, particularly in cold, winter months. Good drainage is the answer. Adding drainage materials such as broken shards, sand, grit and ash helps lighten soils, as does regular application of organic compost and organic mulches, which are slowly incorporated and improve soil condition. Top-dressing beds with gravel also protects plants rotting from water lying around their crowns.

Raised Beds and Planted Walls

These give outstanding opportunities for creating well-drained sites. Incorporate drainage materials when building the beds and walls by adding hardcore across the bases, topped with gravel and finished with a good depth of friable compost. Mediterranean plants love this free-draining environment. Raised beds can begin at around 20cm and accommodate plants of varying heights, from low-growing, creeping perennials and small bulbs to taller species. They are convenient for both the elderly and disabled, bringing plants to a convenient height for working or viewing without bending. Beds can be formal or informal, have a top-dressing of gravel or other attractive mulch, and incorporate a few larger boulders or other decorative features. If retaining walls have a smooth top they are convenient for sitting on.

Walls are better suited to low-growing, creeping plants. Double cavity walls filled with drainage

A terrace garden in course of construction on a steeply sloping hillside in Shropshire. The first layer is retained by a substantial brick wall or concrete wall. The second layer, with railway sleepers, is firmly fixed with wooden posts.

material and compost are ideal for plants growing along the top. A dressing of gravel chippings makes an attractive finish. Plants can be inserted into walls to cascade down the sides, while stonecrops, *Sedum* and *Sempervivum* are particularly suited to growing between the stones.

Stone or brick are obvious choices for walls and raised beds, but timber or railway sleepers also make strong retaining walls. Whatever the material, it must withstand the weight of the filling.

Extensively terraced gardens, filled with tender plants, overlooking Morecambe Bay, Lancashire. (Photo courtesy of Val Corbet)

Plants for Raised Beds

Convolvulus sabatius.

Francoa sonchifolium.

Convolvulus sabatius, syn. *C. mauritanicus*. 20cm. Perennial with trailing stems, oval leaves and small, purple-blue, trumpet-shaped flowers in summer.

Draba aizoides, **yellow whitlow grass**. 2.5cm. Mat-forming, semi-evergreen perennial with rosettes of bristled, lance-shaped leaves and four-petalled yellow flowers in spring.

Francoa sonchifolia. 75cm. Perennial with lobed leaves and racemes of small pink, red-marked flowers in summer and early autumn.

Genista sagittalis, 8cm. Deciduous, low shrub with winged stems, pea-like, bright yellow flowers in early summer, followed by hairy seedpods.

Geranium clarkei, **'Kashmir White'**. Syn *G. pratense*. 60cm. Rhizomatous perennial with deeply divided leaves and cup-shaped white flowers with pink veins, lasting over a long period in summer.

Nepeta grandiflora. 40–80cm. Aromatic perennial with grey-green foliage and clustered spikes of violet-blue flowers.

Origanum **'Kent Beauty'**. 20cm. Trailing perennial with small, aromatic leaves and short spikes of pink, tubular flowers in summer.

Sempervivum arachnoideum, **cobweb houseleek**. 12cm. Rosettes of evergreen, oval, pale green leaves, flushed red, smothered with cobweb-like hairs. Star-shaped rose-coloured flowers in summer.

Tanacetum densum, subsp. *Amani*. 20cm. Clump-forming perennial with fern-like, grey, hairy leaves and yellow, daisy-like flowers with woolly bracts.

Thymus × *citriodorus* **'Aureus'**. 10cm. Small, oval, evergreen, golden leaves and clusters of tiny, lilac flowers in summer. **'Silver Queen'**, variegated cream or silver leaves.

Geranium clarkei.

Raised beds give an excellent opportunity for creating well-drained sites for drought tolerant plants. Angel Gardens, Shropshire.

This immaculately constructed wall at RHS garden Rosemoor, Devon, is filled with plants that enjoy such a well-drained environment.

Water

The cooling sight and sound of water is an integral part of many Mediterranean gardens. Originally, irrigation channels developed into highly sophisticated pools and reservoirs, which became important aspects in decorative gardens such as those found at the Alhambra in Granada (Spain), the Villa Lante, near Viterbo (Italy), and the Château de Versailles, outside Paris.

Space can be found in the smallest garden for a simple water feature, frothing over pebbles, trickling into a carved basin, or creating formal or natural ponds and fountains.

Pools are another excellent way of reducing lawn area, adding attractive and relaxing elements to the garden, while the sound of water, whether it be of turbulent torrents, tinkling fountains or gentle splashes and drips, enhances the mood. Electrical pumps circulate water, minimizing loss. Solar-powered units are increasingly available, reducing running costs as well as being more ecologically conscious.

Pools can be sunk below ground or raised inside brick or stone walls. Pre-cast shapes are set into suitably excavated holes. Plastic and butyl liners are not as durable, but are effective. Ground must be well prepared and lined, ensuring nothing can pierce the liner. Edges of liners and pre-cast pools are concealed with stones and plants. Sophisticated pools can be created with concrete-lined structures and decorative tiles reminiscent of Mediterranean courtyards. One unforgettable pool in Spain was faced with grey slate that reflected light, making the water look like a sheet of pure silver. In water-wise gardens, low, bubbling water is preferable, as higher, spraying water is quickly lost from evaporation and drift.

Oxygenating water plants achieve a good balance, keeping pools clean and clear, while water lilies, iris, *Zantedeschia* and marginals add colour to the simplest scheme. Fish create further interest, and water in the garden is invaluable for attracting wildlife.

Designing with Water

A formal canal at a garden in Ludlow, Shropshire.

An exotic-looking pool in an Italian style garden in Shropshire.

A carved stone fountain at a garden in Ludlow, Shropshire.

Water drips from a stone trough into a long, narrow canal on the terrace of Stockton Bury Garden, Herefordshire.

Water gently trickles from this large rock onto a bed of pebbles at RHS garden Rosemoor, Devon.

The pool at Highdown Gardens in Sussex, with water lilies, iris and Zantedeschia.

A simple stone basin amidst plants at Preen Manor, Shropshire.

A sheltered pool with carved mask at Kiftsgate Court, Glos.

And of course – don't forget the fish!

8 Getting it Right

They say that when a duck floats serenely across the surface of a pond, its feet are working nineteen-to-the-dozen beneath the water to keep it afloat. Similarly with gardens, it's what happens underneath that counts. You cannot expect wonderful, healthy looking plants if you ignore important areas such as soil quality and drainage.

In their natural environment Mediterranean plants survive with little or no water. Rain that does fall quickly soaks away through parched stones and rock. More northerly climes have higher rainfall, therefore in these areas Mediterranean plants must have excellent drainage to ensure cold water is not held against the roots for long periods of time, causing roots to rot and wither away.

We generally over-water rather than under-water, killing thousands of plants each year, both indoors and out. Surrounded by constant water, roots are unable to breathe and literally drown. Over-watered plants are shallow rooting, and fail to send roots deeply into the ground to find their own sources of water. In turn, this makes them susceptible to wind damage.

Soil

Over millions of years, soil has formed from mixtures of weathered rocks, inorganic and organic materials. It has been eroded away by rain, ice, frost and wind, and built up again. It is a complex substance that also contains living organisms such as earthworms and microscopic bacteria, which all have an effect on its final composition. Base rocks determine soil type. Old

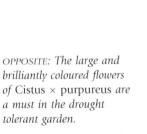

OPPOSITE: *The large and brilliantly coloured flowers of* Cistus × purpureus *are a must in the drought tolerant garden.*

RIGHT: *This dry and arid landscape of parched earth and rocks is typical of Mediterranean regions in summer.*

igneous rocks such as granite are generally acidic, while sedimentary chalk and limestone are alkaline. The top 30cm or so of soil is usually better than underlying levels, having been enriched with decaying plant material and the action of earthworms. Humus slowly builds up from the constant breaking down and regeneration of organic matter, supplying nutrients for plant growth. It adds bulk and increases water retention on sandy soils, giving a more open texture that aids drainage on clay. Increasing the quality of humus improves the overall quality of the soil.

It is not necessary here to go into lengthy discussions about the merits of different chemical compositions, but testing kits are readily available for detailed analysis of your garden soil. In general, the plants you are able to grow indicate the type of soil you have. Most gardeners experiment, often with good results, and it is possible to arrange soil in different parts of the garden to accommodate different types of plants. It simply depends how far you wish to go to achieve the results you want.

Soil quality dictates whether ground is well drained or water retentive. Few of us are lucky enough to have good quality, rich, free-draining loam – happily though, Mediterranean plants flourish in poorer soils. In fact, if too well watered or fertilized they lose their natural characteristics and become fleshy, leaving them susceptible to wind damage and drought. Exactly the thing we are trying to avoid!

Sandy soils are free-draining, quick to dry out in summer and generally lack sufficient nutrients. Gravel and chalk usually have little depth, leaving them unable to hold water. Peaty soils often have little body. Heavy clay soils hold water rather than allowing it to drain away, meaning ground is wet and cold in winter, slow to warm up in spring, and solid in summer. Mediterranean plants prefer well-drained soil that is not too heavy, rich or over-fertilized.

Compost

One of the best ways of improving soil quality is by adding compost. All gardens should have a compost heap, however small. A two-bin system is preferable, where one side breaks down as the other builds up with new composting material. Some local councils supply discounted composting bins, which are a boon to smaller gardens. They look neat and can be slipped into the smallest corner.

Where space allows, it is a simple matter to construct two adjacent 'bins'. Wooden planks, corrugated iron or small mesh wire netting, held between stakes firmly embedded into the ground, are ideal. If three sides are firmly fixed, the fourth can have a double stake on each front edge, to slide in a wood or metal sheet that can be raised or lowered as necessary. Ideally each 'bin' should measure about 1.5m high and be 1.1m to 1.5m wide. If possible, site heaps where they are sheltered from drying winds, which exacerbate heat loss.

Composting materials are good mixes of organic kitchen waste (not bread, cheese or meat, which attract vermin), annual weeds, soft plant material, leaves, grass cuttings, straw, wood ash, and remnants of spent compost from pots. Exclude diseased materials, rose cuttings, brassica waste, perennial weeds such as couch grass, bindweed and celandine, thick layers of grass cuttings, woody refuse, paper or chemically treated materials. Woody material can, however, be shredded and then added to the compost heap.

Build up layers of composting materials and, when the bin is full, cover with an old piece of carpet or heavy duty plastic. It takes about six to twelve months to rot down. There is generally enough residual soil on weeds, but if not sprinkle garden soil on each 25cm layer. Alternate with a sprinkling of chalk to help prevent acidity, which slows down the

Types of soil: (LEFT TO RIGHT) peat; sand; clay.

Building compost heap structures: (LEFT) Basic post and retaining structure; (RIGHT) Well-made wooden box construction, here utilizing waiting compost for growing marrows.

Manufactured plastic composting bin.

Leaves can be raked up and mixed in with the general compost heap or form a heap on their own.

composting process. Turning the heap every few weeks speeds up the process, but is not necessary if you have patience.

When compost heaps are 'working', they generate considerable internal heat, and after a period of time produce a crumbly, black, pleasant-smelling mixture, full of earthworms. Plants love it! When one side of the bin is ready, move the top layer of unrotted material into the second bin, until you reach the compost ready for use. In Mediterranean countries compost requires additional water to help the process, but this is not necessary in cooler countries with sufficient rain.

Farmyard and poultry manure can be used to enrich soil; if already well rotted, it can be dug straight into the soil, but fresher manure should first be composted by adding it in layers to the compost heap. Mediterranean plants do not require rich soil, but other plants appreciate the stronger compost created by the inclusion of manure.

Compost can also be made entirely from fallen leaves. They should be spread into layers interspersed with a good sprinkling of soil. If very dry, a little water should be added to keep the heap moist as you go along. Finish with a final dressing of soil so that leaves do not blow away. Although these heaps take longer to rot down, they have the advantage of containing few weed seeds. When compost heats up some, but not all, weed seeds are killed. Weeds in compost,

Turn this (LEFT) into this (RIGHT)! Regular applications of compost and fine drainage materials can turn heavy clay into soil any gardener would be proud of.

however, are generally annual weeds and can be simply hoed off the ground to go back into the next heap.

Spread compost on heavy soils before winter digging, when the action of weather helps break up the ground. Apply to lighter soils in spring or early summer, and lightly fork in. Compost can be used on its own, or mixed with commercial potting mediums for pots and containers.

Providing your own good, organic compost is a simple and rewarding method of improving soil quality and supplying plants with plenty of nutrients. Chemical additives should be used sparingly, if at all, since purely organic approaches to gardening are by far the best.

Peat

The commercial supply of peat is leading to dangerous levels of erosion in natural peat bogs, which is seriously threatening valuable habitats. We should conserve peat and not use it in our gardens. When peat dries out, it is extremely difficult to get it to retain water again, meaning it is not well suited to Mediterranean gardening. Many commercially produced, peat-free composts are free draining, but can also dry out quickly. Using home made compost is therefore a preferable alternative to commercially produced peat or even peat-free composts.

Lime

Heavy clay soils benefit from applications of lime, which helps to aerate the soil and neutralize acidity.

Hydrated lime improves soil condition, helps break up heavy clay and binds a sandy soil together.

Drainage materials

In their natural environment Mediterranean plants survive in a few centimetres of poor, sun-baked earth. In cooler climates, the advantage of free draining soils is that they ensure water does not lie around plant roots for lengthy periods of time. In areas of heavy clay, compost improves soil condition, but digging in sharp sand or fine gravel also benefits drainage. It might take a few years before clay soils show any noticeable improvement from all this hard work, but it is worth persevering. If soil is particularly heavy and new beds are not too large, remove topsoil, break up the wet clay beneath, and add broken brick, pot shards, ash, gravel, sharp sand, crushed pumice or lava rock (scoria). Mix topsoil with grit and lots of organic compost before spreading back onto the bed. In the worst areas, dig out drainage channels and fill with broken rubble before replacing topsoil.

Mulch

Mulches are made from various organic or inorganic materials, spread across the top of well-weeded, moist soil. They are highly important in drought tolerant gardens as they prevent water evaporation, and protect the soil from erosion, drying winds and sun. In addition to keeping roots cool and moist, they also limit weed growth, which not only saves labour but leaves more water for the plants you had intended growing.

Mulches must allow air through but retain moisture. Organic mulches of around 10cm deep last for a good year or two, gradually being incorporated into the soil and helping to condition it. Inorganic mulches such as pebbles or chippings are attractive and last longer than organic mulches, but do not supply nutrients. They also cost more.

Apply mulches from mid-May to late June, when ground is moist, free from weeds and has had a chance to warm up after winter frosts. Mulches can be varied around the garden depending on availability, appearance and plant requirements. They should be tucked carefully around plants so they do not smother them, and be disturbed as little as possible after laying. When planting or weeding, make sure mulches are pushed back across areas of bare earth. Birds also enjoy rifling through mulches, looking for worms and insects, so again check periodically that there are no bare patches.

Organic Mulches

COCOA SHELLS

Generally need replacing each year as they are slowly incorporated into the soil, but they are efficient, especially if you like your garden to smell of chocolate in the heat! Watering immediately after laying helps settle small particles.

BARK

Between 5 and 10cm of shredded bark provides an effective and attractive mulch. Weeds are easily removed, but make sure bare patches are covered with mulch again so other weeds cannot establish. A thick layer of bark lasts between one and three years, but quality varies. It is advisable to spread both shredded bark and cocoa shells in areas with retaining edges in order to stop them spreading into adjacent areas.

MUSHROOM COMPOST

Good when available, but contains lime so is unsuitable for acid-loving plants and chalky soils.

STRAW

Bales are cheap to buy for breaking and spreading in thick layers beneath plants. Straw can look unsightly, especially when new, but weathered straw is excellent. Straw works well beneath trees and shrubs where foliage hides most of the surface.

SEAWEED

Near the coast, seaweed makes good, economical mulches and soil conditioners. Wash well before applying to reduce salt content, and then spread in thick layers, or compost.

SPENT HOPS

Available in hop- or beer-producing areas, but can smell strong. Good if you do not mind your garden smelling of beer!

STABLE MANURE

Farmyard manure should be part decayed, with a good straw content, otherwise it compacts down, becoming too solid and caustic for plants.

NEWSPAPER, CARPET

Generally unattractive mulches but they can be used. Carpet eventually rots, and newspaper makes a short-term mulch if wetted and laid several sheets thick.

ABOVE: *Bark mulch. A good mulch of bark at the Beth Chatto Gardens, Essex.*

RIGHT: *Straw mulch. This works well where leaves will conceal its rather untidy appearance.*

GRASS CUTTINGS

Mown grass cuttings can be used, but are better composted first. Too thick a layer of cuttings on their own results in plants suffocating in a slimy, green mess. Make sure grass has not been chemically treated before using.

LEAVES AND PINE NEEDLES

Large undecayed leaves should be avoided as they compact, excluding air. Pine needles should be treated cautiously as the resin can be harmful to plants.

WOOD

Small logs or branches make unusual but attractive mulches that also create havens for insects. Wood should be placed close together or overlapped to stop weeds growing through.

Inorganic Mulches

GRAVEL, PEBBLES AND BOULDERS

Come in a range of natural colours, grades and shapes that make attractive, long-lasting mulches, showing plants off to advantage. More expensive than organic mulches, they last longer, but do not add nutrients to the soil. Lay to around 5cm.

SHEETING

Effective for covering large areas but, unless top-dressed with gravel or bark, looks unsightly. Sheet mulches such as black polythene are cheap and suppress weed growth, but do not allow air or rain penetration, while adding compost to the soil becomes almost impossible. Before laying sheet mulches fork masses of compost into the soil and make sure the ground is moist. Black polythene should be 150 gauge and sheets should be laid in strips no wider than 40 to

ABOVE: *Carpet mulch. Generally makes an unattractive, if useful, mulch.*

LEFT: *Wood mulch. An unusual, attractive and ecologically friendly mulch of old branches beneath trees at Bryan's Ground, Herefordshire. (Photo courtesy of Sue Graham)*

Gravel mulch. Plants happily grow in free-draining gravel mulches, as here at RHS garden Rosemoor, Devon.

Stone mulch. Larger stones can look effective but will allow weed penetration. Placing stones on top of gravel would help solve the problem.

60cm, so some rainwater run-off will seep into the ground.

Polypropylene is porous, long lasting and hard wearing, but expensive. Bonded fibre fleeces are long lasting and allow moisture through. All sheet mulches should be pegged firmly to the ground. Plants are placed into the soil through crosswise slits cut into the material, folded open for planting and then moved back around the plant to prevent weed growth.

Sheet mulches are excellent in vegetable gardens, where appearance is not quite so important. They help retain moisture in the soil and effectively suppress weeds.

Wind

Wind is another element creating problems for plants and gardens, but it can be counteracted with judicious placing of windbreaks. Walls are too solid, creating turbulence as wind blows across and down them. Hedges and trees are preferable, especially evergreens, as they filter wind through. Buildings raise temperatures around them by some degrees, which makes these areas excellent locations for growing less hardy plants. But some town gardens, protected by taller houses, are extremely vulnerable to wind currents funneling around buildings and down passageways. Seaside gardens do not generally suffer such severe

Sheet mulch. Sheet mulches are unattractive but a good choice in the vegetable garden, where appearance may not be quite so important.

Plants for Windbreaks

Berberis darwinii. 2m. Evergreen shrub with small, glossy leaves and clusters of rounded orange flowers from mid-late spring, followed by blue berries.

Elaeagnus × *ebbingei* **'Gilt Edge'**. 4m. Evergreen shrub with glossy, grey-green leaves marked with yellow and insignificant yellow flowers in summer and autumn.

Ilex aquifolium, **holly**. 20m. Evergreen shrub or tree with grey bark and spiny-edged, glossy green leaves. Tiny, pink-tinged, white flowers are followed by red or yellow berries in winter. Prune back to check growth.

Ligustrum ovalifolium, **Californian privet**. 4m. Oval, glossy leaves and panicles of small, white, tubular flowers from early to mid-summer, followed by small, black fruits.

Prunus lusitanica, **Portuguese laurel**. 6–10m. Dense, evergreen shrub with oval, glossy green leaves and long spikes of tiny, fragrant white flowers in early summer, followed by purple fruits. Prune to check growth.

Rhododendron ponticum. 8m. Evergreen shrub with dark green leaves and lilac-purple flowers in spring.

Salix caprea, **pussy willow**. Yellow-brown twigs, grey-green leaves and conspicuous grey catkins with golden anthers in spring.

Taxus baccata, **yew**. Red-brown bark and narrow, shiny dark green leaves. Slow growing.

Thamnocalamus spathaceus, **umbrella bamboo**. 4m. Evergreen, clumping bamboo with broad, apple-green leaves, grey culms and light brown sheaths.

Viburnum tinus, **laurustinus**. Evergreen with oval, dark green leaves, pink buds and small, star-shaped, white flowers in winter and spring.

Elaeagnus × ebbingei *'Gilt Edge'*.

Prunus lusitanica, *Portuguese laurel*.

Ilex aquifolium, *holly*.

At Long Cross Garden, Cornwall, the judicious use of trees and hedges acting as windbreaks has created numerous sheltered pockets for plants.

frosts as inland gardens, making the growing of tender species simpler, but they are often tormented by strong, salt-laden winds that scorch and kill new growth. Well-placed windbreaks offer efficient solutions while also providing sheltered pockets for tender plants.

Long Cross, a restored Victorian garden in north Cornwall, thrives in England's most notoriously windy area. Here, winds deposit about 50kg of salt on every acre each year. The garden has made effective use of carefully sited, salt tolerant trees and shrubs for windbreaks. Many plants at Long Cross also have leathery or shiny leaves, affording further protection from salt. Even in severe gales parts of the garden are completely calm, and many frost tender, Mediterranean species grow happily.

Windbreaks are also necessary in exposed hillside gardens inland that do not have the advantage of milder, seaside climates. The creators of a newly developing garden on the high, barren, windswept slopes of Shropshire's Clee Hills have planted windbreaks that will afford plants the necessary protection as they mature.

Dunge Valley Hidden Gardens, high in the

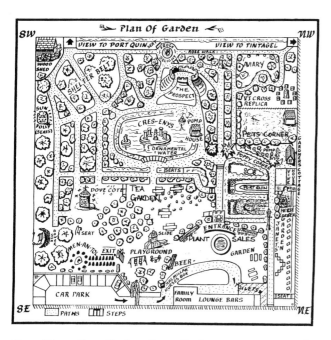

Plan of Long Cross Garden, Cornwall, showing arrangement of windbreaks to shelter plants from heavily salt-laden sea winds. (Reproduced by kind permission of James and Sharon Bishop)

Pennines, even had problems trying to establish windbreaks, given the severe winters experienced in that part of the country. They erected a giant net, 20m wide and 6.5m high, to stop searing winter winds defoliating even the hardiest plants. With this protection, windbreaks finally established themselves and it was possible to remove the net. Here, experience has shown that low growing trees provide the best windbreaks, since roots of taller trees are damaged by continuous wind movement. They support larger trees, such as *Eucalyptus*, by inserting a dry mix of stones, sand and cement around the roots. Now the gardens are filled with rare and tender plants, including many Mediterranean species.

Wind is extremely drying, exacerbating moisture loss from plants and soil. Existing trees indicate the direction of prevailing winds. Shelter belts should be constructed on the windward side of the garden. They provide effective protection to a distance of around ten times the height of the screen and reduced protection to twenty times the height of the screen. When planting, also bear in mind the shadows cast by windbreaks.

Angel Gardens has been recently created high on the windswept slopes of Clee Hill, Shropshire. Newly planted windbreaks of Taxus baccata *are already establishing to form protection for tender and drought tolerant species.*

Salt Tolerant Windbreaks

Atriplex **species**. Greyish white, hoary leaves.

Choisya ternata, **Mexican orange**. 2.5m. Rounded, ever-green shrub with aromatic, leathery foliage and clusters of fragrant white flowers in spring and autumn.

Cupressus macrocarpa, **Monterey cypress**. 20m. Fast growing evergreen with sprays of scale-like, aromatic, green leaves. Brown cones.

Escallonia **'Apple Blossom'**. Evergreen glossy, dark-green leaves and pink flowers from early to midsummer.

Euonymus japonicus. 5m. Evergreen, upright shrub or small tree with shiny, medium-sized leaves, light or dark green or with some variegation depending on variety.

Griselinia littoralis. 6m. Evergreen upright, dense shrub with bright green, oval, leathery leaves and inconspicuous yellow flowers in late spring.

Hippophae rhamnoides, **sea buckthorn**. Silver foliage. Plant both male and female forms to produce bright orange berries.

Pinus nigra maritima, **Corsican pine**. 30m. Fast growing, narrowly conical with grey-green, stiff leaves and yellow-brown cones.

Pinus pinaster, **maritima pine**. Grey-green needles.

Pyracantha × **'Watereri'**, **firethorn**. 3m. Dense, evergreen, spiny shrub with small, dark green, glossy leaves and clusters of small, cup-shaped white flowers in early summer, followed by red berries.

Tamarix gallica. Deciduous tree or shrub with purple new shoots, tiny, blue-grey, scale-like leaves and slender racemes of pink flowers in summer. *T. ramosissima* **'Rosea'**. Slender branches with small, dense leaves and rose-pink flowers. *T. tetrandra*. Light pink flowers.

Choisya ternata.

Pyracantha × Watereri.

Tamarix ramosissima.

9 Mediterranean Gardens in Cool Countries

Mediterranean countries cradled some of the first gardens. Many influential ideas arising from practical planting solutions tried and tested in these gardens subsequently spread across the world. Mediterranean plants, gardens and practices are now common around the globe, in hot climates as well as cooler, more northerly latitudes such as Austria, Denmark, northern France, Germany, Sweden and Switzerland.

In Germany, large numbers of Mediterranean plants are grown at Westpark, Munich, in conservation-conscious borders. Palmengarten Botanical Gardens, Frankfurt am Main, has gravel beds filled with drought tolerant plants, and a special Mediterranean species section. Switzerland's Gartenwerke Nursery stocks Mediterranean climate species, listing plants' frost tolerance levels, including amongst many others: St Bernard's lily, *Anthericum liliago*; *Ballota pseudo-dictamnus*; numerous *Cistus*, *Eryngium*, *Kniphofia*, *Lavandula* and *Salvia* species; *Olearia* × *haastii*; *Pistacia lentiscus*; and *Thalictrum flavum ssp. glaucum*. Nurseries world-wide offer plants, advice and information, as new Mediterranean gardens appear everywhere.

Western parts of Britain usually have milder winters, while temperatures are generally a little lower on the eastern side. But Mediterranean gardens can be found in most counties – even in areas considered far too inhospitable, such as the Yorkshire Moors, the Pennines, Northumberland and the Scottish Highlands. Traffic roundabouts, motorway service areas and gardens around public buildings are planted to follow water-wise rules, as local councils and individuals create low maintenance beds filled with drought tolerant plants, mulched with gravel.

Rainfall in Essex averages 50cm a year, with soil generally an impoverished mix of sand, stones and clay. But Essex has renowned dry gardens, filled with Mediterranean plants. RHS Hyde Hall, Chelmsford, established their outstanding dry garden in 2001. Some 4,000 plants represent about 1,000 drought tolerant species and cultivars in a wonderfully naturalistic setting. Beth Chatto's gravel garden near Colchester has wide, sweeping beds made on the site of a compacted old car park, which are full of colour, even in

OPPOSITE: Colourful collections of Mediterranean plants at Kiftsgate Court, Gloucestershire. Even in cooler climates, stunning effects can be easily created.

RIGHT: This Lavatera olbia *thrives happily in Denmark. (Photo courtesy of Lars Vestergaarde)*

the severest droughts. Cambridge University Botanic Garden's dry garden is designed to illustrate the principles and inform about the benefits of water conservation. None of these gardens received any additional water once established. In Norfolk, East Ruston Old Vicarage, Norwich, has wonderful gardens filled with tender species. Borde Hill, West Sussex, has a specially designed Mediterranean garden as well as an Italian garden and Greek bank.

We expect milder parts of Britain such as Cornwall to support tender plants, but Glendurgan, Falmouth, made headlines when *Agave americana* sent up giant flower spikes in 2004, unusual even for this county. Headland Garden at Polruan has collections of *Agave, Aloe, Cactus, Crassula, Echeveria, Lampranthus, Sedum* and succulents. Lamorran House, St Mawes, an outstanding 'English' Mediterranean garden reminiscent of the great Italian Riviera garden at La Mortola, has Mediterranean plants in an outstanding setting: *Acacia dealbata; Aloe; Citrus; Lagerstroemia indica; Olea europaea; Pistacia lentiscus; Punica granatum; Cordyline,* palms and succulents.

Stockton Bury, Herefordshire, is a superb example of the scores of specialist gardens that grow tender Mediterranean plants. A true plantsman's garden, hundreds of carefully tended, rare and beautiful plants appear at every turn.

Much further north, RHS Harlow Carr, Harrogate, Yorkshire, has countless Mediterranean plants among their collections. *Echium pininana* grow outside at Burton Agnes Hall, Driffield. Sledmere House has Mediterranean borders, while rare Mediterranean plants thrive at Sleightholmedale Lodge, North Yorkshire. We have already mentioned Dunge Valley Hidden Gardens, high in the Pennine peaks, but further north still, in Northumberland, Bide-a-Wee Cottage has tender, drought tolerant species; Chester's Walled Garden, a Mediterranean garden, and Herterton House have many tender, Mediterranean plants.

Travelling into Scotland, Castle Kennedy, Stranraer, grows *Callistemon* species and many Chilean plants, including an avenue of monkey puzzle trees, *Araucaria araucana. Embothrium coccineum,* and the tallest *Pittosporum tenuifolium* in Britain. Inverewe on the west coast benefits from the warmth of the Gulf Stream and is renowned world-wide for its tropical and

Ballota pseudodictamnus: *one of the many Mediterranean plants grown at Gartenwerke Nursery, Switzerland.*

Unusual even for Cornwall, Agave americana *flowers in the National Trust garden at Glendurgan in 2004.*

RHS garden Hyde Hall, Essex, showing a corner of the
outstanding dry garden created in 2001.

Beth Chatto's renowned gravel garden in Essex.

*The plan for the
Mediterranean Garden
at Borde Hill, Sussex,
designed by Robin
Williams. (Reproduced
by kind permission of
Robin Williams and
Associates, and
Andrewjohn and Eleni
Stephenson Clarke,
Borde Hill Gardens)*

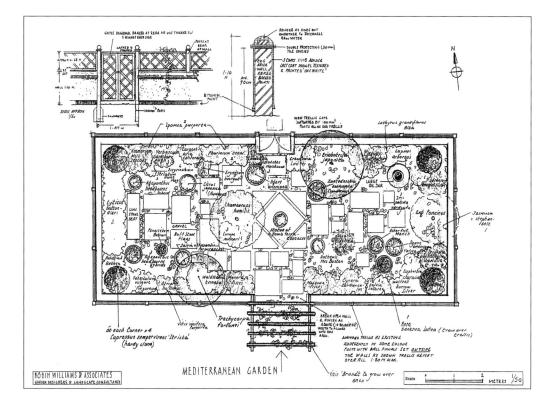

ABOVE: *Warmed by the Gulf Stream, the National Trust garden at Inverewe, on the west coast of Scotland, is a treasure house of tender and drought tolerant plants from around the world, including all the Mediterranean climate regions.*

BELOW: *Grasses and tender species thrive in the borders of Bide-a-Wee Cottage, Northumberland.*

ABOVE: *Stockton Bury Garden, Herefordshire: a wealth of rare and unusual, tender and drought tolerant plants at every turn.*

BELOW: *Colourful Mediterranean borders at the University of Dundee Botanic Garden, Scotland.*

Mediterranean plants. In the east, Dundee Botanic Gardens, Tayside, has well-stocked Mediterranean gardens. Even the Castle Of Mey, perched on the northernmost coast, where gales sweep your feet away, grows many tender species behind protecting walls.

Bodnant Gardens, Wales, has outstanding collections including *Arbutus*, *Cistus*, *Cupressus sempervirens*, *Embothrium*, and numerous tender shrubs, climbers and Mediterranean plants. Further down the coast, Portmeirion has Mediterranean plants and palms. In Northern Ireland, Castle Ward grows *Cordyline*, *Embothrium* and palms amongst its numerous plants; Mount Stewart has *Clianthus*, *Cyclamen*, *Mimosa*, *Phormium* and *Pittosporum*. In the Irish Republic, Earlscliffe has amazing collections of plants from Australia, Chile and South Africa as well as the Mediterranean. Turning to the southernmost areas of the British Isles, the Channel and Scilly Islands are noted for the tender plants that grow there, particularly in the gardens of Tresco Abbey.

Even if you consider you do not have a 'Mediterranean' garden, it is almost certain that many plants you grow originated in Mediterranean climate regions. Now new introductions of tender and exotic species are increasingly available, while garden publications extol the virtues of exotic and drought tolerant gardens. Many of these plants grow well given a little winter protection; some like to be taken indoors during the coldest months. Others, however, happily survive outside for years, with no protection whatsoever.

Embothrium coccineum, Chilean firebush, has adapted to *cooler climates and thrives across Britain.*

For example, we associate citrus trees with Mediterranean regions. Further north, they are planted in large pots, and taken into 'limonaia' during winter. Citrus were considered too tender for more northern latitudes, but were collected as novelties by some large estates, which kept trees in orangeries, placing pots outside in summer. Now citrus trees are readily available everywhere.

Although most overwinter with the protection of a greenhouse or conservatory, for decades some fruiting citrus trees have grown in Britain, outside, in the ground, year round. Numerous London gardens have

The grapefruit tree at Chelsea Physic Garden, London, was grown from a pip. Some years ago, as quite a large tree, it was planted in a sheltered corner of the garden, where it bears edible fruit year after year. (Photo reproduced by kind permission of Chelsea Physic Garden)

Although it does not produce fruit, this pomegranate tree, Punica granatum, *at the University of Dundee Botanic Garden, Scotland, thrives and flowers well outside.*

Olive trees, Olea europaea, *now grow across Britain and some even produce fruit. Chelsea Physic Garden's tree carries a large crop, and this tree at The National Trust garden at Ickworth, Suffolk, also fruits.*

The National Trust Garden at Buscot Park, Oxfordshire, has a walled garden filled with colour in summer, box-edged beds of herbaceous and tender plants, vegetables and fruit trees, while the citrus ring has huge pots of orange and lemon trees.

lemon trees. At Chelsea Physic Garden, a long-established grapefruit tree happily grows outside, bearing edible fruits. They also have a pomegranate tree and a hefty, fruiting olive. Pomegranate trees? In Cornwall possibly, but they happily survive outside in Scotland as well! Bitter orange, *Poncirus trifoliata*, grows in Liverpool. Established olive trees thrive across the country: Ickworth House, Suffolk, has a large fruiting olive; Wales a whole olive orchard!

When Mediterranean climate plants first arrived here, they were cosseted in vast, ornate conservatories. Over time many found their way outside where they thrived. Now gardeners regularly grow tropical and sub-tropical as well as Mediterranean species, and increasing numbers of these exotics also over-winter outside.

The garden at the National Herb Centre, Oxfordshire, has numerous silver and grey-leaved species.

A plant's basic requirements are warmth, food, light and water. Given these, and the correct environment, they grow. We can change certain aspects of our gardens to encourage plants that would not normally flourish: for instance, growing lime-hating plants in chalk and limestone areas, or vice versa, by digging out and replacing soil. Hard work, but it is possible. Mediterranean gardens can be established with minimum effort, and filled with drought tolerant species, saving time, labour and water. The above examples show gardens across the country already do this to great effect.

When designing Mediterranean gardens in cooler climates, we must consider other aspects as well as the plants. Good drainage, shelter, windbreaks, aesthetic appearance and colour are all important. Mediterranean colours are sun-faded, bleached-out blues, greys, greens, honey, terracotta, burnt umbers, earth reds or gleaming white. (Iron oxide incorporated into cement creates faded earth tones and many natural coloured paints are available).

A garden does not have to be permanently green to be attractive. Numerous Mediterranean plants come in shades of silver-grey and blue-green. Many are evergreen, but also bear flowers and berries, for year round colour and interest. Evergreens are essential for lush colour and cover in the winter garden.

Mediterranean shrubs are often mound forming, so plants that can be clipped to imitate this are useful: for example buckthorn, *Rhamnus alaternus*; box, *Buxus sempervirens*; common privet, *Ligustrum vulgare*; *Santolina pinnata*; and yew, *Taxus baccata*. Species from other climate regions such as Australia, California, Chile and South Africa are also readily available.

We must also consider the garden's aspect, nearby buildings, climatic conditions, soil, views (or lack of them), balance, scale and proportion.

Evergreens and grey and silver-leaved species of drought tolerant plants provide colour throughout the year, as shown here in the dry garden at RHS garden Hyde Hall, Essex.

Winter colour is provided by various evergreen trees at RHS garden Rosemoor, Devon.

Euphorbia acanthothamnos *forms a rounded shrub with honey-scented flowers and spiny rays from the previous year.*

Plants can be clipped to emulate mound-forming, Mediterranean shrubs, and box, Buxus sempervirens, *is particularly attractive when closely trimmed as here, at Brook Cottage, Oxfordshire.*

LEFT AND ABOVE: If you are unable to go out, go up! In Bridgnorth, Shropshire, two houses that open directly onto the street have created colourful displays of climbing plants, hanging baskets and window boxes.

Small Gardens

How small is small? Small is a window box, over-flowing with colourful plants. If you are unable to go out, go up! Houses without any garden can be trans-formed into oases of colour, brightening dull streets by placing pots around the door, trellis for jasmine, roses or honeysuckle, hanging baskets and window boxes.

Tiny yards need not be dull, dingy and claustro-phobic. High walls add privacy and romantic intimacy, creating peaceful sanctuaries, prized since ancient times. Small, enclosed spaces are generally degrees warmer. White or pale coloured walls, together with touches of soft blue on woodwork or doors and simple paved floors, reflect light. Moorish influences can be adapted well to small spaces and vistas can be created with *trompe-l'oeil* scenes. Formal designs work well in small gardens, appearing neat and calming.

Brightly painted, Portuguese or Spanish ceramics add colour. Pots overflowing with palms, *Pelargonium*, *Ipomoea*, lavender and scented plants and herbs supply lush vegetation and perfume. Scent is important in small spaces, evoking memories of hot, herb-scented hillsides. Aromatic leaves of *Artemisia*, *Cupressus*, *Lavandula*, *Myrtus*, *Nepeta*, *Rosemarinus*, *Salvia* and *Santolina* are invaluable.

Banish lawn. With little space for mowing – or storing machines – substituting other surfaces are obvious solutions. Instead, let plants creep between stones, cascade over walls, or scale buildings. Many Mediterranean plants evolved tiny leaves or needle points to conserve water. These add delicate, ethereal touches, perfect for small gardens. One or two larger leaved plants add contrast and structure, while chang-ing levels create interest, even in small spaces.

The cooling sight and sounds of water are histori-cally important elements of Mediterranean gardens. Incorporate a bubbling water feature, pool or trough, while a small fountain freshens the air in enclosed spaces.

Shade is necessary, providing a place to retreat from the relentless sun (in the Mediterranean anyway, if not always in cooler countries!) Tiny, shady arbours smoth-ered with vines or perfumed climbers can shade a com-fortable seat. No room for garden furniture? Top low walls bounding raised beds with long, flat stones, soft-ened with padded cushions. Tiny details, such as a short length of stone balustrade, carved pillar, classical urn, statue set into a niche, or a colourful umbrella, add interest and atmosphere.

For impact, limit plant colours. Try the following combinations: blue or white with silver; red and orange with dark green; golden evergreens are permanent

ABOVE LEFT AND RIGHT: *Two tiny gardens, packed with Mediterranean plants, at Boscastle, Cornwall.*

RIGHT: *Tiny details add interest and atmosphere, such as this sculpture, 'Icon', tucked between plants in a small Northumberland garden.*

BELOW: *This minute yard in Devon is sheltered and bright with colour from a simple display of hanging baskets and tender plants in pots.*

137

The brick wall around this tiny tiled terrace at RHS garden Hyde Hall, Essex, incorporates a seat and beds of herbs and drought tolerant species.

reminders of sunshine, even on dull winter days. Soft blue or grey-green mixed with earth colours such as terracotta, ochre, grey and brown, cream or white, are relaxing. Hot coloured flowers add warmth as well as making plants appear closer, while lighter colours create illusions of space.

Walls and fences constrict. Create impressions of space by painting in pale colours, or camouflage with reed or bamboo panels. Mirrors reflect light and add depth, but must have air circulation and waterproofing. Include one or two tiny features to draw the eye.

Careful planning is essential in small spaces, since using an uncluttered approach to design and materials maximizes the feeling of space. Mediterranean plants fit particularly well.

Medium Gardens

Increased space allows more scope for replacing lawn with a terrace, parterre, plants or pond. If you must have 'green', experiment with lawn substitute plants (See chapter 5). Parterres or knot gardens with gravel or plants make excellent lawn replacements. Hedges of box, *Buxus sempervirens*, and *Rosemary officinalis* add that Mediterranean feel plus aromatic perfume, particularly after rain, while the delicious perfume of lavender evokes the Mediterranean as no other plant can.

For a simple, easy maintenance design, try a small terrace near the house, opening onto a formal parterre filled with gravel or plants. Box or bay, clipped into

Variegated leaves and golden evergreens are permanent reminders of sunshine, even on dull winter days. Herterton House, Northumberland.

The delicious perfume of the Lavender Garden at Johnson Hall, Staffordshire, evokes the Mediterranean as almost no other plant can.

A simple plan for an Italian style garden. Lawn is replaced by soft-toned gravel with low, clipped box parterre and Italian cypress, Cupressus sempervirens 'Stricta'. A narrow, stone-walled border round the boundary is planted with lavender, which fills the garden with perfume in summer and is clipped into a low, grey-leaved hedge for winter. Colours are simple and effective, the greens of box and cupressus contrasting with the pale pink climbing roses against the wall, the stone urns of pink pelargoniums, and the border of purple lavender.

dome or cone shapes, add height, as do slim Italian cypress, *Cupressus sempervirum* 'Stricta'. A central pot of flaming red *pelargonium* can be echoed on each corner. Potted citrus trees look wonderful. Surround a parterre with paved or gravel paths, and, if space allows, add a border against the garden boundary for a low hedge of lavender or rosemary, backed by climbing roses. A small, centrally placed pond also works well in parterres.

Informal designs include gently winding borders, or island beds, filled with drought tolerant plants. Mix in low maintenance grasses or introduce natural-looking sweeps of grasses, prairie-style; patios can have creeping plants and shady arbours. Small trees add height and year round interest. Mix flowers, fruit, shrubs and vegetables together – especially attractive when space is at a premium. Think French potager!

This tiny terrace opens onto an elegant parterre of low, clipped box filled with flowers, at Leeds Castle, Kent.

A mist of gently swaying grasses delicately frames drought tolerant plants in the long grass border at RHS garden Harlow Carr, Yorkshire.

A series of 'rooms' with different characteristics have been created at Angel Gardens, Shropshire. Enclosed gardens round the house open onto the 'Terrace Garden', which leads to an ornamental pool, summerhouse garden, and wide sweeping lawns dissected by island beds and new hedges, which will eventually enclose further 'rooms'.

The pink and mauve border at RHS garden Hyde Hall, Essex.

Large Gardens

The sky is the limit with larger gardens, literally, where there is ample opportunity to plant tall trees that would swamp smaller gardens. Create 'rooms' with different characteristics, or colour-schemed themes. Include shrubberies, drought tolerant borders, herb gardens and parterres. Patios can be grander and not limited to one near the house; pergolas can be longer and larger, there is more space for terraces, raised beds and walls, and possibly a kitchen garden with vegetables and fruit.

In large gardens it is impractical to remove lawn completely, but enlarging beds or creating new island beds, patios and pools minimizes lawn area. Some lawn can be naturalized. This encourages wild flora and fauna and needs mowing only once or twice a year.

Design interesting paths edged with scented plants or create a narrow path between lavender or chest-high hedges of rosemary, for a delicious perfume as you walk through. Steps can be wider and more extravagant. In cooler climates summer evenings are often chilly, if not downright cold. Patio heaters help, but for a lavish touch build an outdoor fireplace on the patio, providing luxurious warmth. Add comfortable garden furniture and continental touches with decorative gates and ironwork. Raised beds and terraces create differing levels; build a secluded summerhouse, floored with coloured Spanish tiles; include a statue or two, or groups of containers full of colourful plants.

Eating *al fresco* is very Mediterranean and very popular. Even small spaces can incorporate a barbecue, whether of commercial design or simply stacked breeze blocks, topped with a paving slab, edged with bricks to contain charcoal.

Warm, sheltered walls give greater scope for growing tender species. Trees and hedges create shade as well as protection, and space allows for wider choices of hedging plants and topiary. Larger plants add architectural backbone, but do not necessarily need to be dense. Bamboos and pampas grass, open and fragile in appearance, provide moving screens rather than solid blocks. Concentrate on small numbers of larger plants rather than hundreds of smaller ones, and avoid gardens becoming sprawls of unrelated elements. Unify, but provide focal features.

The larger the garden the more maintenance required. Grouping plants depending on their water-wise requirements is an even greater consideration where it is more important to simplify maintenance and conserve water.

Larger gardens also offer unlimited opportunities for even wider collections of interesting drought tolerant plants; perhaps room to experiment with a few more tender, borderline species, which may well survive given protection during their first couple of years. Larger gardens also provide scope for enticing, adventurous journeys from one area to another, with the promise of hidden secrets.

ABOVE: A corner of the sweeping mixed shrub and herbaceous border at Hall Farm, Shropshire.

RIGHT: Cortaderia species, pampas grasses, create useful, tall, but gently waving, fragile-looking screens.

Bark of Prunus serrula *looks as if it has been burnished to a shining brown.*

Winter Gardens

In their natural state, gardens in Mediterranean countries lie dormant during summer. In northerly latitudes, summer is the main flowering season and gardens lie dormant in winter. But gardens can still be full of colour and interest in winter. Many Mediterranean plants have attractive evergreen foliage in shades of grey, silver, red and gold, giving interest throughout the year, including winter. Trees often have beautiful bark. Winter-flowering shrubs add wonderful fragrance. Tiny bulbs flower from autumn to spring.

Evergreen *Euphorbia characias* is statuesque; *Eryngium giganteum*, Miss Wilmott's Ghost, contrasts with *Phyllostachys aurea*, while insignificant flowers of *Elaeagnus pungens* 'Maculata' perfume the garden. Blue, evergreen *Sesleria heufleriana* has soft, rounded seed-heads. You could also plant the dark green *Rubus tricolor* or the silver and dark green *R. cockburnianus* with its blue-white shoots; *Chionochloa conspicua* 'Rubra' has shades of silver, greens, bronzes and browns. All make fine shows in the winter garden – and do not forget to include a sheltered corner with some perfumed plants, for relaxing on milder, sunny winter days.

Acer griseum *has red, attractively peeling bark.*

Galanthus nivalis, *snowdrops, begin flowering in November.*

The dry garden at RHS garden Hyde Hall, Essex, incorporates excellent drainage with crushed stone and sharp sand mixed with top soil and organic compost. Begun in 2001 and now well established with more than 4,000 plants, representing 740 species and cultivars of drought tolerant plants, the garden thrives with no additional water in an area renowned as one of the driest in Britain.

Dry and Gravel Gardens

These are low maintenance, well-drained and attractive mediums for Mediterranean plants. Informal designs work particularly well in gravel gardens, giving a naturalistic appearance, although gravel also adapts well to formal designs. South- or west-facing sites are warmer and preferable for growing tender species. Natural, muted colours of chipped stone, in a range of colours from white, cream and grey through to brown and black, change depending on whether they are wet or dry. Shingle, smoothed and rounded by the action of water, comes in mixed, natural shades. All show plants off to perfection. Be cautious of brightly coloured aggregates, which can look incongruous, detract from plants and create glare in sunlight. Loose materials are versatile and simple to lay in curving shapes. A quick rake-over soon restores their order, but it can also change texture and appearance. Other materials include crushed granite, slate or marble.

Materials range in size from 10 to 20mm. Smaller grades and pea shingle look attractive, but larger grades stay in place more easily. Calculate around 15kg for a 1cm depth per square metre. Use a minimum depth of 5cm, although up to 15cm or 20cm is preferable for plants. The deeper the gravel, the less likelihood of tenacious weeds forcing through or annual weeds

Beth Chatto's Gravel Garden, Essex, was begun in 1991 on the site of an old car park of compacted sand and gravel over clay. The soil was first broken up before incorporating home-made compost. Plants were well soaked before planting and then given a final watering. Later the garden was mulched with 12mm gravel to a depth of 2–5cm.

Larger grade pebble mulch in the dry garden at RHS garden Hyde Hall, Essex, is simple to lay in curving shapes.

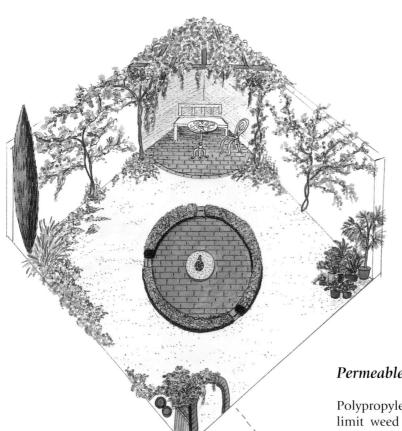

A small courtyard with white walls has been turned into a low maintenance gravel garden. Clipped box hedges surround a circle of mellow brick with central, bubbling water trickling over pebbles. Bricks form the floor of the tiny, creeper-covered arbour, just large enough to hold a small bench and table. Climbing roses and a single cupressus add height and drought tolerant species are planted directly into gravel to wander and seed where they please. The creeper-clad entrance screens a small utility area, dustbin, plastic compost bin and tiny store for garden tools. A collection of ceramic and terracotta pots add bright splashes of colour outside the main window of the house.

establishing, while weeds that do take hold are easily removed.

Ground must be well prepared and weed free, eliminating coarse weeds such as docks, thistles and couch. On heavy clay, mix topsoil with good compost, sharp sand or other coarse materials to aid drainage. Rake the site level and allow up to two weeks for it to settle; remove weeds as they appear. Small, loose materials require retaining boundaries to stop spreading into surrounding areas. Wooden battens or stone kerbing, set in place before laying the aggregate, are ideal.

For small areas, spreading can be kept simple by buying material in polythene sacks. Larger areas require bulk deliveries, meaning aggregate is dumped at the nearest access point to the road, needing speedy removal if likely to cause a hazard. Do not simply barrow gravel into another enormous pile elsewhere, creating further work. Disperse loads around the prepared area, or shake directly from the barrow, spreading a depth of material as you go. When spreading is complete, rake level and if necessary water to remove surface debris and dust. Particularly dirty gravel may require thorough washing before laying.

Permeable Membrane

Polypropylene type sheets, laid onto prepared ground, limit weed growth, although they are not necessary with deeper aggregates. Level the area and lay membrane smoothly, pushing edges into narrow, v-shaped trenches. Overlap joins by at least 2cm, securing with ground staples every 1m. Cut small, crossed slits into the membrane, insert plants into prepared holes, then draw material back round, cutting or folding away surplus. Spread gravel to a minimum depth of 5cm. Rake level, pushing gravel between plants but taking care not to smother them. Small plants can be protected with an upturned flower pot while the spreading takes place.

Planting

Planting is best undertaken before spreading shallow gravel. Container or pot-grown plants require thorough soaking to ensure root balls are wet through. Dig holes large enough to accommodate root balls easily. Mix soil with organic compost, including grit or sharp sand for drainage if necessary. Place plants into holes, carefully spreading out roots. Fill with soil, easing it between the roots. Gently shaking plants helps soil to settle and removes air gaps. Plant to the original depth of soil in the pot, bearing in mind levels will settle slightly. Firm and water well. On free-draining ground, small depressions around plants act as reservoirs, channelling moisture directly to roots. When planting is finished spread a layer of organic compost before adding gravel.

When inserting plants into existing gravel, clear a small area, mixing as little soil as possible with the gravel. Plant into prepared holes and carefully rake gravel back around plants. With deeper depths of gravel, plants generally have enough soil around root balls to establish and they can be placed directly into gravel. Disturb gravel gardens as little as possible once established.

Varying grades of mixed gravel and stone create different textures and effects. Add interest with larger rocks, boulders, pieces of driftwood, or a tree stump. An extremely simple and easily maintained garden can be created from gravel or shingle planted with sweeps of grasses. For a warm appearance choose natural coloured shingle with reds, brown and golden-toned grasses. Cooler effects are achieved with blue-grey gravel and blue and blue-green plants.

Gravel gardens require watering until established, but then happily survive without additional supplies. They are well drained, full of colour from wide ranges of drought tolerant species, easily maintained and are becoming increasingly important ecologically.

Plants for Gravel Gardens

Abutilon vitifolium. 4m. Grey-green, toothed and lobed leaves and cup-shaped purple-blue flowers in late spring and early summer.

Achillea **'Moonshine'**. 60cm. Perennial with feathery, silver-green leaves and flat heads of yellow flowers in summer.

Artemisia abrotanum, **southernwood**. 1.5m. Finely divided, aromatic, grey-green leaves and clusters of small, yellow flowers in summer. *A.* **'Powis Castle'**, masses of aromatic finely cut, silvery foliage.

Asphodelus albus, **asphodel**. 1m. Tufts of narrow, green leaves and spikes of star-shaped white flowers. *A. lutea*, yellow flowers.

Cistus ladanifer. 2.5m. Sticky stems and rough leaves with large, open, cup-shaped flowers with a dark red spot at petal base.

Eryngium amethystinum. 60cm. Branched stems and spiny, divided leaves with small thistle-like blue flowers and darker blue bracts.

Euphorbia characias, *subsp characias*. 1.5m. Upright, evergreen shrub with narrow, grey-green leaves and dense spikes of purple-centred, yellow-green flowers in spring and early summer.

Helianthemum nummularium, **'Amy Baring'**. 15cm. Spreading evergreen shrub with narrow grey-green leaves and a succession of open, yellow flowers, with orange centres, in summer.

Phuopsis stylosa. 30cm. Mat-forming perennial with narrow, pointed whorled leaves and drooping umbels of pink, funnel-shaped flowers in summer.

Salvia **'Trebah'**. 65cm. Shrubby perennial with dark green leaves and lilac-tinged. White flowers in summer and autumn.

Tulbaghia cepacea. 40cm. Bulbs with long, slender leaves and loose umbels of pale mauve flowers in summer.

Achillea *'Moonshine'*.

Euphorbia characias *subsp* characias.

Salvia *'Trebah'*.

10 Classical Italian and French Country Style

We are unable to transfer Mediterranean gardens, plus climate, into our northerly latitudes, however much we crave that extra sunshine. Nor, out of context, would these gardens sit happily in our environment, even if we could. In cooler climates we aim for the essence of those countries, using their plants and ideas, with the added bonus that we achieve water and labour saving gardens as well. Drought tolerant plants require good drainage: good drainage equates to gardens that use gravel, shale or stone. Drier gardens support Mediterranean plants.

Neither are we able to include information about all Mediterranean climate region countries. For the sake of this book, we must limit ourselves to the better-known areas, the ones that have had most influence and adapt most readily to Britain.

French and Italian gardens have been popular for centuries. Travellers taking the 'Grand Tour' discovered plants and ideas for their own gardens. These were adopted on a grand scale in the eighteenth and nineteenth centuries, but many ideas are still attractive today. Replacing large sections of lawn with paved terraces or parterres still carries great appeal, for example. Even small areas can incorporate a simple 'knot' of low box.

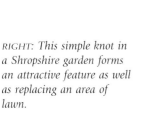

RIGHT: *This simple knot in a Shropshire garden forms an attractive feature as well as replacing an area of lawn.*

OPPOSITE: *An imposing, plant twined pergola at the RHS garden, Hyde Hall, Essex.*

147

Classical Italian

Italian Renaissance gardens are timeless. Images of great villas with wonderful architecture, carefully tended acres, landscape vistas, evergreen hedges and classical styles are brought to mind when we think of them. This style became highly fashionable in Britain, where the symmetry of box parterres and terraces set amidst cypress avenues, pleached walks, topiary, statues, garden urns and fountains, appealed to many.

Traditionally, Italian gardens have few flowers, but the greenery is superb; trees frame distant views, the garden blends into countryside and the landscape enhances the garden, making a cohesive whole. Arcaded loggias are cool in the heat. Cascades, pools and extravagant fountains shower silver droplets. Perfumes of jasmine and box pervade the air. Gardens are based around neatly clipped, evergreen forms that look as beautiful in winter as summer. Less formality came with the surrounding *bosco*, a hunting forest that also offered shade.

Italian Gems

There are many fascinating gardens in Italy, most famously those at Isola Madre, Isola Bella, La Landriana, the Villa d'Este, Villa Carlotta, Giusti Gardens, Boboli Gardens, Villa Gamberaia, Villa Cetinale, Villa Medici, Villa La Pietra, Villa Rufolo and Villa Cimbrone. There are also, of course, thousands of exquisite, anonymous, private gardens.

Southern Italy has dramatic scenery and coastlines, with islands such as Capri, Ischia, Sardinia and Sicily scattered across an azure sea. All have important gardens where Mediterranean species thrive in the equable climate. La Mortella, the fabulous garden on Ischia of Sir William Walton, the late composer, and his wife Susana is a steeply sloping site on volcanic rock. La Mortola, (Giardini Botanica Hanbury), near Ventimiglia on the Italian Riviera, was created by Sir Thomas and Daniel Hanbury, who, from 1867, established a world-renowned collection of native and exotic plants. It is as famous now as it was then. Italy also has the two oldest botanic gardens in Europe, at the University of Pisa, 1543, and the University of Padua, 1545.

Italian Style in Britain

Many great British gardens were built in the classical Italian style with green avenues, topiary and parterres of clipped hedges filled with flowers, herbs or roses. Powis Castle, Wales, is an outstanding example of an Italianate terraced garden. Four massive terraces, each almost 180m long, are carved into the hillside; stone balustrades are decorated with classical urns and

The National Trust's Powis Castle, Wales, is a magnificent example of an Italianate terraced garden with four massive terraces, each almost 180m long.

ABOVE: *A modern Italianate garden in Ludlow, Shropshire. The main lawn is divided by an avenue of immaculately clipped hedges pierced with simple, standard white rose trees.*

RIGHT: *Mary and Andy Poole's Italian-style garden in Shropshire. (Photo courtesy of Gill Guest.)*

BELOW: *Tapeley Park, Devon, also has Italianate terraces.*

ABOVE AND LEFT: An Italian courtyard garden near Bridgnorth, Shropshire, has neat parterres around a central pool, and niches with lion masks and carved figures.

Pots of citrus trees at The Dower House, Morville Hall, Shropshire.

Herterton House, Northumberland: (ABOVE LEFT) Silver-leaved pear; (ABOVE RIGHT) The new parterre showing peg and line markers; (RIGHT) Cloistered arches of the grotto.

exquisite lead figures of shepherds and shepherdesses. Topiary was an important element, and although some has been lost, massive domes of rolling, immaculately clipped yew and box still survive.

A modern Italianate garden in Ludlow, Shropshire, has two long clipped hedges punctuated by simple, standard white rose trees forming an avenue in the centre of the main lawn. A small, herb-filled parterre frames an elegant stone terrace. Side gardens leading off at right angles have classical stonework, water canals and paths edged with lavender. At the far end, a huge mulberry remains from the silkworms used in the once important glove industry of the town. Another Shropshire garden, on a grander scale, is an Italian idyll of topiary hedges, trees, arbours, herbaceous borders, roses and acclaimed modern sculptures.

Nearby, an Italian courtyard garden, quartered by parterres of roses, has raised terraces with wrought iron railings leading to intricate, high, arched entrance gates. The opposite wall supports a series of niches containing statues, above raised beds. An elevated stone terrace looks back across the garden at a carved wellhead, which spouts water into a stone trough.

In Northumberland, Frank and Marjorie Lawley of Herterton House have created magnificent gardens high on a wind-blasted hillside. Hedges form windbreaks for numerous Mediterranean species. Divided into 'rooms', there are delightful knot gardens and parterres. A grotto, enclosed behind cloistered arches reminiscent of an Italian monastery, opens onto a burgeoning physic and herb garden dominated by an

exquisite silver willow-leaved pear, *Pyrus salicifolia pendula* 'Bostock'. Part of the 'nursery' area now forms the basis of a large, new parterre. The first box cuttings of *Buxus* 'Suffruticosa' were planted in 2003 and will form

Stone steps edged with low clipped hedges fit well into an Italian theme at Kiftsgate Court, Gloucestershire.

Clipped evergreens and a simple touch of pale blue Agapanthus *at Bide-a-Wee Cottage, Northumberland.*

weaving hedges between stone paths. To create an intricate parterre, it is always advisable to plan it on paper before pegging it onto the ground.

Italian Inspiration

Italian gardens are traditionally 'green', but some flowering plants are acceptable. Evergreen foliage comes in many colours – grey, silver, light and dark green, bronze or gold. Introduce geometrically clipped topiary, domes, balls, spirals or cones. Good plants include bay, box, cypress, holly and yew. Cut a 'window' through an evergreen hedge, framing a distant view, or train ivy round a large wire hoop, forming a circular 'window'. Gold-leaved shrubs and variegated ivies create 'sunshine' in shady corners.

Add pots of clipped trees like slim, Italian cypress or incorporate other features such as balustrades, honey-coloured paving, sand or gravel paths, simple stone steps bordered with pot plants, large orna-

mental pots, classical vases, marble or sandstone busts, statues or urns set into niches, decorative wrought metalwork, stone wellheads, circular pools, water troughs and fountains.

Italian pergolas (the word comes from the Latin *pergola*, a projecting roof) have stone or brick columns supporting wooden beams. Smother with climbing plants such as jasmine, roses, vines or wisteria, underplanted with scented herbs, lavender or rosemary. For something different, pile railway sleepers two deep on either side of the pergola, forming a seat or bench to support collections of potted plants.

Limit flower colours to one or two shades to achieve harmony. Glowing red pelargoniums make effective foils to greenery. Pots of citrus trees are traditional, either as specimen trees, forming an avenue, incorporated into a parterre or lining a terrace. Some overwinter in protected or milder areas, but if unsure, move inside. If space allows, build a small stone pavilion, grotto or cloister, or paint a mural. Whatever the scale, small or grand, Italian style adapts well to cooler climates.

Plants for the Italian Garden

Acanthus mollis, **bear's breeches**. 2m. Pinnately lobed, toothed and spiny, dark green leaves and long spikes of white, flushed mauve, hooded, tubular flowers in summer.

Buxus sempervirens, **common box**. 1–8m. Multi-stemmed shrub or tree (var. *arborescens*) with small, ovate, green leaves, paler beneath.

Clematis armandii. Early flowering, evergreen climber with dark green foliage and highly perfumed, single white flowers.

Cupressus **species, cypress**. Evergreen coniferous trees with scale-like leaves and globose to oval cones. *C. sempervirens*, Italian cypress. 40m. Slender, columnar, dark green, evergreen trees. *C. arizonica 'Glauca'*, blue tints.

Daphne mezereum, **Daphne**. 1.7m. Sweet scented, white or purple flowers in early spring on bare branches, followed by narrow, green leaves.

Eucryphia × *intermedia* **'Rostrevor'**. 8m. Evergreen, upright tree with simple and pinnate, glossy, dark green leaflets and open, nodding white flowers in late summer.

Jasminum officinale. Deciduous climber with clusters of sweetly perfumed white flowers in summer. J. polyanthum, semi-evergreen, white flowers, underside of petals flushed pink.

Ilex aquifolium, **holly**. 25m. Evergreen glossy, dark green, undulating leaves with spines. Tiny white or pale pink flowers and bright red berries in winter. 'Fructu Luteo', yellow berries. 'Aureamarginata', golden-edged leaves.

Laurus nobilis, **bay**. 3–15m. Small tree or shrub with dark green, oblong ovate leaves, used for flavouring.

Lonicera caprifolium, **Italian honeysuckle**. Highly perfumed (especially in evening), oval leaves and whorled heads of creamy white flowers, followed by red berries.

Myrtus communis, **myrtle**. 5m. Erect, branching shrub with aromatic, shiny leaves and small, fragrant white flowers.

Acanthus mollis *var.* latifolius.

Rosmarinus officinalis, **rosemary**. 2m. Evergreen, aromatic shrub with small, green, needle-like leaves, white beneath, and blue flowers in spring. 'Albus', white flowers. 'Majorca pink' and 'Roseus', pink flowers.

Santolina chamaecyparissus, **cotton lavender**. 10–50cm. Grey-white shrub with small, crowded leaves and dark yellow flowers in summer. 'Lambrook Silver', silver leaves. 'Little Ness', small, compact. Clip into shape or leave to flower.

Taxus baccata, **yew**. 15m. Heavily branched, domed tree with small, glossy, dark green, linear leaves and red fruits.

Trachelospermum jasminoides. Creamy white climber with jasmine-like, perfumed flowers and narrow, dark green leaves.

ABOVE: Jasminum officinale, *common jasmine.*

RIGHT: Eucryphia × intermedia *'Rostrevor'.*

Elements for the Italian Garden

Classical statues add beauty and style.

Evergreens add year round colour, shape and texture.

Soft-toned peonies flank a stone trough at Stockton Bury Garden, Herefordshire.

A secluded terrace surrounded by greenery.

The beautiful colours and perfumes of honeysuckle twine around and enhance hedges, arbours and pergolas.

A stone bench amidst shrubs and climbing Vitis vinifera *'Purpurea'.*

Ethereal flowers of Eucryphia glutinosa *'Plena'.*

Classical, weathered stone balustrade.

Neatly clipped trees give restrained shape and form.

A terracotta urn adds a stylish touch as well as a focal point.

155

French Country Style

Italian influences flowed into France, combining with ancient countryside and farming traditions. Romantic fairy-tale châteaux have wonderfully landscaped parks and gardens, huge terraces, magnificent pools and fountains, and intricate *parterres de broderie*. Trees and hedges of poplar, cypress and laurustinus protect from the north wind – the notorious mistral, which blows hard in December ... and March ... and July! This climate of strong winds, sudden and torrential storms, and wonderful, burning, bright sunshine has shaped and dominated the countryside, its people, and plants for millennia.

Midday sun filters through layers of trees and shrubs; dark pines, cypress, chestnut, oak and plane. Perfumes of golden mimosa and broom are heavy on the warm air. Arbutus hang their white bell blossoms and red fruits. Lavender fields are a purple scented haze. Acres of golden sunflowers nod in the heat. There are also gaunt, pale silver-leaved olive trees; orchards of delicately blossomed almond, cherry, fig, apple and pear trees; pungent sages, rosemary, thyme and marjoram, picked from mountain *garrigue* and *maquis*, and dried in the sun for bustling, local markets; and, of course, the vineyards with their rich and valuable harvest.

Unlike Italian gardens, French gardens have an abundance of flowers, reflected in the famous flower market in Nice, and acres of sweetly scented blossoms around Grasse for the perfume industry. Gardens are a profusion of colour from roses, climbers, creepers and vines twining houses and walls, herbaceous perennials, and pots filled with luxuriant blooms. Natural, rounded, shapes of hillside bushes such as box, myrtle, phlomis, broom and gorse are emulated in gardens with carefully clipped bushes. Fruit trees are perfectly cordoned or espaliered. Autumn colour is important, with flaming leaves and berries.

French Gems

The balmy climate and fascinating coastline of southern France has long drawn visitors from cooler climates, particularly in winter. Many of these stayed and created remarkable, but very 'English' gardens, such as Major Lawrence Johnson's Serre de la Madone,

Trees and hedges protect from the north wind. Bolfracks Garden, Tayside.

Lavender fields with their purple scented haze. Snowshill Lavender, Worcestershire.

Arbutus hang their white bell blossoms and red fruits.

A simple rose shown to perfection against a green hedge.

Menton; La Chèvre d'Or, Nice; Villa Noailles, Grasse (English and Italian influences); William Waterfield's expertly planned and planted Le Clos du Peyronnet, and countless other wonderful gardens.

French style was recreated in other countries such as Germany, with the Royal Gardens of Herrenhausen, Hanover; Sanssouci Palace, Potsdam, and the UNESCO World Heritage site of Augustusburg at Brühl, outside Cologne.

French Style in Britain

Numerous examples of French style in Britain include Mount Edgcumbe Garden, Cornwall, a Regency French garden (which also has Italian, modern American and New Zealand sections); Oxburgh Hall, Norfolk, a French style parterre; Wrest Park, Bedfordshire, an 'English Versailles', and Waddesdon Manor, Bedfordshire, a Renaissance-style chateau and garden with an extravagantly planted parterre.

In Scotland, the massive, château-like Dunrobin Castle, Sutherland, hangs above French style gardens, backing onto the exposed coastline of the Dornoch Forth. Stone steps descend through terraces filled with herbaceous plants, many of Mediterranean origin. Intricately designed parterres contain fruit, flowers and herbs, in the French *potager* style, while wooden obelisks scramble with climbers and roses, and beds are edged with low cordon apple trees.

French Inspiration

French châteaux have flights of elegant steps running between stone terraces edged with balustrades or formal, clipped hedges. These contrast with intricately woven parterres tapestried into smooth turf, bordered with stonework, lavender, box or santolina, filled with an abundance of flowers and sweetly perfumed roses. Emulate this style in larger gardens, setting aside areas for formal terraces and parterres of colourful flowers. Intermingle fruit, flowers and vegetables. Even grand châteaux favoured designs that wove utility and beauty together.

In southern France gardens have become cornu-copias of abundance. Intensively planted and cropped beds of rich soil are edged with dry stone walls, box

ABOVE: *The elegant, château-like Dunrobin Castle, Sutherland, Scotland. The terraced gardens were designed in 1850 by Charles Barry, architect of the Houses of Parliament.*

BELOW: *The round parterre with clipped greenery, bedded out with glowing red dahlias.*

ABOVE: *The long garden has three parterres surrounding the fountains. Two are traditionally bedded out while the central area mixes flowers, fruit and vegetables, hedged with low, cordoned apple trees. The wooden obelisks are adorned with climbing roses and clematis.*

hedging or herbs, and contain assortments of vegetables, including artichokes, cardoons, tomatoes, peas, beans, cabbage, coloured kales, asparagus, melons, pumpkins and espaliered fruit mixed with nasturtiums, alliums, roses, sweet peas, lavender, heliotrope, sunflowers and aromatic herbs. 'Companion planting' in this way offers plants greater protection from disease and pests. This French *potager* style is ideal for modern gardens, however small, and our French inspiration is more accessible if drawn from these sun-baked plots, nestling around picturesque villages in the south, rather than from grand, sophisticated estates.

Beds can be slightly raised with low, stone walls or wooden battens. Fill with rich compost and edge with box, dwarf lavender, parsley, chives, strawberries or low metal railings. Mix rows of vegetables, fruit, flowers and herbs. Construct attractive supports for beans or climbing plants, from hazel or willow branches; make or buy decorative pillars or obelisks. Divide individual beds with sanded or slabbed paths.

The design and number of beds depends on space available. Small gardens could have one main square bed, each side forming a triangle of plants, crowned by

Low, cordoned apple trees edge potagers at Dunrobin Castle.

RHS garden Rosemoor, Devon has a beautifully designed and extremely productive potager, filled with an abundance of vegetables, fruit and flowers.

ABOVE: Tropaeolum speciosum *clambers through hedges, its brilliant red flowers making a wonderful contrast against the green.*

LEFT: Hampton Court Vankampen Gardens, Herefordshire, has a large, intricately designed potager in the old walled garden. Productive beds overflow with colourful vegetables, fruit and flowers. (Photo courtesy of Sue Graham)

a central pillar of roses or climbing beans, edged with low, uniform hedging. Surround this with a path and, if space allows, a narrow, raised bed against the garden boundary, planted in similar style. Achieve height with standard or shrub roses, *Cupressus*, or climbing plants. *Tropaeolum speciosum* looks particularly attractive when its brilliant red flowers are shown to perfection, climbing through dark green, clipped hedges.

With more space, and rectangular gardens, place four beds in a square, or circular format, divided by paths. The central axis has a pillar of cascading roses or vines, garden vase, statue or small pool. Arches at the entrance to each path are smothered with climbing beans or golden hops, *Humulus lupulus* 'Aurea'. Add balance with clipped trees of box or bay on corners. In long, narrow gardens, place beds in a line, perhaps two and two, with a central feature such as a raised pool or statue on a slightly wider path dissecting the two series of beds.

In large gardens, potagers form one element in the overall design. In bigger beds, flowers and vegetables can be divided by rows of lavender. Pollarded trees such as plane, *Platinus x acerifolia*; or tightly clipped hedges of yew, *Taxus baccata*, hornbeam, *Carpinus betulus*, or *thuja* look elegant. Pollarding stops trees growing too tall, and encourages larger leaves, which provide more shade, while tight clipped hedges bring

A newly planted olive tree in a London garden.

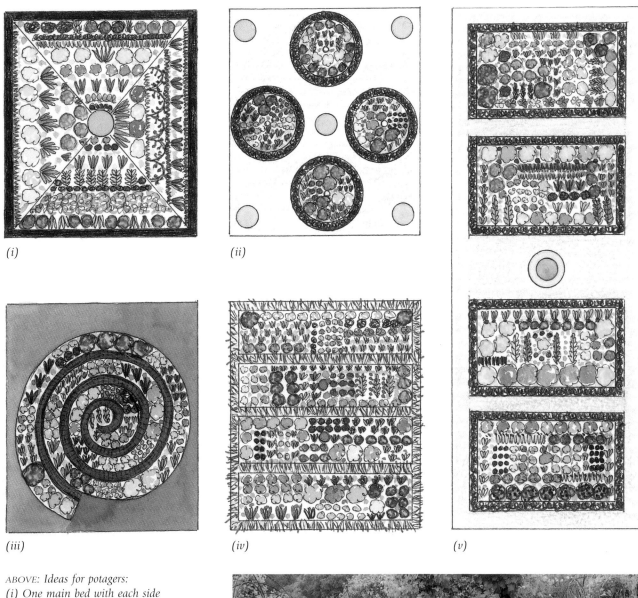

(i)   *(ii)*   *(v)*

(iii)   *(iv)*

ABOVE: *Ideas for potagers:*
(i) One main bed with each side forming a triangle.
(ii) Circular beds set into paving.
(iii) A long, narrow garden can be laid out formally with four beds and a central pool.
(iv) In larger beds flowers and vegetables can be divided by rows of lavender or other herbs, which can be clipped into shape during winter.
(v) This spiral design gives easy access to all sides of the borders for harvesting.

RIGHT: *A collection of various thyme species create a focal point at RHS garden Rosemoor, Devon.*

Apple trees supply delicate blossom in spring and a welcome harvest in autumn.

Beds edged with Santolina chamaecyparissus, *cotton lavender, and filled with herbs at RHS garden Rosemoor, Devon.*

Potager beds edged with woven hazel panels at RHS garden Rosemoor, Devon.

Archways of climbing beans are good to look at and simple to harvest. Hundred House Hotel, Shropshire.

(*ABOVE LEFT*) *Peppers;*
(*ABOVE RIGHT*) *Aubergine;*
(*RIGHT*) *Courgettes, cucumbers
and gourds trail through hedges.*

strong structure to the garden. Carve an intricate parterre into the lawn, with a central pool or fountain, filling beds with bulbs, perennials, lavender, herbs and roses. Olive trees were often under-planted with lavender, grey-green foliage making a wonderful foil against the purple flowers. Plant a truffle tree! Truffles are highly prized and expensive, growing throughout Europe between sea level and 2,000m. They even grow in Britain, but we never look for them. Hazelnut trees are specially impregnated with spores and within four to six years you could be gathering your own truffles.

French country houses are white, ochre or terracotta. Echo these colours on walls and add touches of blue or green paint on woodwork. Decorative, metal grilles on walls or windows are also very French. Golden-coloured stone paving near the house can have creeping plants growing between the slabs, or groups of pots filled with Mediterranean species. Include tomatoes, peppers and aubergines to continue the *potager* ideal.

Create a focal point with pots containing a collection of one specific species, such as thyme. For a soothing and relaxing garden limit colours to soft pastels, but for something more dramatic choose exuberant expanses of vivid colour.

Hedges and clipped trees form architectural features in French gardens as well as providing protection for flowers. Almond, cherry, apple, pear or plum supply

Include glowing red creepers in the French garden for autumn colour: (ABOVE) Parthenocissus tricuspidata, Virginia creeper; *(LEFT)* Pyracantha rogersiana.

delicate white and pink blossoms in spring, as well as welcome harvests in autumn. In small gardens try to incorporate one or two decorative trees, but in larger gardens include whole orchards, under-planted with spring bulbs and flowers. *Tamarisk* are attractive trees with feathery branches and tiny, pink flowers, as well as being salt tolerant for coastal areas. *Cercis* species have delicately coloured leaves in spring and good autumn colour. Various specimen trees can be grown inside low, trimmed box hedges.

Grand French châteaux often had massive lakes, fountains and canals, but French country style is more suited to quiet, reflective pools, gently flowing fountains, or water trickling into a stone basin. A small pool filled with blue and yellow iris is effective, as are pure, white *Zantedeschia*.

We do not think of France without thinking vineyards – and wine, so train vines against the house, pergola or arbour, creating shade as well as luscious fruit. Include glowing red creepers or berries for rich, autumn colour.

For somewhere to relax with that glass of wine, you need furniture. It can be of sophisticated metal or wire forms, with brightly coloured umbrellas for shade, or simple stone benches softened with cushions. For sheer luxury on the patio, relax on an elegant French day bed draped with white linen and strewn with colourful rugs and cushions.

A French style bench at RHS garden Rosemoor, Devon.

Plants for the French Garden

Arbutus unedo, **strawberry tree**. 10m. Evergreen tree or shrub with rough bark and glossy, dark green leaves and small, urn-shaped white flowers in autumn and winter, together with round, strawberry-like fruit.

Cynara cardunculus, **cardoon**. 2m. Large, divided, silver-grey leaves and blue-purple, thistle-like flowers in summer.

Euonymous europaeus, **spindle tree**. 3m. Deciduous shrub or small tree, narrowly oval, green leaves with good autumn colour. Inconspicuous green flowers followed by red fruits, which split showing orange seeds.

Fragaria × *ananassa*, **strawberry**. Ovate leaflets and small, open white flowers in spring followed by edible red fruits.

Helianthus annuus, **sunflower**. 5m. Fast growing, small, medium or large annual with oval, serrated leaves and yellow to brown, daisy-like flowers with darker centres. *H. salicifolius*. 2–3m. Narrow, willow-like leaves and branching stems bearing small, yellow, daisy-like flowers.

Heuchera **'Palace Purple'**, **alum root**. 45cm. Clump-forming perennial with heart-shaped, purple leaves and sprays of small, bell-shaped white flowers in summer.

Juniper communis, **juniper**. 10m. Red brown to grey, smooth bark, dark green, needle-like leaves and small, dark blue cones. Numerous cultivars from dwarf, prostrate, spreading and columnar in shades of grey-green and gold.

Brassica oleracea acephala, **kale**. Hardy, edible, crinkled or plain leaved vegetable with green or purple colouring. 'Tall Green Curled', medium height, dark green leaves; 'Dwarf Green Curled'; 'Thousand Headed'; 'Cottager's', purple leaves.

Lavandula stoechas, **French lavender**. 100cm. Evergreen, bushy shrub with narrow grey-green leaves and fat heads of minute, dark purple flowers topped by purple bracts in late spring and summer.

Lilium candidum, **madonna lily**. 2m. Lanceolate leaves and fragrant, funnel-shaped, white flowers with yellow bases in summer.

Origanum vulgare **'Aureum'**. 8cm. Perennials forming dense mats of small, aromatic, yellow-green leaves, and small, mauve flowers in summer.

Parthenocissus tricuspidata, **Virginia creeper**. Rampant climber, leaves turning brilliant red in autumn.

Phaseolus vulgaris, **French bean**. Dwarf or climbing annual with pink, white or purple flowers and long edible pods.

Viola odorata, **sweet violet**. 7cm. Spreading, semi-evergreen perennial with heart-shaped leaves and slender stems bearing sweetly scented, flat-faced, blue, violet or white flowers in late winter and spring.

Roses

Climbers: Bouquet d'Or, fragrant copper-salmon; Château de Clos Vougeot, fragrant dark crimson; Lawrence Johnston, semi-double yellow; Mermaid, single creamy yellow; Souvenir de la Malmaison, pink. **Ramblers**: Mme Sancy de Parabere, fragrant soft pink; René André, apricot yellow; R. banksiae banksiae, fragrant double white, and R. Banksia lutea, double yellow. **Shrub**: Blanc double de Coubert, pure white; Roseraie de L'Hay, wine-purple; Zepherine Drouhin, deep pink; **Old roses**: Albas, Centifolias, Damasks, Gallicas and Moss roses. **Bush**: Madame Louise Laperriere, deep crimson; Michèle Meilland, amber-pink, and L'Aimant, coral pink.

Helianthus annuus, *sunflower*

Arbutus unedo *fruits turn bright red.*

Cynara cardunculus, *cardoon.*

Elements for the French Garden

The wonderful fragrance and colour of lavender.

Campanula prefer well-drained soil and sun.

Herbs are a must, such as the colourful and pungent Origanum vulgare.

Soft-toned asters provide good autumn colour in French-style gardens.

Lilies have beautiful flowers in a range of glorious colours and shapes.

Paeonia 'Bowl of Beauty', has exquisite pink petals and masses of golden stamens.

Viburnum opulus 'Xanthocarpum'. Yellow fruit and good autumn colour.

An attractively shaped stone bench.

Include vegetables as well as fruit and flowers. Cucurbita pepo, vegetable marrow, or summer squash.

A good potager of mixed vegetables and flowers.

Long borders at the French style, Dunrobin Castle, Sutherland.

11 Spain, Greece and Other Mediterranean Climate Regions

Spain: the Perfect Climate

Spain attracts millions of visitors and is urbanizing fast to accommodate them. Its hot summers and mild winters are often described as the perfect climate. Gardens are always in flower and rain is welcome, by gardeners at least, to moisten sun-baked earth.

Spain's Story

The Muslim conquest of Spain in AD711 had a massive impact on design, and led to the introduction of ornate gardens of terraces, orchards and aviaries. Water was greatly prized: ponds, fountains and cascades were artfully contrived so that cooling sights and sounds enhanced the landscape. Water was utilized to great effect in the unforgettable Alhambra, Granada, with gently tinkling fountains and pools reflecting blue sky, horseshoe arches, polychromatic brickwork and intricate inscriptions of delicate Moorish architecture. Granada and Seville were significant horticultural areas under the Moors, and Cordoba an important centre of

botanical knowledge in the tenth century. Gardens developed through the centuries – Italian renaissance gardens were briefly in favour, for example. New plants and ideas, including palm trees, were introduced from expeditions and conquests, and these travelled on into Europe.

Northern Spain has fertile soil, a mild, almost frost-free climate and abundant rainfall. Central regions have short, baking summers, long, cold winters, scant rainfall and arid landscapes. Southern Spain enjoys mild winters, hot dry summers and temperatures that can rise to 45°C in Seville and Cordoba.

Spain, a country of dazzling white, russet-tiled buildings, villages clinging to precipitous hilltops,

OPPOSITE: A simple pot immediately evokes that 'Mediterranean' feeling. This one is actually pictured at the RHS garden at Hyde Hall, Essex in south-east England.

RIGHT: Water was an important element in Spanish gardens with cooling fountains and reflective pools. (Photo courtesy of Sue Pendleton)

Gleaming white houses and terracotta roofs of a typical Spanish hilltop village.

Vivid colours of Bougainvillea, *so typical of Spain and other Mediterranean countries.*

ancient castles, Moorish architecture, colourful ceramic tiles, pierced stonework, burnt red earth and vividly coloured plants, *Bougainvillea, Poinsettia,* pink-blossomed almond trees, vines, olives and citrus (although, sadly, the latter require heavy irrigation). Irrigation is rampant in gardens surrounding massive new developments – the ever-spreading rash of golf courses, public parks and private gardens – in an attempt to keep them green and blooming throughout the year, with resultant ecological problems. Spain has hundreds of attractive, native species that happily grow with little or no water. Gardens of the future must, of necessity, limit such massive irrigation.

Spanish Gems

At Elche, the garden of El Huerto del Cura has up to 400,000 *Phoenix dactylifera*, reputedly planted by the Phoenicians about 300BC. The Jardín del Parterre, Aranjuez, has a small parterre dating to the mid-sixteenth century and a larger, eighteenth-century French-style parterre. El Jardín de Monforte, Valencia, is a formal garden from the mid-nineteenth century with clipped box, cypress and myrtle, parterres, Carrara marble statues, a spectacular wisteria twined round an iron pergola and an abundance of plants including bulbous species.

The Balearic Islands have a temperate climate with important public and private gardens, including the historic Raxa and Alfabia on Mallorca. The islands have numerous endemic plants including the beautiful *Paeonia cambessedesii*.

Spanish Style

Despite Spain's wonderful, historical gardens, Spanish design has not travelled across Europe in the same way as that of French and Italian gardens. An occasional Spanish-style villa sits incongruously in the British countryside. Canals and fountains influenced by the Alhambra form water features in some gardens. We utilize Spanish plants, and palms now grow in British gardens, but actual 'Spanish' gardens are few. Compton Acres, Dorset, includes a Spanish water garden and Ugbrook Park, Devon, a Spanish garden.

Spanish Inspiration

Spanish style can be introduced without looking out of place. Exuberant, brightly coloured plants can be set against brilliant white walls, with touches of terracotta, pierced stonework and Moorish influenced tiles set in paths and patios (early designs were geometric, since naturalistic shapes of plants or people were forbidden). All add touches of the Spanish Mediterranean to a garden. Also effective are mosaics used in paving, walls,

The amazing Agave americana *heads up to flower in a Mallorcan garden.*

Paeonia cambessedesii, *endemic to the Balearic Islands, flowers in late spring.*

Spanish-style water canal and pavilion in the gardens at David Austin Roses, West Midlands.

Sculpture, such as this group of stone figures by Pat Austin, fits well with the Spanish theme.

table tops or stone benches. Incorporate still pools for reflections, or long, narrow canals edged with low, arching jets of water. Modern sculpture fits well.

Decorative ironwork includes grilles or balconies cascading with colourful plants: *Fuchsia, Pelargonium,* Petunia, nasturtiums (modern hybrids carry flowers well above foliage). Pergolas wreathed with climbing plants create shade. Grasses add form and movement, evoking dry landscapes. Bright, soft cushions can be placed on relaxing sun loungers. Add accents of vibrantly coloured Spanish pottery, ceramic planters – and, of course, palm trees.

Cacti and succulents thrive in Spain, where specimens as tall as houses can be found. With 2,500 species, cacti form one of the largest families of succulents in the world, with a unique system of water storage. Most require winter protection in Britain, but some survive outside, given shelter and perfect drainage. Build raised beds, filled with open, gritty, free-draining mediums, such as pumice, scoria, grit or gravel. Many succulents benefit from purely inorganic mediums, others appreciate peat or coir mixed in. Try *Aeonium, Aloe, Agave, Echeveria, Lampranthus, Sedum, Sempervivum* and *Yucca*. Collections look well grouped in pots, which can be taken indoors in winter. Sharp, fine spines are ferocious – not good plants with children around.

Tiny courtyards can be adapted beautifully to Spanish style, painted white, filled with colourful plants in ceramic containers, with a potted palm or two. Common ivy, *Hedera helix*, is a Mediterranean native. Smaller leaved ivies can be trimmed and golden, variegated species add that sunshine feel.

Portugal

Portugal is 'greener' than Spain, with hot summers and mild winters, wetter in the north, dryer in the south. Rugged landscape means many gardens are terraced and intimate, incorporating ideas from Roman, Moorish and Christian cultures. *Azulejos*, ceramic tiles, are important forms of decoration; large water cisterns offer reflections; French-style parterres and topiary are popular. Rustic Portuguese ceramics add colour and interest.

ABOVE: Agave americana *happily growing in Beth Chatto's gravel garden, Essex.*

LEFT: *This decorative wrought-metal wellhead at Brook Cottage, Oxfordshire, would fit beautifully with a Spanish theme.*

Plants for the Spanish Garden

Acacia dealbata, **mimosa**. 30m. Evergreen with silver-green, bipinate leaflets and clusters of fragrant, globose, fluffy yellow flowers.

Callistemon citrinus, **bottle brush**. Lemon-scented leaves and bright crimson flowerheads in summer.

Campsis grandiflora, **Chinese trumpet vine**. 10m. Woody-stemmed climber. Oval, toothed leaflets and red or orange, trumpet-shaped flowers in summer and autumn.

Cistus species. Evergreen shrubs with long successions of short-lived, showy flowers.

Gazania 'Orange Beauty'. 20cm. Silver-green leaves and rich orange flowers

Hyacinthoides hispanica, **Spanish bluebell**. Clump-forming bulb with strap-shaped, glossy leaves and loose spikes of bell-shaped blue, pink or white flowers in spring.

Hibiscus syriacus 'Blue Bird'. Deciduous shrub with lobed leaves and open, red-centred, lilac-blue flowers, late summer and early autumn.

Paeonia cambessedesii, **Mallorcan peony**. 45cm. Perennial with attractive foliage, dark green above, and undersides, veins and stems flushed red. Pink flowers with golden anthers in spring.

Prunus dulcis, **almond**. 8m. Deciduous tree. Open, pink flowers appear in spring before pointed, toothed leaves. Fruit in a hard shell with velutinous covering.

Spartium junceum, **Spanish broom**. 3m. Deciduous shrub with dark green stems and golden flowers, summer to autumn.

Campsis grandiflora, *Warwickshire.*

Callistemon citrinus, *Surrey.*

Hibiscus syriacus *'Blue Bird', Worcestershire.*

Elements for the Spanish Garden

A dry, gravel border of colourful, drought tolerant plants.

Delosperma sutherlandii *must have well-drained soil.*

Great sweeps of drought tolerant plants in Beth Chatto's dry gravel garden.

Peony flowers are followed by shiny, black or red seeds.

Succulents require dry, well-drained conditions.

Colourful seeds pods of Cercis siliquastrum, Judas tree.

174

Hibiscus syriacus, *enjoy well-drained soil.*   Puya alpestris, *from Chile.*   *African daisies,* Arctosis *and* Gazania.

A beautiful display of Spanish bluebells. Hyacinthoides hispanica.

Bladder Senna, Colutea arborescens. *Shrubs with pea-like, red-tinged, yellow flowers and attractively swollen seed pods.*

Abutilon × suntense *has saucer shaped white or blue flowers, and enjoys a sheltered wall.*

Greece and its Islands

Despite Greece and its islands having the richest floral diversity of any European country, it does not have the same culture of historical private gardens. However, one only has to look at Greek frescoes and pottery to see exquisitely portrayed plants and flowers. Towns grew larger and people began creating gardens around their houses, although these were exceptions rather than the rule. Today, Greece is steadily building a new tradition of great, modern gardens.

Summers are generally very hot, often with no rain, and strong winds. Winters are cold, temperatures can fall below freezing, with rain and sometimes snow. Spring and autumn are temperate months when gardens and countryside burst into bloom. Large tracts of arid, rocky hillsides have shallow soil over bare rock. Fertile plains are cradled between rugged peaks. Although coastal frosts are rare, high mountains carry snow for many months.

Hillsides are scarred with ancient terracing that absorbed the heat of winter sun, warming the soil. Terraces helped prevent erosion and facilitated cultivation, and stone walls offered some shade and protection. Production of food crops was important, including tomatoes, peppers, avocado, fruit, olives, vines and citrus.

Greek Style in Britain

Borde Hill Gardens, Sussex, has a 'Greek bank' planted with native Greek species. Also in Sussex, the late Sir Frederick and Lady Stern's garden at Highdown has many Greek plants and bulbs collected on expeditions by E.K. Balls. Thriving on almost pure chalk, many, such as the tiny *Anemone blanda*, naturalized everywhere. In Nottingham a Mediterranean garden on sandstone includes numerous Greek species. With no conservatory or greenhouse, tender plants, including pomegranate, over-winter on a sheltered, south-facing

North terraces, Sparoza, Greece. The garden, begun by Jaqueline Tyrwhitt in 1965, is now headquarters of The Mediterranean Garden Society. Photograph courtesy of Jennifer Gay.

Here at Highdown, Sussex, the garden of the late Sir Frederick Stern, Greek species adapted well to growing in little more than pure chalk.

ABOVE: *A well-shaped terracotta urn bursting with colourful plants at RHS garden Rosemoor, Devon.*

RIGHT: *A magnificent hanging basket at Leeds Castle, Kent.*

patio. Plants include *Campsis grandiflora, Carpobrotus edulis, Datura, Dracunculus vulgaris, Fritillaria graeca, Hibiscus syriacus, Medicago arborea, Olea europa, Pancratium maritimum*, and *Sternbergia lutea*. Historically, Greek gardens were favoured too: in the 1740s 'Capability' Brown laid out a Grecian valley and William Kent designed Grecian temples at Stowe, Buckinghamshire.

In Greece, 'gardens' are often collections of assorted pots of every shape, size and description, containing vegetables and flowers. Cans, oil drums, ancient clay jars, disused kitchen pans – in fact, anything that will hold plants! Gathered near the house, precious water from washing or dishes can be saved for plants. To add a Greek touch to a garden you could tuck in a small classical statue, stone seat or piece of decorative marble. Modern statues can be aged with yoghurt, sour milk or by being buried for a few months.

Group containers around doors or against steps. A tiny paved courtyard can have one single pot containing a specimen tree, or larger groupings of containers and plants, as space allows. Utilize weird and wonderful containers, or keep them all uniform. Window boxes and hanging baskets allow vertical displays of cascading plants, while climbers bound up frameworks of canes or twigs. Large containers hold trees and shrubs. Include a tiny water garden in an old sink or

wooden tub, filled with marginal plants and miniature water lilies.

Use your imagination and visit garden centres or salvage yards for massive selections of chimney pots, barrels, baskets, grow bags, hanging baskets, sinks, troughs of wood, metal or stone, trugs, tubs, tyres, urns, wheelbarrows, water cans, cisterns or window boxes. There are as many different materials as there are containers: cast iron, clay, copper, glass-fibre, glazed porcelain, lead, plastic, stainless steel, stone, reconstituted stone and wood. The wonderful colours of weathered clay pots or old oil jars are difficult to surpass, gradations of colour depending on where they were made.

Cacti and succulents grow well in pots and are simple to move during winter: *Aloe, Echeveria, Sempervivum, Kalanchoe, Sedum, Crassula, Opuntia*. Many tender species can be grown with a little winter protection.

Container gardening is 'instant gardening'. An ever-changing selection of plants creates colour and interest throughout the year with bulbs, annuals, half-hardy annuals and biennials. Perennials, trees, shrubs, ever-

LEFT AND ABOVE: A good sense of humour at RHS garden Harlow Carr, West Yorkshire. Toilet pans find another use, as do old boots.

greens and topiary trees form permanent displays. Containers are ideal for growing Mediterranean plants as they can provide ideal drainage. Pots are easy to move to create new arrangements, brighten dull areas, hide unsightly manhole covers or pipes, create focal points or add instant colour.

Pots and containers, however, require quite intensive maintenance. Dead-heading keeps plants trim, encouraging new growth and flowers. Feeding depends on the plants being grown. Winter displays are not fed between late summer and early spring; spring bulbs and biennials do not require feeding, but summer bedding plants need regular feeding. Plants easily absorb liquid fertilizers, while slow-release granules, sticks and pills are increasingly popular. Measure accurately, mix well and distribute evenly, following manufacturers' instructions. Both over- and under-fertilizing are damaging. Regular weeding

Filled with drainage material and free-drained compost, this old bath makes an unusual receptacle for plants.

keeps plants tidy, removes competition for valuable water and nutrients, and helps keep away pests and diseases.

Watering is of paramount importance, especially in summer where pots often require watering at least twice a day (especially porous clay pots, which absorb more water than glazed or plastic containers). Compost should not become waterlogged, and check watering does not wash away soil, exposing roots. Placing pots near entrances makes reusing household grey water easy, but be sure to eliminate strong detergents, grease or food particles that rot, causing offensive odours and damage to plants. Stand pots in saucers filled with gravel and water from the bottom once established. This also increases moisture circulation around the plants. Misting is beneficial, keeping plants clean, but never mist in strong sunlight.

Composts should be free draining but water retentive. Additions of perlite, vermiculite or water-retaining granules can help quality. Special composts suit individual plant requirements, such as ericaceous compost for *Camellia* and *Erica*. Make sure containers have adequate drainage holes, add a layer of broken crock, followed by a layer of pea-shingle, before filling with well-mixed, friable compost.

Insert plants to the height of the soil in the original pot and thoroughly soak root balls *before* planting. Place larger plants in containers before filling with compost, then pack compost around, firm and finish about 2cm below container rims.

Dressing the surface with shingle looks attractive,

This collection of succulents survives happily all year outside in a hilltop garden in Shropshire.

helps preserve moisture and prevent weed growth. Ground cover plants such as *Ajuga*, *Arabis* and *Thymus* species are attractive additions to larger pots containing trees or climbers. Create scented seats by planting low chimney pots or troughs with chamomile or thyme.

Containers set directly onto the ground provide havens for slugs, ants, earwigs and wood lice, while wooden containers rot. Supporting pots on small blocks encourages air flow and better drainage. Mount heavy containers on low, wheeled platforms to facilitate moving.

An old stone trough filled with low-growing herbs at The National Herb Centre, Oxfordshire.

Plants for Pots

Spring/summer

Brachycome iberidifolia. Half-hardy, blue or white, daisy-like flowers.

Epimediums. Attractive leaves and clusters of flowers in late spring and early summer. Dry soil.

Nerium oleander. Shrub with narrow leaves and white, pink or red flowers. Winter protection.

Pelargonium, zonal, ivy-leaved or scented. Different leaf, flower forms and colours.

Lobularia maritima, **sweet alyssum**. Clusters of tiny scented white or mauve flowers.

Winter

Bellis perennis, **daisy**. Rounded leaves and white, pink or red petalled flowers.

Cheiranthus cheiri, **wallflower**. Narrow leaves and scented, four-petalled flowers.

Crocus species, and other bulbs such as *Eranthis hyemalis*; *Galanthus nivalis*; *Iris reticulata*, *I. danfordiae*; *Muscari*; miniature narcissus, tulip species and lilies.

Viola × **'Wittrockiana', pansy 'Universal Mixed'**. Rounded leaves and brightly coloured, flat-faced flowers.

Skimmia japonica **'Rubella'**. Bright red flower buds in winter open to white flowers with yellow anthers in spring.

Climbing and trailing

Helichrysum petiolare. Tender arching trailer with rounded, downy, white leaves.

Humulus lupulus **'Aureus', golden hop**. Climber with yellow, hop-like leaves.

Ipomoea tricolour, **morning glory**. Climber with bright blue, funnel-shaped flowers.

Lapageria rosea, **Chilean bellflower**. Glossy, leathery leaves and pendant pink, magenta or white flowers, for a sheltered corner.

Tradescantia fluminensis. Green, purple or variegated leaves.

Evergreens

Buxus sempervirens **'Suffruticosa'**. Small, dark green, shiny leaves.

Chamaecyparis lawsoniana **'Ellwoodii'**. Dark green, slow-

Pots of Nerium oleander *dominate the terrace at Kiftsgate Court, Gloucestershire.*

Brightly coloured Pelargonium *always look attractive in pots.*

Crocus *species adapt happily to both naturalizing or growing in containers.*

Lapageria rosea, *Chilean bellflower.*

Ipomoea tricolour.

Buxus sempervirens. *Snowshill Manor, Worcestershire. (The National Trust)*

Herb planter, RHS garden Harlow Carr, West Yorkshire.

Asphodeline lutea, *yellow asphodel, with tall spikes of star-like yellow flowers and grassy leaves.*

Dracunculus vulgaris, *Dragon Arum, a spectacular plant with a rather unfortunate odour.*

growing, columnar tree. *C. pisifera* 'Boulevard'. Silver-blue, cone-shaped.

Euonymus fortunei. Variegated leaves.

Hebe × *franciscana* **'Variegata'**. Rounded, cream edged leaves, with mauve flowers in summer. Sheltered position. *H.* × *andersonii* 'Variegata'. Cream and green leaves, for large containers.

Thuja orientalis **'Aurea Nana'** = **platycladus orientalis**. Golden foliage, compact, rounded shape.

Herbs and food plants

Hanging baskets, containers and specialist planters are ideal for herbs, fruit and vegetables, including aubergines, courgettes, cucumbers, small lettuce, peppers and tomatoes. Strawberries and fruit trees all grow well in containers.

In larger gardens include rustic poled pergolas or arbours, a 'lawn' of *Achillea millefolium*, or low-growing chamomile, which can be trimmed like grass, and plants such as acacia, *Allium, Anemone, Asphodelus, Cydonia, Dracunculus, Echium, Fritillaria, Gladiolus, Iris, Mandragora, Paeonia, Punica* and *Salvia*.

Aubrieta deltoidea, *native to Greece and around the Aegean, has adapted well to the British climate, although it still enjoys a rocky habitat. Here it has naturalized on this stone wall in Shropshire. Many cultivars have been developed, both single and double, in a range of blue-purple shades.*

Elements for the Greek Garden

Showy red pomegranate flowers.

An elegant stone vase.

A large old, terracotta jar.

Triteleia laxa 'Queen Fabiola', thrives in dry soil and hot sun, ideal at the base of a wall.

Phuopsis stylosa, with heads of tiny, perfumed, purple flowers.

Stone troughs make excellent containers for drought tolerant species.

Giant alliums make a striking show in the late spring garden.

A white painted planter overflowing with delicate flowers.

Osteospermums, available in shades of white, yellow, pink and mauve.

Anemone coronaria, from the Mediterranean, enjoy full sun and light sandy soil with summer drought.

A small statue adds an authentic touch to the Greek garden. The Hundred House, Shropshire.

South Africa

The winter rainfall belt in South Africa is situated around the south of Western Cape province. The country boasts thousands of species of indigenous plants and bulbs, playing a vitally important role in world plant heritage. The Kirstenbosch gardens, Cape Town, founded in 1913 to study and preserve the country's rich floral heritage, are world renowned, with collections of bulbs, *Cycad*, *Erica*, *Protea*, ferns, succulents and Cape endemics. South African species are readily available for gardens world-wide, including outstanding bulbous species.

South African Inspiration

Ventnor Botanic Garden, Isle of Wight, has a South African garden on south-facing terraces of local stone, which includes bulbous species of *Agapanthus*, *Diascia*, *Kniphofia*, *Osteospermum*, *Pelargonium* and *Watsonia*.

Another South African garden has developed on a housing estate near Plymouth. The garden is south facing and free draining, allowing maximum light and warmth during winter. David Fenwick concentrates specifically on African species and well-drained beds are filled with collections of plants, many grown from seed or cuttings. Larger plants offer protection for smaller, tender species, and cuttings ensure any plants

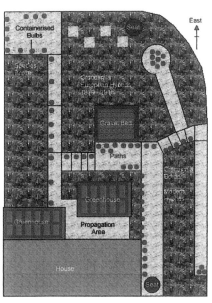

ABOVE LEFT AND LEFT: David Fenwick's African Garden in Plymouth, crammed with tender species, most of which happily survive the British winter. (Photographs courtesy of David Fenwick)

ABOVE RIGHT: Plan of the African garden, Plymouth. (Reproduced by kind permission of David Fenwick)

damaged by frost are replaced. Of more than 1,000 different varieties, only 15 per cent come indoors during winter. There are National Collections of *Amarylis*, *Crocosmia* with *Chasmanthe, Eucomis, Galtonia, Freesia* (*Anomatheca* Group) and *Tulbaghia*. David recommends planting 'half-hardy' South African bulbs much deeper than generally accepted, providing frost protection during winter. He plants *Crinum* up to 1m; Watsonia 35cm; *Zantedeschia* 30cm, and *Eucomis* and some *Crocosmia* over 15cm. Beds are well mulched and David employs an effective groundcover/mulch of succulents such as *Lampranthus* and *Delosperma*, or plants like *Diascia* and *Pelargonium grossularioides*. Planted from cuttings, these form thick mats giving protection to bulbs below. Although frost kills 50 to 75 per cent of this 'mulch' annually, old plants are replaced with new cuttings in spring. Low walls and raised beds are painted dark green, absorbing more warmth in winter, keeping soil a degree or two higher, as well as complementing the plants.

North Africa

Although bordering the Mediterranean Sea, North African countries always seem to have a more exotic ambience. Garden design is influenced by the arid landscapes, whitewashed, stuccoed houses, mud bricks, domed mosques and intricate mosaics. Intimate enclosed courtyards are decorated with coloured, glazed tiles in natural designs of flowers and fruit. Water was sacred and gardens were adorned with still pools and channels reflecting the sky, and gentle fountains cooling the air. Early gardens developed along agrarian lines incorporating fruit, flowers, vegetables, herbs, gourds and vines. In countries where temperatures rise to 45°C, trees such as *Cupressus*, evergreen hedges, cork oak and fruit trees add essential shade. Exquisite, well-irrigated, formal and informal gardens are richly planted, green oases filled with carnations, honeysuckle, lilies, iris, jasmine, marigolds, narcissus, zinnias and hundreds more exotic blooms, with pungent perfumes of flowers and spices filling the air. Important native bulbs include *Crocus*, *Muscari*, *Narcissus* and *Tulipa*. Tulips became highly desirable, especially forms with elongated, pointed petals, and huge beds were filled with rare specimens. The bulbs were also traded for vast sums. Colourful roses grown across pergolas provided petals that could be used for flavouring food and for oil in perfumes. Orchards of figs, olives, vines, pomegranate, and palms strung with luscious dates also abound. We grow many North African plants, especially bulbous species.

The beautiful flowers of Algerian iris, Iris unguicularis, *flower in Britain between December and April.*

Delosperma sutherlandii forms thick, colourful mats, useful when these plants are used as a natural 'mulch' to protect tender bulbs which are growing beneath them.

To introduce North African elements, include smooth, reflecting pools or gently playing fountains; stuccoed white walls adorned with climbing plants and vines; small pavilions decorated with glazed tiles; arched gateways; hand-crafted pottery or copper containers for plants; palms; fruit trees, pomegranate and figs; colourful shrubs; jewel-bright flowers; weatherproof rattan furniture. *Hedera maroccana*, Moroccan ivy, provides attractive ground cover and is tough, withstanding drought as well as cold.

A Selection of
South African Plants

Kniphofia rooperi

Eucomis comosa

Zantedeschia aethiopica

Crinum × powellii

Regal pelargonium

Agapanthus campanulatus

Crocosmia citronella

Nerine bowdenii

Galtonia candicans

Schizostylis coccinea

187

California, Chile, Australia and New Zealand

It seems incongruous to group the vast and incredible areas of coastal California, central Chile, southern and south-western Australia together, but they do not necessarily have distinctive styles that can be transported into Britain. They do, however, provide vast ranges of glorious plants, many of which happily adapt to cooler climates: *Acacia*, asters, *Araucaria araucana*, monkey puzzle tree, *Brugmansia*, *Ceanothus*, *Cordyline*, *Cornus*, *Crinodendron*, *Embothrium*, *Eschscholzia*, *Eucalyptus*, *Fuchsia*, *Helichrysum*, *Lapageria*, *Leptospermum*, *Matthiola*, *Nicotiana*, *Olearia*, *Phlox*, *Phormium*, *Plectranthus*, *Romneya*, *Salvia*, *Trillium* and *Yucca*, to name only a very few.

LEFT: Salvia involucrata.

ABOVE: Phormium tenax.

LEFT: Cordyline australis *at Leeds Castle, Kent.*

Carol Valentine's steep garden in California, designed by Isabelle Green, representing landscape as viewed from a plane. (Photograph courtesy of Sue Pendleton)

Small desert-like areas look good in colder climates, using stones, boulders, sand or gravel. Sweeps of grasses provide year round, 'prairie-like' illusions. Dry riverbeds of shale offer attractive, well-drained areas for plants. A garden near Belsay, Northumberland, moulded 80 tons of imported topsoil to represent the curves and banks of a dried-out riverbed. Various grades of stone and rock with chunks of bog oak added texture and colour, while plants were chosen for their rusty and bronze colours: *Ajuga, Carex comans, Digitalis ferruginea, Euphorbia characias* subs. *wulfenii* 'Purple and Gold', *E. griffithii* 'Dixter', *Gladiolus papilio, Sedum* and dusky poppies. A second gravel garden uses shale, river sand and silver-blue toned plants, including *Amelancher* and *Eucalyptus gunnii*, enhanced by decking and blue-grey lath fencing.

California has many outstanding gardens, including the world famous Huntington Gardens, San Marino. Isabelle Greene designed a sloping garden with three integrated terraces, very effectively representing 'landscape' as seen from a plane. Divided into sections using blocks of drought tolerant plants and variously coloured succulents, rocks form a 'river' and a slab of polished black granite gives highly effective glints of 'water'. Even unplanted sections fit well and become integral parts of this scheme.

Australia has given us many plants for drought tolerant gardens, while Chile has provided all manner of exotic-looking species, which have adapted well to cooler regions. All of these countries have supplied plants that are invaluable in our Mediterranean, drought tolerant gardens, providing wonderful colours, textures and shapes year round.

Winter in Trevor Nottle's garden, Walnut Hill, Australia.

189

Plants from the Americas and Australasia

Zauscheneria californica

Sisyrinchium striatum

Carpenteria californica

Calycanthus occidentalis

Acacia retinodes

Phlox paniculata

190

Rhodochiton atrosanguineum

Olearia 'Waikariensis'

Tropaeolum polyphyllum

Liatris spicata

12 The Bare Necessities: Maintenance and Garden Care

We all aspire to achieving beautiful gardens. It is an added bonus when they are easy to maintain, as Mediterranean gardens can be. All gardens, however, require some maintenance to keep them in peak condition and Mediterranean gardens are no exception.

Plants

Condition

Gardens always look better when plants are healthy. Of necessity drought tolerant plants must be strong to survive in their native surroundings. Regular dead-heading improves appearance, strengthens plants and encourages new flowers. Remove dead or diseased growth and compost or burn. Check for pests and treat accordingly. Do not let piles of rubbish and weeds accumulate: they may harbour disease. Clear autumn leaves to the compost heap. Regular weeding keeps gardens tidy and allows more moisture and nutrients to reach the plants. When planting check root balls are thoroughly soaked and plant in autumn to establish with winter rain. Check taller plants are stable after high winds. Stake or support plants where necessary.

OPPOSITE: *The beautiful flowers of* Agapanthus – *African lily – come in many shades, from pale to deepest blue as well as white.*

RIGHT: *Plants are well maintained and healthy in Beth Chatto's Essex garden.*

Drainage

The main problem in colder climates is that drought tolerant plants get too much water rather than too little. By providing good, basic drainage, this problem is largely eliminated. Water, held around roots for lengthy periods, causes roots to rot, while in cold

weather it freezes, further damaging plants. Drainage is vitally important for drought tolerant plants in cooler, northern climates where we do get rain.

Mulches

Mulches help retain moisture in the soil and create cool root runs for plants. They also limit weed growth, cutting down on another onerous chore. Obviously weeds still grow – even if we covered everything with 2m of concrete weeds would still grow somehow. Weed seeds have difficulty penetrating mulches, however, and those that do are easily removed. After planting or weeding, make sure mulch is carefully raked back around plants so soil is not exposed, inviting weeds to return. Similarly, check birds do not leave exposed soil after scratching around for insects. Renew mulches when wearing thin to keep gardens tidy and stop weed seeds establishing, causing problems later.

Beth Chatto's garden in Essex is a perfect example of all the principles of good, drought tolerant gardening: (TOP) Well-mulched beds filled with healthy, drought tolerant plants; (BOTTOM) Collections of pots grouped near the house for ease of maintenance.

Pots and Containers

Containerized plants need regular water, but if surfaces of pots are mulched this helps retain moisture for longer. Raising pots slightly above ground helps eliminate slugs, snails and woodlice finding comfortable homes beneath them. Use small blocks of wood, or purpose-made blocks or wedges from garden centres. Always clean containers thoroughly before replanting. Group near water sources for ease of maintenance.

Water-wise Gardens

Using drought tolerant plants massively reduces use of water in the garden, as well as long hours spent watering during summer. When plants are grouped according to their water-wise requirements, watering is further limited to only those few plants that really need it.

Pests, Diseases and Garden Hygiene

Happy plants are healthy plants. If they are strong and grow well, they are far less likely to attract pests and diseases than if they are weak and struggling.

Garden hygiene is important. Do not leave rotting piles of weeds and rubbish around to act as breeding grounds. Check plants for damage. Remove diseased material as quickly as possible and burn rather than compost it. Use crop rotation where appropriate. Make sure tools are well maintained and clean, so that diseases and pests are not transferred around the garden.

Keep a watchful eye and be ready to deal with pests when they appear. Simply removing by hand the first few aphids can forestall a plague.

Some plants encourage beneficial insects into the garden, such as hoverfly larvae, which chomp through aphids *ad infinitum*. Hoverflies are particularly attracted to yellow flowers. By encouraging them into the garden through the planting of yellow flowers, you create a very effective, perfectly natural, 'biological' control, causing no harm to anything but the aphids, and costing nothing. It is sad that many people consider hoverflies nothing more than small 'wasps' and they are reviled and feared in the same way. Ladybirds and their larvae are also gluttons for aphids but most of us love these shiny red bugs.

Certain insects attract birds into the garden and will soon be picked off. Feed and encourage birds so

It is important to encourage beneficial insects into the garden.
(TOP) *A hoverfly heads for the yellow centre on this hollyhock flower, and they adore sunflowers.*
(BOTTOM) *This bee hunts for nectar amongst the lavender. Bumble bees are under threat and we should do all in our power to encourage them into the garden.*

they snack on slugs, snails and other harmful pests. Ponds attract frogs and toads, who also enjoy tasty slugs.

However careful we are, some pests inevitably creep into our gardens, and it is always frustrating to find a favourite plant suddenly hosting aphids or mildew. Strike a balance between needing to obliterate everything nasty and smothering plants and gardens with noxious chemicals.

Often our first reaction is to reach for the pesticide to treat whatever bug has suddenly appeared. However, we are becoming increasingly aware of the damage chemicals and pesticides can do and now have access to many effective organic and biological controls. Use chemicals only as a last resort. They might destroy pests more quickly and easily but can have long-term, damaging effects on animals, people and the planet.

At one time garden chemicals included such perilous substances as arsenic and cyanide. In the same way these were discontinued, the use of many modern chemicals has been restricted because of the toxicity. Today's chemicals are safer, but they still contain noxious substances, and must be treated with caution since many have dangerous side-effects. You are advised to follow manufacturers' instructions precisely. Although modern herbicides and pesticides are kinder to wildlife than previously, they are still a danger to many creatures we want to encourage into our gardens. Kill the good bugs and nature's balance is quickly lost, giving bad bugs a free run with their predators eliminated. Maintain a balance and encourage the garden to look after itself.

Insecticides

For both indoor and outdoor use, to kill a wide range of pests, or target specifics. Some must not be used on edible crops, others require crops are left for a certain time before harvesting. Systemics are absorbed by the plant before being ingested by the insect; others kill on contact with insects. Handle chemicals with care, mix and apply exactly according to manufacturers' instructions; label and store clearly and safely and do not leave cans or sprays of ready mixed chemicals lying around where they might cause a dangerous hazard.

Fungicides

For fungal infections either on contact or as systemic, they are generally used as preventatives rather than cures. Some fungal diseases are affected by weather and are possible to predict. Others may have been reoccurring problems for years, building up spores in the soil. Make sure the fungicide used is suitable for the problem.

Biological Controls

Generally target very specific pests, so varying controls are introduced to counteract different problems: microscopic mites for thrips; small parasitic wasp species for whitefly, mealy bugs and scale; nematodes for vine weevils and slugs; bacterium against caterpillars; pheromone traps for troublesome moths.

Biological controls are particularly effective under glass but are now also available for outside use. Generally from warmer countries, most, if not all, die during our winter months, but this technology is still in the early stages and it is always a concern we could unleash some unwanted insect to cause havoc in future generations. Again, maintaining nature's balance is key: upset that and we pay a high price, even though it may not be immediately evident. Introducing rabbits into Australia seemed like a good idea at the time – until they almost took over the country!

Biological controls are not cheap. They can be detrimentally affected if chemical pesticides have previously been used, as the effects can last for some time after chemical sprays are discontinued. Some species used as controls have wings, so treated plants need covering with protective nets until predators have established themselves and found their food source.

Problem Check List

Aphids

Spread quickly, covering plants in a short time. There are also root aphids. All aphids distort growth and reduce a plant's strength, making it susceptible to viral diseases and other pests.

Aphid nymphs shed their skins and these tiny white specks are often the first noticeable sign of infestation. Sooty mould is also associated with aphids as it thrives on their sticky secretions. Encourage hoverflies, ladybirds and lacewings into the garden. Treat with insecticide, or use organic treatments such as soft soap, derris or pyrethrum; biological controls may also be used.

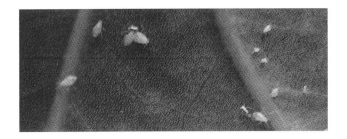

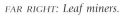

LEFT: *Aphids.*

RIGHT: *Ladybirds control greenfly.*

FAR RIGHT: *Leaf miners.*

Birds

Some birds cause problems, such as blackbirds on fruit or bullfinches with buds, but we are losing such vast quantities of native birds that we should be protecting them rather than considering the small amount of damage they cause as anything but a minor inconvenience. Fruit nets and cages protect soft fruit. Check, too, that mulches have not been disturbed.

Botrytis

Grey mould on plants in damp conditions. Remove and burn infected material, use fungicide and practise good garden hygiene.

Caterpillars

Damage plants and leaves. Use grease bands on trees, insecticide, or pick off by hand.

Earwigs, Forficula auricularia

Brown insects around 18mm long with pincer-like rear ends. Nocturnal and harmless, except when severe infestations damage plants. Earwigs eat aphids and codling moth eggs. Treat with insecticide, if necessary; small flower pots stuffed with straw or rolled newspaper placed in borders attract earwigs for easy disposal.

Froghoppers, Philaenus spumaris

Yellow-green nymph in 'cuckoo-spit', frothy bubbles on stems or leaves. Unsightly but not harmful. Remove by hand.

Frost

Blackens leaves and stems, damaging early flowers.

Remove unsightly growth, but hardy plants generally recover. Mulching helps protect plants, or apply a protective layer of straw, bracken or horticultural fleece in particularly vulnerable areas. Take cuttings of exceptionally tender species so replacements are available.

Fusarium Wilt

Attacks roots causing black patches on stems and leaves and possibly light-coloured, fluffy growth. Remove and burn infected plants and remove or sterilize surrounding soil. Avoid growing vulnerable plants as many resistant varieties are available.

Honey Fungus

Caused by *Armillaria* fungus, which attacks woody plants. In advanced stages honey-coloured fungi appear at base of plants in autumn, and white threads creep through bark. It is difficult to control, but try removing and burning infected plants. Bamboos, box, Cotinus, Hebe, Romneya and yew all have good resistance.

Leaf Miners

Conspicuous, light marks trailing across leaf surfaces denote insects burrowing inside. Treat with insecticide or pick off and destroy infected leaves.

Leatherjackets

Greyish-brown maggots, about 3–5cm, larvae of cranefly (daddy-long-legs). Use soil insecticide or destroy larvae when found.

Lily Beetle, Lilioceris lilii

Red beetles, around 6mm long, and larvae covered in

ABOVE: *Lily beetle,*
Lilioceris lilii.

ABOVE RIGHT: *Mice damage bulbs and seeds.*

black excrement eat leaves and flowers. Use insecticide or remove by hand.

Mealybugs

Colonies of sap-sucking insects covered with white, cotton wool-like substance, on leaves and stems. Cacti are susceptible. Use insecticide, organic insecticidal soap or biological control.

Mice and Rats

Damage bulbs and seeds. Spring traps are efficient. Humane traps are available. Poison baits are effective but dangerous, and must be kept away from children, birds and other animals.

Pollen Beetles

Various species, black or dark green, around 2mm long, infest flowers. They generally cause little damage, but can be a problem in cut flowers. Stand flowers in water in a shed or garage, near but not against an open window, for a few hours and beetles should clear.

Powdery Mildew

White, powdery, fungal growths on leaves. Remove infected material, wash plants or use fungicide.

Rain

Good drainage eliminates most problems, although heavy rain can damage plants. Remove damaged material before it rots, attracting other diseases.

Red Spider Mite

Various species of almost microscopic mites denoted by fine webbing. Some strains are resistant to insecticides. Use biological controls.

Rust

Various fungi causing rust-coloured spots. Remove and burn infected material or use fungicide, but check as not all are suitable.

Scale Insects

Various kinds, noticeable on stems and undersides of leaves. Use insecticidal spray on newly hatched nymphs or biological control.

Slugs

Can live above or below ground and are difficult to eradicate. Remedies include saucers of beer and upturned, halved grapefruit skins hidden beneath greenery at food sources. Both need regular checking and removal of pests. Slug baits or biological controls.

Snails

Inverted plant pots, with one side slightly elevated, tucked into borders provide 'homes', although not safe houses, for snails. A circle of gravel or ash around plants or borders helps prevent slugs and snails crossing. Use bait judiciously, encourage birds or use biological control.

Scale insects.

ABOVE: *Vine weevil,
Otiorhynchus sulcatas.*

ABOVE: *Woodlice,* Oniscus
asellus.

Sooty Mould

Black or grey mould associated with aphids. Control by treating aphid infestations.

Vine Weevil, Otiorhynchus sulcatus

Grubs and adults cause damage. Use insecticidal spray, dust, remove by hand, or try biological control.

Whitefly

Adults look like white dust. Use insecticide, organic pesticide or biological control.

Wind Burn

Browning of leaves and shoots after severe weather. Plants generally recover.

Wireworms

Thin, orange larvae, around 2.5cm long with three pairs of short legs, attack root crops. Soil insecticide or destroy by hand when seen.

Woodlice, Oniscus asellus

Small grey-brown, segmented bodies that can roll into a ball. Live in rotting vegetation, wood or beneath stones. They are generally only a problem with young seedlings. They live on, and dispose of, decaying vegetation.

A rough rule of thumb is that bugs that move quickly are good, those that move slowly are bad. So resist zapping everything that moves!

Garden Check List

Fences, Hedges and Boundaries

Maintain regularly to keep in good order. Treat wooden fences with proprietary preservatives when necessary. Hedges and trees may require trimming or pruning. Give gates an annual scrub, coat of paint or wood preservative treatment. Oil hinges.

Fertilizers

Nothing beats good, home-made, organic compost. In nature, drought tolerant plants have to be tough to survive. In general they should not be heavily fertilized, since this alters their whole attraction: they become sappy and susceptible to wind and disease.

Give gates an annual scrub, coat of paint or wood preservative treatment, and oil hinges.

Maintain wooden structures and treat with suitable preservative. Archway at Angel Gardens, Shropshire.

Furniture and Wood

Wide varieties of furniture are available made from many different materials. If possible store under cover during winter. Wash covers if necessary and store cushions and awnings, making sure they are completely dry and will not attract mould. Wash metal and plastic with warm, soapy water, using a small brush if intricate designs trap dirt, and then dry. Clean wooden furniture and apply specific preservative that will not damage clothes. Repair wooden structures such as gates, arches or pergolas in winter and treat with timber preservative.

Plant Supports

Fix trellises and frameworks securely to walls. Light wires also make good plant supports when securely fastened to walls or buildings. Obelisks, arches and pergolas should be of sound construction and well maintained. Construct simple wigwam supports of natural twigs, branches or bamboo canes. Purpose-made plant supports can be placed around plants in early spring, enabling plants to grow through. Wooden

garden structures require regular maintenance with timber preservative, but first check this is compatible with plants. Make sure hanging baskets, containers and window boxes are securely fixed.

Poisons

Many garden chemicals have adverse effects on humans and animals, and some can prove fatal. Extreme care must be taken with handling and storing all chemicals, keeping them well out of reach of children and pets. Keep one can specifically for pesticides or weedkillers and make sure it is clearly marked. Take care when mixing or transferring chemicals. Wipe up spills and dispose of chemical containers safely. Make sure spray drift or run off does not contaminate other areas, ponds or waterways.

Many plants contain toxins that affect humans or animals, ranging from mild skin or eye irritations to death. It is safer to treat all plants with caution. A few offenders include: *Aconitum*, *Amarylis*, *Brugmansia*, *Buxus*, *Colchicum*, *Datura*, *Euonymus*, *Euphorbia*, *Fremontodendron*, *Helleborus*, *Ipomoea*, *Laburnum*, *Lantana*, *Mandragora*, *Nerium oleander*, *Ornithogalum*, *Prunus laurocerasus*, *Ricinus*, *Robinia*, *Spartium junceum*, *Zantedeschia*.

Pruning

Many trees and shrubs do not require excessive pruning, but dead or diseased wood or tangled branches can be carefully removed. Others are improved by pruning for a good basic framework or to encourage flowers. Make clean cuts with sharp secateurs or a pruning knife, beginning opposite a healthy bud and cutting up at an angle to finish just above the bud.

Certain shrubs such as *Buddleja davidii* require cutting back hard to produce stronger growth. Pruning ornamental dogwoods encourages brightly coloured, new growth. Some clematis, generally large flowered species, require cutting back in autumn; others, such as *C. Montana*, are left to climb at will. Prune roses, thinning weak wood and training new shoots.

Long-established trees often require removal of dead wood and care should always be taken to avoid accidents. Cut dead and diseased branches back to healthy tissue, and lateral branches flush with the main branch. Cut surfaces should slope down to facilitate rainwater run off. When removing branches ensure they do not tear from the trunk, exposing good tissue and causing open wounds. Cut heavy branches in two or three

Plant supports can be highly sophisticated or very simple.
ABOVE LEFT: *Supports for roses with decorative wooden stakes and hooped iron.*
ABOVE RIGHT: *Decorative wooden poles for climbing roses.*
RIGHT: *Purpose-made wire supports for herbaceous plants.*
BELOW: *A simply constructed support of twigs.*

Many plants are toxic and should be treated cautiously.
ABOVE: Helleborus orientalis. Hellebores and mandrake were used as both narcotics and poisons in Ancient Greece.
ABOVE LEFT AND LEFT: Mandragora officinarum, mandrake, has pale green flowers, followed by orange fruits. When uprooted the screams of the plant are said to kill those who hear them.
OPPOSITE: The Dry Garden at RHS Hyde Hall, Essex.

Regularly sweep paths and patios, removing dead leaves and plant material, which could harbour disease.

sections and make sure falling branches do not pose a danger. Carefully trim wounds and when dry, apply a sealing agent. Most trees are pruned during winter but some, such as *Prunus*, are pruned in late spring and early summer to reduce risk of infections.

Stonework

Make sure paving and walls are well constructed and check at least once a year to ensure structures are sound. It is far better to replace one stone than wait for the wall to fall down. Regularly sweep paths and patios, removing dead leaves and plant material, which could harbour disease.

Tools and Equipment

Investing in a basic set of quality, stainless-steel tools pays dividends. Spend a few minutes on cleaning and maintenance after use and they will last a lifetime. Make sure they are suitable to your needs and are of the correct weight.

Topiary

Slow-growing, evergreen trees with small leaves, such as *Buxus* species or *Taxus*, are ideal for topiary. Patience is required since topiary can take years, although most garden centres now sell wire frames, or plants in pots, already trained onto frames to simplify the process. Topiary can be as simple as a small, trimmed ball or cone of box, to enormous hedges of intricate design. Even massive, fully clipped and trained pieces are avail-able to buy, although at considerable cost. Trim low-growing hedges, such as box, in spring and autumn to keep looking immaculate.

Water

Make sure ponds are safe with children around. Even a few centimetres of water can be dangerous, so safety is of paramount importance where water is concerned

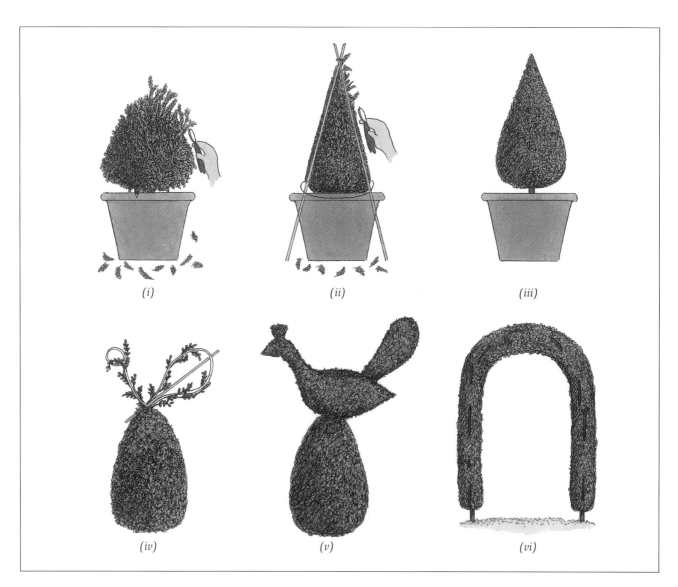

Creating a simple topiary cone:
(i) Young trees are trimmed in August.
(ii) Using a framework of canes and wire as a guide, cut the cone shape the following year.
(iii) Having achieved the shape, clip as required to keep a tidy outline.
(iv) To trim a peacock shape: when the bush is sufficiently grown attach a simple wire frame and start tying in shoots.
(v) Over a period of time train and trim the shoots to fill the frame.
(vi) A basic arch is formed from two trees trained and tied into a wire frame at the top.

in the garden. When a good balance is achieved between plants and fish, ponds virtually look after themselves.

Plants need water, however minimal the amount; this even includes cacti, although they have adapted to surviving with very little. Water helps with photosynthesis and supplying nutrients. All plants require water until established. After this, drought tolerant plants survive on little or no water. In cooler climates, with regular rain, additional watering should not be necessary. In fact plants need good drainage to channel excess rain away from their roots.

Irrigation systems are increasingly sophisticated and certainly of benefit in drought ravaged countries. Most of these countries, however, also grow many native, drought tolerant plants that happily grow with little or no water, and these species should be encouraged in gardens. Irrigation systems should always be well maintained, effective, and have suitable control devices so that water is not wasted. Safeguard against run off and disable automatic systems during periods of rain.

When watering is necessary, limit to early morning or late evening when sunlight will not cause water to evaporate away. Give occasional heavy soakings rather than frequent small amounts of water, which penetrate no further than the first centimetre of soil.

Weeds

Eliminate strong, perennial weeds when preparing beds and apply mulch to help keep weeds at bay. Annual weeds are easily removed from loose materials. Check regularly and re-cover exposed areas with mulch. Hand weeding or hoeing is preferable to chemical treatments, but if necessary use a selective weedkiller, making sure it does not damage surrounding plants. Weather conditions, time of year and soil type all affect the efficiency of herbicides. Follow manufacturers' instructions rigorously. Systemic herbicides are absorbed by the plant and subsequently kill it, while other types work on contact.

Growing strong, drought tolerant plants, working with nature rather than against it, will help us to achieve a good balance and attractive, healthy gardens that are a joy to work and relax in.

Water is a delightful element in any garden. The lake at the Beth Chatto Gardens, Essex, covers a large area, but even a tiny fountain adds interest and the relaxing sight and sound of water.

ABOVE: *Mawley Hall, Shropshire.*

Plants for Mediterranean and Dry Gardens

Heights and minimum temperatures are only a general guide and should not be relied on implicitly.

Bulbs, corms and rhizomes

Allium cernuum. 70cm. Native to North America. Clump-forming bulb with long, semi-erect basal leaves (smelling of onions), and stems bearing nodding umbels of up to 30, cup-shaped, pink or white flowers in summer. Well-drained soil and open, sunny situation. Plant in autumn and propagate from seed in autumn or division in spring, but best left undisturbed.

OPPOSITE: RHS gardens contain wonderful collections of drought tolerant plants. This is Hyde Hall, in Essex.

Allium flavum. 10–30cm. Fully hardy. Clump-forming bulb with narrow, linear leaves (smelling of onions), and slender stems bearing loose umbels of up to 30 bell-shaped yellow flowers on arching stems. Well-drained soil and open, sunny position. Best left undisturbed, but can be propagated by division in spring or by seed in autumn.

Allium scorodoprasum, syn A. *jajlae*, sand leek, Spanish garlic. 90cm.

Fully hardy. Native to eastern Europe, the Caucasus, Turkey and northern Iran. Clump-forming bulb with long, narrow leaves, sheathing the stem, and dense umbels of many tiny, pink or purple flowers, sometimes replaced by bulbils. Well-drained soil and full sun. Propagate by division in spring or seed in autumn.

Anemone blanda, windflower. 5–10cm. Tuberous perennial with divided, toothed, three-lobed leaves and single stems bearing flattish, narrow-petalled flowers in white, pink or blue. Humus rich, well-drained soil in sun or shade. Best left undisturbed, but can be divided in spring after flowering.

Anemone coronaria. 5–25cm. Native to Mediterranean regions of Spain, France, Greece, Turkey and Algeria, also Central Asia. Tuberous perennial with divided, parsley-like foliage and stiff stems, each bearing a shallowly cup-shaped flower in shades of red, pink, blue, purple or white with prominent dark stamens, in spring. Well-drained soil and sun.

Arisaema candidissimum. 15cm. Native to W. China. Tuberous perennial with stiff stems bearing pink striped, green and white cowl-like spathes followed by semi-erect, three-lobed leaves. Humus-rich soil with underlying moisture and sun or part shade. Propagate by offsets in spring or seed in spring or autumn.

Crocus tommasinianus. 10cm. Spring-flowering corm with erect, narrow, basal leaves with a central white line. Slender, funnel-shaped flowers in shades of lilac and violet with orange anthers. Well-drained soil and sun. Naturalizes well. Propagate by division or seed in autumn.

Anemone pavonina. 30cm. –10°C. Native to Mediterranean regions from France eastwards to Turkey. Tubers with finely divided leaves and slender stems bearing solitary, cup-shaped flowers in early spring. Variable flower colours, pink, violet, purple or scarlet, and occa-sionally white or yellow. Well-drained soil and sun, dry in summer. Propagate by fresh seed or division.

Crocus species. 5–10cm. Spring-flowering corms with slender basal leaves and central white line. Rounded or funnel-shaped flowers in shades of white, cream, yellow, blue or mauve. Well-drained soil and sun. Plant corms in autumn or propagate from seed or division in autumn.

Crocus 'Zwanenburg Bronze'. 2.5–8cm. Spring-flowering corm with narrow leaves and white central line. Flowers deep yellow with bronze marking outside petals. Well-drained soil and sun. Propagate by division or seed sown in autumn.

Eranthis hyemalis, syn. *E. cilicicus*, winter aconite. 5–10cm. Clump-forming tubers with divided leaves and open, cup-shaped, yellow flowers backed by dissected leaf-like, green bracts. Well-drained, humus-rich soil in shade, but not too dry. Divide clumps immediately after flowering or sow seed in autumn.

Fritillaria meleagris, snake's head fritillary. 30cm. European native from Croatia and southern Russia to Poland, central France and southern Britain. Bulb with slender stems and narrow, grey-green leaves carrying heavily chequered, bell-shaped, pendant flowers in shades of pink-purple or white in spring. Well-drained soil that dries out slightly in summer, and sun or half shade. Naturalizes well. Propagate by seed in autumn and winter, or offsets in summer.

Cyclamen coum subs. *coum*. 10cm. Early spring flowering tubers with dark green, rounded leaves, marked with silver and flushed red on reverse. Carmine-coloured flowers have five reflexed petals with darker mouths. Humus-rich, well-drained soil in sun or part shade. Propagate from seed sown in late summer or autumn.

Freesia species. 30cm. Native to South Africa. Corms with long, slender, sword-shaped leaves and leafless stems bearing loose spikes of very fragrant, funnel-shaped flowers in spring or summer. Good for cutting. Well-drained soil and sun. Propagate by seed in spring or offsets in autumn.

Galtonia candicans, summer hyacinth. 1–1.2m. Native to South Africa. Bulbs with strap-shaped, semi-erect, grey-green basal leaves and a stem bearing up to 30 pendant white flowers in late summer or autumn. Fertile, well-drained, but not dry soil, in full sun. Dies down after flowering. Propagate by offsets, or seed sown in spring.

Gladiolus tristis, marsh Afrikaner. 40–150cm. 0°C. Native to Western Cape, South Africa. Narrow, often spiralled leaves and slender stems bearing narrowly bell-shaped, six-petalled, creamy yellow flowers, perfumed at night, often tinged green, flushed and dotted red-purple. Peaty sandy soil dry in summer but some winter moisture.

Muscari armeniacum, grape hyacinth. 15–20cm. Spring-flowering bulb with long, narrow, semi-erect leaves and dense spikes of small, fragrant, blue, bell-shaped flowers with constricted mouths and a narrow, notched rim. Well-drained soil and sun. Plant in autumn, propagate by seed in autumn or divide bulbs in late summer.

Paeonia cambessedesii, Mallorcan peony. 45cm. Native to eastern Mallorca and Menorca. Clump-forming perennial with attractive purple-tinged stems and lanceolate leaflets, carrying single, deep rose-coloured flowers in spring. Rich, well-drained soil and sun. Easily grown, but requires protection from late frosts. Propagate by root cuttings in winter or seed in autumn.

Iris unguicularis, syn. *I. stylosa*, Algerian iris, winter iris. 20cm. Rhizomes with tufts of strong, narrow, evergreen leaves and short-stemmed, perfumed, lilac-blue flowers with yellow marking on the three beardless falls. Flowers late autumn to spring and excellent for cutting. Sheltered south- or west-facing position. Divide rhizomes in late summer when necessary.

Muscari latifolium, grape hyacinth. 25cm. Spring-flowering bulb with strap-shaped, grey-green leaf and a dense spike of small, bell-shaped flowers. Upper flowers pale blue, lower flowers dark, blue-violet. Well-drained soil and sun. Plant in autumn, propagate by seed sown in autumn or divide bulbs in late summer.

Paeonia mascula subs. *mascula*. 25–60cm. Clump-forming perennial. Deeply lobed green leaves with from 9 to 21 leaflets and single, red-carmine flowers with bosses of golden anthers in early summer. Rich, well-drained soil and sun. Propagate by seed in autumn.

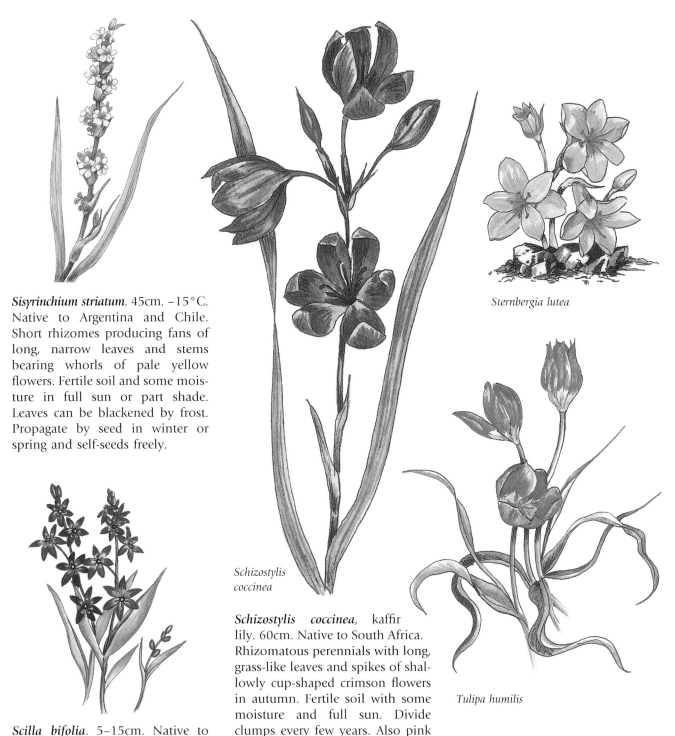

Sternbergia lutea

Schizostylis coccinea

Tulipa humilis

Sisyrinchium striatum. 45cm. −15°C. Native to Argentina and Chile. Short rhizomes producing fans of long, narrow leaves and stems bearing whorls of pale yellow flowers. Fertile soil and some moisture in full sun or part shade. Leaves can be blackened by frost. Propagate by seed in winter or spring and self-seeds freely.

Scilla bifolia. 5–15cm. Native to central and southern Europe. Spring-flowering bulb with narrow, strap-shaped. basal leaves, and single-sided spikes of star-shaped, blue, mauve, white or pink flowers. Well-drained soil and open situation in sun or part shade. Propagate by seed in autumn or divide bulbs in late summer.

Schizostylis coccinea, kaffir lily. 60cm. Native to South Africa. Rhizomatous perennials with long, grass-like leaves and spikes of shallowly cup-shaped crimson flowers in autumn. Fertile soil with some moisture and full sun. Divide clumps every few years. Also pink and white forms.

Sternbergia lutea. 6cm. Native to Mediterranean regions. Bulbs with strap-shaped, basal leaves and large, yellow, crocus-like flowers in autumn. Good drainage, full sun and summer drought. Best left undisturbed.

Tulipa humilis. 20cm. Native to eastern Turkey, northern Iraq and north-west Iran. Bulbs with grey-green leaves and variable flowers from pale pink, red and purple with central blotch, which can be yellow or black. Well-drained soil. Propagate from seed in autumn or spring.

Tulipa sprengeri

Asphodeline lutea, yellow asphodel. 150cm. –15°C. Native of the Mediterranean area from central Italy to Romania, Greece and Turkey, east to Trabzon. Fleshy rooted, clump-forming perennial, stems covered in narrow, grey-green, grass-like leaves with large bracts and dense spikes of yellow, star-shaped flowers in spring. Well-drained soil in full sun. Propagate by seed in autumn or division in spring, though be careful not to damage roots.

Tulipa sprengeri. 30–45cm. Native to north-west Turkey; almost extinct in the wild, although easily cultivated. Late-flowering bulb with long, narrow, grey-green leaves and narrowly oval, orange-red petalled flowers, tapered at the base. Outer three petals have buff-yellow backs. Well-drained soil and full sun. Naturalizes well, increases rapidly and easily grown from seed.

can become invasive, with upright, hairy stems, and rough, hairy, narrowly oval leaves. Branching racemes of open, cup-shaped deep blue flowers in early summer. Well-drained soil and sun, dislikes winter wet. Propagate by root cuttings in winter.

Herbaceous

Anthemis tinctoria. 1m. –25°C. Native to Europe, Turkey and the Caucasus, western Syria and Iran. naturalized in the British Isles and North America. Clump-forming, evergreen perennial with crinkled, fern-like foliage, masses of daisy-like flowers in summer in shades of yellow or cream. Propagate by basal cuttings in spring or late summer. Well-drained soil and sun, good on chalk.

Anchusa azurea. 50cm. –15°C. Native of Europe from France, Spain and Portugal and eastwards, North Africa and Turkey, eastwards to Iran and Arabia, into Central Asia. Basal rosetted perennial that

Aubrieta deltoidea. 10–15cm. Fully hardy. Native to Sicily and Asia Minor. Spreading, mat-forming or trailing perennial with small, hoary-green leaves and short, terminal spikes of cross-shaped flowers with rounded petals in shades of purple, rose and lilac in spring. Well-drained soil and sun, enjoys lime and dry banks. Numerous hybrid cultivars. Plant between September and March and trim back plants after flowering to maintain bushy habit. Propagate by seed during spring, greenwood cuttings in summer or basal cuttings in late summer and autumn.

Centaurea montana, perennial cornflower. 60cm. −20°C. European native from the Ardennes in Belgium, south to the Spanish Pyrenees, east to Poland and Croatia. Perennial with creeping rhizomes and lax stems, spreading into large patches. Undivided, silky leaves and thistle-like flower-heads with narrow ray petals in shades of blue, white, mauve or pink throughout summer. Well-drained, moist soil in sun or partial shade. Propagate by seed or division in spring or autumn.

***Cerinthe major* 'Purpurascens'**. 60cm. Mediterranean regions and Portugal. A spreading, upright winter annual with dark, blue-green bracts almost enclosing

tubular, deep purple flowers. Propagate by seed in autumn or spring; self-sown seeds often survive mild winters. Good in a gravel garden.

Cheiranthus cheiri, wallflower. 20–60cm. Evergreen, bushy perennial, with lance-shaped leaves and heads of very fragrant, four-petalled flowers in spring, in white, yellow, orange and bronze. Short lived and generally treated as biennial. Propagate by seed sown in spring.

Convolvulus cneorum. 50cm. −10°C. Native to Mediterranean regions. Slender silver-grey leaves and open, trumpet-shaped, white and pink flowers. Well-drained, fertile or poor soil and full sun. Propagate from softwood cuttings in late spring and summer or seed in spring.

Convolvulus sabatius syn *C. mauritanicus*. 10cm. −5°C. Native to north-west Italy, Sicily and north-west Africa. Prostrate perennial with slender stems bearing silver-grey leaves and masses of small, pale-blue, open, trumpet-shaped flowers throughout summer. Good in walls or pots. Poor, well-drained soil and sun. Propagate by seed in spring.

Cynara cardunculus, cardoon. 2m. −10°C. Native to south-western Europe, from Portugal to southern France, Italy, Greece and North Africa. Deeply dissected, long grey-green leaves up to 1m, often with spines. Flower heads are similar to an artichoke, with tight, spreading bracts opening to a mass of purple stamens. The fleshy leaf bases of the basal rosette of leaves are edible when blanched. Well-drained soil in full sun. Propagate by division in spring or autumn.

Delphinium staphisagria. 1m. Native to Mediterranean regions. Perennial or biennial with shiny, deeply divided leaves, and spikes of short-spurred, purple-blue flowers in late summer. Well-drained soil and sun. Propagate by seed.

Dictamnus albus var. 'Purpureus', burning bush. 1m. Native to Spain, east to Italy and Germany, and across to Turkey, the Caucasus and western Himalayas. Upright, clump-forming perennial with leaves divided into leaflets and stiff spikes of scented, star-shaped flowers from pale pink to purple, with long stamens, in early summer. Highly aromatic leaves that may be set alight in hot weather. Fertile, well-drained soil and full sun. Propagate by fresh seed in late summer. Dislikes disturbance.

Euphorbia amygdaloides var. *robbiae*, wood spurge. 80cm. –15°C. Native from European Turkey to north-western Anatolia. Creeping underground rhizomes form large spreading patches of red-tinged, woody stems with distinctive rosettes of semi-evergreen, narrowly oval, leathery, dark green leaves on non-flowering stems. Flowering stems carry pale green, cup-shaped bracts in spring and summer. Moist or poor dry soil in partial shade or full sun. Not long lived but seeds easily. Propagate by basal cuttings in spring or summer or division in spring or autumn. Milky sap can cause skin irritations.

Diascia cordata. 15–30cm. Native to South Africa. Prostrate perennial with heart-shaped leaves and slender stems bearing terminal clusters of flat-faced, spurred, rose-pink flowers in summer and autumn. Humus-rich, well-drained soil and some moisture. Propagate by seed in autumn, softwood cuttings in spring or semi-ripe cuttings in summer.

Eryngium × **oliverianum**, sea holly. 45–60cm. Upright perennial with deeply toothed, heart-shaped, basal leaves and strong, upright stems bearing rounded, blue-mauve, thistle-like flowers in summer. Well-drained soil and sun. Sow seed in autumn.

Euphorbia characias subs. *wulfenii*. 1.8m. –10°C. Native to Mediterranean regions, Greece and Turkey. Upright, evergreen shrub with biennial stems and clusters of grey-green leaves, followed by spikes of yellow-green bracts the following spring. Well-drained soil and sun. Persistent low temperatures are a danger, especially when wet. Propagate by division in spring or autumn, seed in autumn or spring and basal cuttings in spring or summer.

Euphorbia griffithii 'Fireglow'. 1m. –20°C. Native to Bhutan. Bushy perennial with underground rhizomes and annual stems with linear or lanceolate mid-green leaves with an orange midrib. Terminal umbels of red or orange, cup-shaped bracts containing small flowers. Well-drained but moist soil in sun or slight shade. Propagate by division in spring or early autumn, seed in autumn or spring and basal cuttings in spring and summer.

Galega officinalis, goats rue. 1.5m. Native to central and southern Europe, the Caucasus, Turkey, Lebanon and east to Central Asia

Geranium clarkei
'Kashmir White'

Geranium endressii

Geranium macrorrhizum

and Pakistan. Lax stems and leaflets in four to ten pairs and spikes of pea-like flowers from white to purple. Well-drained soil and sun. Sow seed in autumn. Plants require staking.

Geranium clarkei 'Kashmir White', syn *G. pratense* 'Kashmir White'. 45–60cm. –20°C. Native to Kashmir. Rhizomatous perennial forming thick clumps with divided leaves and loose clusters of white, pink-veined, open, cup-shaped flowers during summer. Well-drained soil, part shade or sun. Propagate by division.

Geranium endressii. 45cm. –15°C. Native to south-western France and north-west Spain. Carpeting, rhi-zomatous, semi-evergreen perennial with small, divided leaves and cup-shaped, deep pink flowers in summer. Well-drained, moist soil, partial shade or sun. Propagate by division.

Geranium macrorrhizum. 30–50cm. –15°C. Native of the southern Alps in France and Italy and the south-eastern Carpathians in Romania, south to Greece. Fleshy, underground rootstock forming thick rhizomes growing into dense, weed-smothering mats. Semi-evergreen, divided aromatic leaves, and loose clusters of pale pink, magenta or white flowers. Damp or dry ground, shade or sun. Propagate by division in autumn or spring.

Geranium × magnificum, cranesbill. 45cm. Underground rhizomes form spreading mats with divided, lobed, hairy leaves and clusters of prominently veined, cup-shaped, deep violet-blue flowers in summer. General soil, not water-logged, sun. Propagate by cuttings or division in autumn or spring.

Geranium × oxonianum **'Thurston-ianum'**. –15°C. Thick mounds of divided, deep green leaves and slender stems bearing narrow-petalled, deep pink flowers from June to September. Recorded since before 1914 and now found wild in some parts of Britain. Well-drained soil, shade or sun and drought tolerant. Propagate by division.

Geranium phaeum, mourning widow. 60–80cm. –20°C. Native to Europe from the Pyrenees and Alps, east to the Czech Republic, Croatia and western Russia. Now naturalized in many places, partic-ularly eastern Scotland. Thick rhi-zomes form large clumps with soft, lobed leaves often spotted dark red and stems bearing clusters of small, reflexed petalled, maroon to almost black flowers in late spring. Propagate by division or cuttings.

Geranium psilostemon syn. *G. armenum*. 1.2m. –20°C. Native to north-eastern Turkey and the south-western Caucasus. Strong-growing, clump-forming perennial with deeply toothed and lobed leaves that turn red in autumn. Numerous cup-shaped single, magenta flowers with black centres in summer. Propagate by division.

Geranium phaeum

Geranium × oxonianum 'Thurstonianum'

Glaucium flavum, horned poppy. 30–60cm. Native to the Mediterranean, Black Sea and European coasts, as far north as Norway. Slow-growing biennial with generally hairy, lobed, grey-green leaves and open, poppy-like bright yellow flowers in summer and early autumn. Fertile, well-drained soil and sun. Propagate from seed sown in spring. Excellent plant for gravel gardens.

Helianthus decapetalus, sunflower. 1.5m. Native of the Appalachian mountains, eastern North America. Creeping rhizomes and woody stems with ovate leaves and flat-faced, golden yellow flowers with numerous petals in late summer and autumn. Well-drained soil and sun. Can become invasive and is best divided and replanted each year in autumn or spring.

Heuchera sanguinea. 50cm. –20°C. Native to southern Arizona and northern Mexico. Clumps of rounded, lobed leaves and slender stems bearing numerous, small, red flowers in summer. Well-drained soil and sun or part-shade. Propagate by division in spring or autumn, taking younger, outer portions.

Hypericum olympicum 'Citrinum'. 15–30cm. –15°C. Native to Greece. Deciduous tufts of upright stems with small, oval, grey-green leaves and terminal clusters of cup-shaped, pale yellow flowers in summer. Well-drained soil and full sun. Propagate by softwood cuttings in summer.

Helleborus foetidus, stinking helle-bore. 45cm. Clump-forming, ever-green perennial with dark green, deeply divided leaves and panicles of cup-shaped, apple-green flowers in winter and early spring. Petals edged with dark red. Well-drained but water-retentive soil. Seeds freely and seed can be planted in spring.

Hypericum calycinum, rose of Sharon. 50cm. –25°C. Native to southern Bulgaria and northern Turkey. An evergreen or semi-ever-green, suckering shrubby plant, stems bearing solitary, bright yellow flowers in summer and autumn, with masses of stamens having orange anthers. Excellent ground cover and tolerates poor soil, drought and shade. Well-drained soil and sun. Propagate from softwood cuttings in summer or division in spring.

Lamium galeobdolon, syns *Gale-obdolon luteum*, *Lamiastrum galeob-dolon*, yellow archangel. Native to Europe from Ireland east to European Russia, south to Spain, northern Turkey and the Caucasus. Creeping perennial with upright stems bearing rounded to pointed leaves and whorls of yellow flowers. Well-drained soil and sun or shade. Can become invasive. Propagate by division in early spring or autumn.

Lamium maculatum. 15–40cm. Native in most parts of Europe, northern Iran, the Caucasus and Turkey. Creeping, mat-forming, non-flowering stems and upright flowering stems with mid-green leaves, often with white markings. Pinkish-purple flowers. Partial shade or full sun. Propagate by division in autumn or early spring, or stem tip cuttings of non-flowering shoots in mid-summer.

Lampranthus spectabilis. 30cm. –3°C. Native to South Africa. Spreading, bushy, perennial succulent with narrow, grey-green leaves and daisy-like flowers, which can be cerise or yellow. Very well-drained soil, dry in summer and full sun. Propagate by stem cuttings in spring or autumn.

nial, often grown as annual, with winged stems, lance-shaped, wavy-edged leaves and clusters of papery, tubular calyx in a range of colours in summer and autumn. Well-drained, sandy soil and sun. Propagate by seed in spring or autumn.

Lamium orvala, deadnettle. 30cm. Clump-forming perennial with mounds of mid-green leaves, sometimes with central white stripes. Clusters of pink or purple flowers in late spring and early summer. Well-drained but moist soil in sun or partial shade. Dislikes too much winter wet. Propagate by division in autumn or spring, or by stem-tip cuttings from non-flowering shoots in summer.

Lathyrus cyaneus. 30cm. Native to the Caucasus. Perennial with linear to lanceolate leaflets and racemes of up to fifteen blue-lilac flowers in summer. Well-drained soil and full light. Propagate by seed in autumn.

Limonium sinuatum and cultivars. 45cm. 7–10°C. Native to southern Portugal and the Mediterranean, but now also found wild in other parts of the world. Bushy peren-

Mandragora officinarum, mandrake. 5cm. Fleshy-rooted perennial with rosettes of crinkled, dark green leaves and funnel-shaped flowers in yellowish-mauve, followed by large round, shiny, greenish-yellow fruits. Humus-rich, well-drained soil and sun or part shade. Propagate by seed in autumn. Does not transplant well.

Monarda didyma 'Cambridge Scarlet', bergamot. 1.5m. –25°C. Native to eastern North America. Aromatic plant with upright stems with softly hairy or smooth leaves, and terminal flower heads of showy, red-tinged bracts and bright red corolla. Well-drained soil, sun and tolerates dry conditions. Propagate by division in spring.

Nicandra physaloides 'Violacea', shoo fly. 130cm. Native to Peru. Erect, branching hardy annual with wavy-edged, ovate leaves and solitary, blue-mauve, bell-shaped flowers. Both flowers and fruit have attractive purple calyces. Deep, well-drained soil with some moisture and full sun. Propagate from seed sown *in situ*, or under glass in spring, planting out when there is no danger of further frost.

Nigella damascena, love-in-a-mist. 50cm. Native to southern Europe. Hardy annual with deeply divided,

feathery leaves and flat, blue or white flowers surrounded by feathery bracts. Inflated capsule seed pods. Well-drained soil and sun. Self-seeds freely. Propagate from seed sown in spring.

Osteorpsermum 'Cannington Roy'. 15–30cm. Evergreen perennial with linear, toothed, grey-green leaves and daisy-like flower heads with darker centres. Pink tipped petals open white, maturing to mauve. Well-drained soil and sun. Propagate by semi-ripe cuttings in summer.

Nepeta grandiflora, catmint. 1m. –20°C. Native to the Caucasus. Lightly hairy stems with heart-shaped to oval leaves with rounded toothed edges and long spikes of hooded, lavender-blue flowers in summer. Well-drained soil and sun. Propagate by softwood cuttings in spring or summer or division in spring.

Osteospermum
'Cannington Roy'

Pelargonium 'Royal Oak'

Pelargonium 'Royal Oak'. 1m. 1°C. Native to South Africa. Evergreen, scented pelargonium with softly hairy, irregularly lobed leaves and purple marking along main veins. Large, pale pink flowers with darker blotches on upper petals. Well-drained soil and sun. Propagate by soft wood cuttings from spring to autumn.

some moisture, and sun or semi-shade. Propagate by division in spring or autumn.

Salvia guaranitica syn *S. ambigens*. 1.5–3m. Native to Brazil, Uruguay and Argentina. Upright perennials with ovate to cordate leaves and spikes of hooded, deep blue flowers with indigo blue calyx, in summer and autumn.

Polygonum amplexicaule syn. *Bistorta amplexicaulis*, knotweed. 1m. −20°C. Native from Afghanistan to south-western China. Perennials forming large clumps of tall stems with clasping, oval to heart-shaped leaves and spikes of bright red flowers in late summer. Well-drained soil with

Salvia greggii. 1m. −5°C. Native to southern Texas and south to central Mexico. Evergreen, thin, woody-based stems with narrowly oblong leaves and racemes of pinkish-red flowers. Fertile, well-drained soil and sun. Propagate by softwood cuttings in summer or seed in spring.

Salvia patens. 60cm. −5°C. Native to central Mexico. Erect, branching perennial with oval leaves and whorls of large, blue, hooded flowers in summer. Fertile, well-drained soil and sun. Propagate from seed or cuttings in summer, so tubers can establish before winter.

Vinca major, greater periwinkle. 45cm. Native to northern Mediterranean regions from south-west France to Italy and Croatia. Trailing, rooting stems to around 2m with glossy, ovate, evergreen leaves and open, five-petalled, blue-purple flowers from late spring to autumn. Any soil but not too dry, sun or shade. Propagate by division from autumn to spring or semi-ripe cuttings in summer.

Salvia × *superba*. 60–90cm. Much branched perennial with lanceolate to oblong leaves and long, slender racemes of two-lipped violet or purple flowers with purple-tinged calyx in summer and autumn. Fertile, well-drained soil and sun. Propagate by seed or division in spring, and softwood cuttings in summer.

Tanacetum vulgare, tansy. 120cm. Native to Europe and temperate Asia. Aromatic perennial, with finely cut leaves and woody stems bearing dense corymbs of button-like, yellow flowers. Can become invasive, so divide clumps regularly to keep in check. Well-drained soil and sun. Propagate by division.

Zauschneria cana, California fuchsia. 60cm. −10°C. Native to California. Woody-based perennial with several stems bearing narrow, hairy, grey-white leaves and bright orange-red, fuchsia-like, tubular flowers from late summer to autumn. Well-drained soil and full sun. Propagate by side-shoot cuttings in summer, seed or division in spring.

Salvia 'Van Houttei'. 1.5m. Tender shrubby perennial with oval to heart-shaped leaves and racemes of bright red flowers with red calyx in late summer and autumn. Well-drained soil and sun.

Verbena bonariensis. 1.5m. 1°C. Perennial with basal leaves and tall, upright stems bearing tight clusters of rose-pink flowers in summer and autumn. Well-drained soil and sun. Propagate by seed in autumn or spring.

Trees and Shrubs

Carpenteria californica. 2.7m. –5°C. Native to California. Evergreen shrub with broad, lanceolate, dark green leaves and large, white, fragrant, saucer-shaped flowers with yellow anthers in summer. Best as a wall shrub, but generally recovers from the base if damaged by frost. Deep rich, moist but well-drained soil in full sun. Propagate by seed in autumn, or softwood cuttings in mid- to late summer.

Cercis canadensis 'Forest Pansy', eastern redbud. 14m. Native to North and Central America. Deciduous spreading tree or shrub with small, pink, pea-like flowers appearing before heart-shaped, red-purple leaves. Deep, fertile, well-drained soil and full sun.

Cercis siliquastrum, Judas tree. 10m. Spreading, deciduous tree with heart-shaped, green leaves and profuse clusters of pink or cerise, pea-like flowers growing directly from old wood, in mid-spring, followed by long, purple-red seed pods. Fertile, well-drained soil and full sun. Dislikes being transplanted, so buy young trees or grow species from seed in autumn and cultivars by budding in late summer.

Choisya ternata, Mexican orange blossom. 3m. –10°C to –15°C. Native to Mexico. Dense, rounded, evergreen shrub with trifoliate, aromatic, mid- to dark green, glossy leaves and flat-topped clusters of small, fragrant, white flowers in late spring to early summer and often again in autumn. Fertile, well-drained soil in full sun or shade. Drought tolerant and can be clipped into shape. Propagation from softwood cuttings in summer. C. 'Sundance' has yellow leaves.

Cistus ladanifer. 2.5m. –10°C. Native to southern France, Spain, Portugal and North Africa. An open, upright evergreen shrub with narrow, sticky, dark green leaves and large, open, saucer-shaped white flowers, often with red blotched petals at the base, and golden stamens, borne in profusion throughout summer. Well-drained soil and full sun. Does not transplant well. Propagate by seed in autumn, green or softwood cuttings in summer, cultivars and hybrids by cuttings.

Cistus parviflorus. 1m. –10°C. Native to south-east Italy, Greece, eastwards to southern Turkey and Cyprus. Dense evergreen shrub with oval, grey-green leaves and small, open, saucer-shaped pale pink flowers in early summer. Well-drained soil and full sun. Propagate by seed in autumn, or greenwood cuttings in summer.

Daphne sericea   *Crinodendron hookerianum*

Cornus kousa. 7m. Fully hardy, deciduous tree or shrub with oval, glossy, dark green leaves that turn red-purple in autumn. Conspicuous white bracts surround insignificant flowers in early summer and can be followed by strawberry-like fruits after hot summers. Fertile, well-drained soil in sun. Propagate by softwood cuttings in summer or seed in autumn.

Crinodendron hookerianum, syn *Tricuspidaria lanceolata*, lantern tree. 3m. –10°C. Native to central Chile. Evergreen shrub or tree with narrow, dark green leaves, silver beneath. Pendant, lantern-like crimson-red flowers, on mature wood, in spring and early summer. Fertile, moist, but well-drained, acid soil in shade or semi-shade with shade at base. Propagate by softwood cuttings in early summer.

Daphne sericea. 1.1m. 10°C to –15°C. Native to Sicily, Italy, Crete, western and southern Turkey, Syria and the Caucasus. Upright or rounded evergreen shrub with obovate or narrow-elliptic, glossy, dark green leaves and highly perfumed clusters of pale rose-coloured, tubular flowers in spring and sometimes again in autumn. Well-drained soil and sun. Variable hardiness. Propagate by semi-ripe cuttings in summer or by fresh seed.

Ficus carica, fig. 10m. –10°C. Native to Turkey and the Middle East. Shrub or tree with deeply lobed leaves and rounded to pear-shaped, edible fruits. Humus-rich, heavy but well-drained soil. Grows well in a pot, restrict roots or it becomes invasive at the expense of fruit. Can produce two crops, one in summer and one in autumn.

Ficus carica

Lantana camara 'Arlequin'

Lantana camara 'Arlequin'. 1–2m. 5°C. Native to tropical America. Evergreen shrub with bristly stems and ovate, lightly toothed, wrinkled leaves. Small, tubular, five-lobed flowers are in terminal clusters with pink buds that open to pale yellow, turning almost immediately pink again. All parts of the plant are toxic. Fertile, well-drained soil and light. Pot-grown specimens need to be well watered when in full growth, lightly at other times. Propagate by semi-ripe cuttings in summer or seed in spring.

Laurus nobilis, sweet bay. 12m. Evergreen trees with aromatic, narrowly oval, leathery green leaves (culinary uses). Small, pale yellow, star-shaped flowers in spring are followed by oval green, then black, fruits. Fertile, well-drained soil in sun or semi-shade and some shelter is an advantage. Propagate by seed in autumn or semi-ripe cuttings in summer.

Lavandula angustifolia 'Hidcote', lavender. 1.5m. Evergreen, bushy shrub with aromatic, narrow, grey-green leaves and dense spikes of fragrant, purple flowers in

Laurus nobilis

summer. Good for hedging. Fertile, well-drained soil and full sun. Propagate from semi-ripe cuttings in summer.

Lavandula angustifolia 'Hidcote'

Lavandula latifolia, syn *L. spica*, spike lavender. Native to the Mediterranean from Spain and North Africa to Croatia. Narrow grey-green leaves and stems bearing heads of linear-lanceolate bracts and minute flowers in summer. Fertile, well-drained soil and full sun. Propagate by semi-ripe cuttings in summer.

Lavandula multifidia. 1m. –10°C. Native to Italy, Sicily, North Africa, Spain and Portugal. Evergreen, rounded, sub-shrub with much divided leaves and erect, branching stems with slender spikes often branched at the base. Small fertile bracts and blue-violet flowers. Well-drained soil and full sun. Propagate by semi-ripe cuttings in summer.

Lavandula **'Munstead'**, syn *L. angustifolia* 'Munstead', lavender. 60cm. Compact, evergreen, bushy shrub with narrow, aromatic, grey-green leaves and dense spikes of small, fragrant blue flowers in summer. Well-drained soil and full sun. Propagate by semi-ripe cuttings in summer.

Lavatera olbia. 3m. Native to south-west Europe, including Italy and Sicily, and west to Spain, Portugal and North Africa. Semi-evergreen, woody-based shrub with three- to five-lobed lower leaves and three-lobed upper leaves. Clusters of short-stalked, pink, hollyhock-like flowers born in profusion from summer until cut back by frost. Well-drained soil and sun. Propagate with softwood cutting in spring and summer.

Phlomis fruticosa, Jerusalem sage. 2m. –10°C. Native to Mediterranean regions. Evergreen shrub with sage-like, grey-green leaves and whorls of hooded, yellow flowers. Dry, well-drained soil and little or no summer water. Propagate by softwood cuttings in summer or seed in autumn.

Prunus dulcis, almond. 9m. –10°C. Native to Syria and North Africa, but naturalized in Mediterranean regions. Spreading deciduous tree with pointed and toothed lanceolate leaves that appear after the pale pink flowers in late winter and early spring. Oval, velutinous fruit. Well-drained soil and full sun. Propagate by grafting or budding.

Lavandula stoechas, French lavender. 50cm. –10°C. Native to Mediterranean regions. Bushy, evergreen shrub with narrow, grey-green leaves and dense spikes with fertile bracts tinged purple and dark purple flowers. Fertile, well-drained soil and sun. Propagate by semi-ripe cuttings in summer.

Prunus dulcis

225

Rosmarinus officinalis, rosemary. 2m. Upright, evergreen shrub with narrow, aromatic leaves and two-lipped, blue-purple flowers in spring and often again in autumn. Used for flavouring food and makes a good hedging plant. Well-drained soil and full sun. Prune hedges after flowering and cut woody plants back to healthy wood in spring. Propagate from semi-ripe cutting in summer.

Santolina chamaecyparissus, cotton lavender. 50cm. –15°C. Native to Mediterranean regions. Dense, rounded, evergreen shrub with finely toothed, grey-white leaves and thin stalks bearing small, round yellow flowers in summer. Well-drained, open soil and full sun. Propagate by softwood cuttings in early summer or semi-ripe cuttings in late summer, and trim plants back in spring to keep in shape.

Senecio greyi, *Brachyglottis greyi*. 1–2m. –15°C. Native to New Zealand. Spreading, evergreen shrub with rounded, grey-green leaves and large terminal corymbs of daisy-like, bright yellow flowers in summer. Well-drained soil and full sun. Propagate by semi-ripe cuttings in summer.

Climbers

Akebia quinata, chocolate vine. 10m. –15°C. Native to Japan, China and Korea. Evergreen or semi-evergreen, woody-stemmed twining climber. Leaves have five

rounded leaflets. Flowering in late spring with purple-brown inflorescence, male flowers at the apex and female flowers at the base. Any soil and sun or shade. Good for pergolas and walls and will grow in east- or north-facing positions. Propagate by seed in spring or autumn or semi-ripe cuttings in summer.

Campsis grandiflora syn. *Bignonia grandiflora*, Chinese trumpet vine. 6m. –10°C. Native to eastern China. Strong, woody-stemmed, deciduous climber with pinnate leaves with from seven to nine leaflets and hanging clusters of bright orange-red, or pinkish, open, trumpet-shaped flowers in late summer or autumn. Requires warm summers to flower really well. Fertile, well-drained soil, moist in summer. Propagate by layering in winter or semi-ripe cuttings in summer.

Ipomoea multifida syn *I. × sloteri*, cardinal climber. 3m. 5°C. Hybrid raised around 1910. Annual, twining climber with narrowly segmented leaves and small, bright crimson, trumpet-shaped flowers, shallowly lobed at mouth, in

Ipomoea multifida   *Passiflora caerulea*   *Trachelospermum jasminoides*

summer. Humus-rich, well-drained soil. Propagate by seed in spring.

Passiflora caerulea, passion flower. 10m. Evergreen or semi-evergreen, fast growing, woody-stemmed, tendril climbers with palmate leaves. Pale creamy green flowers with central coronas of showy blue or purple-banded filaments, in summer and autumn, followed by egg-shaped orange fruits. Fertile, well-drained soil and sun or semi-shade. Propagate by seed in spring or semi-ripe cuttings in summer.

Trachelospermum jasminoides, star jasmine. 9m. –10°C. Native to southern China, Vietnam, southern Japan and Korea. Evergreen, woody-stemmed, twining climbing shrub with simple leaves and highly perfumed, jasmine-like white flowers and pink, bean-like fruits. Well-drained soil and sun or semi-shade. Propagate by semi-ripe cuttings in late summer or autumn, or seed in spring.

Tropaeolum speciosum, flame creeper. 3m. Twining, herbaceous climber with creeping rhizomes. Blue-green lobed leaves and small, brilliantly scarlet, spurred flowers with red calyces, in summer followed by bright blue fruits. Well-drained soil and sun, but roots in shade. Propagate by seed or tubers in spring.

Tropaeolum speciosum

Gardens Reference

The gardens, nurseries and societies listed below are all of interest in the context of this book. There are many more gardens we could have included if space allowed. For full details of these and hundreds of other gardens, see the *RHS Garden Finder*, by Charles Quest-Ritson and the National Gardens Scheme 'Yellow Book'. Opening times are only a general guideline and must be confirmed before visiting. Most gardens also arrange visits by appointment.

Gardens Open for Viewing

Abbotsbury Sub-Tropical Gardens, Weymouth, Dorset, DT3 4LA. Tel. 01305 871387. Open 10.00–6.00 or dusk, daily, all year except 25 and 26 December and 1 January. Mediterranean and sub-tropical plants including, eucalyptus; loquat; palms and pittosporum.

Acton Round Hall, Acton Round, Much Wenlock, Shropshire. Open occasionally under National Gardens Scheme. Mediterranean climate species.

The African Garden, 96 Wasdale Gardens, Estover, Plymouth, Devon, PL6 8TW. Tel. 01752 301402. www.theafricangarden.com. Phone for appointment times. Specializing in South African plants.

Angel Gardens, Springfield, Angel Lane, Bitterley, Ludlow, Shropshire. Tel. 01584 890381. Open 2.00–5.00 Saturdays, Sundays, Wednesdays, May to September. Mediterranean climate region species.

Benmore Botanic Garden, Dunoon, Strathclyde, PA23 8QU. Open 10.00–6.00 daily April to September; 10.00–5.00 March and October. Tender Mediterranean and Chilean plants.

Benthall Hall, Broseley, Shropshire, TF12 5RX. Tel. 01952 882159. The National Trust. Open 1.30–5.30 Tuesdays,

Wednesdays and bank holidays, April to September. Mediterranean collections.

Beth Chatto Gardens, Colchester, Essex, CO7 7DB. Tel. 01206 822007. Open 9.00–5.00 Monday to Saturday, March to October. 9.00–4.00 November to February. Closed Sundays. Dry and gravel gardens. Wide selection of Mediterranean plants.

Bicton Park Gardens, Budleigh Salterton, Devon, EX9 7BJ. Tel. 01395 568465. Open 10.00–6.00 (5.00 in winter) daily, except Christmas Day. Mediterranean, Italian and American gardens.

Bide-a-Wee Cottage, Stanton, Netherwitton, Morpeth, Northumberland, NE65 8PR. Tel. 01670 772262. Open 1.30–5.00 Wednesdays and Saturdays, April to August. Tender plants.

Birmingham Botanical Gardens, Westbourne Road, Edgbaston, Birmingham, West Midlands, B15 3TR. Tel. 0121 1860. Open 9.00–7.00 (or sunset) daily, all year except Christmas Day. Mediterranean plants and garden, tender plants.

Bodnant Gardens, Tal-y-Cafn, Colwyn Bay, Clwyd, LL28 5RE. Tel. 01492 650460. The National Trust. Open 10.00–5.00 daily, March to October. Tender and Mediterranean species.

Bolfracks Garden, Aberfeldy, Tayside, PH15 2EX. Tel. 01887 820344. Open 10.00–6.00 daily, April to October. Many Mediterranean species.

Borde Hill Garden, Balcombe Road, Hayward's Heath, West Sussex, RH16 1XP. Tel. 01444 450326. Mediterranean garden designed by Robin Williams, Greek bank, Italian garden.

Brook Cottage, Well Lane, Alkerton, Banbury, Oxfordshire, OX15 6NL. Tel. 01295 670303. Open 9.00–6.00 Monday to Friday, Easter Monday to 31 October. Tender plants, gravel garden.

OPPOSITE: A seat on the terrace at Preen Manor, Shropshire.

Bryan's Ground, Letchmoor Lane, Stapleton, Presteigne, Herefordshire, LD8 2LP. Tel. 01544 260001. Open 2.00–5.00 Sundays and Mondays, April to August. Parterre, Mediterranean climate region species.

Buscot Park, Faringdon, Oxfordshire, SN7 8BU. Tel. 01367 240786. The National Trust. Open 2.00–6.00 Monday to Friday, April to September. Saturdays and Sundays, 2nd and 4th weekends April to September. Italian features, citrus ring.

Cambridge University Botanic Garden, Cambridge, CB2 1JF. Tel. 01223 336265. Open 10.00–4.00 winter, 10.00–5.00 spring and autumn, 10.00–6.00 summer, daily except 25 December to 1 January. Dry garden, Mediterranean plants.

Cannington College Heritage Garden, Cannington, Bridgwater, Somerset, TA5 2LS. Tel. 01278 655000. Open 9.00–5.00 daily, April to October. Collections of rare and unusual plants, Australasian garden.

The Castle and Gardens of Mey, Thurso, Caithness, KW14 8XH. Tel. 01847 851473. Open 11.00–4.30 Tuesdays to Saturdays, 2.00–5.00 Sundays; closed Mondays and between mid-May and end of July and mid-August to end of September. Home of the late HRH Queen Elizabeth the Queen Mother. Ornamental and kitchen gardens on Britain's most northerly coast.

Chelsea Physic Garden, London, SW3 4HS. Tel. 0207 352 5646. Open 12.00–5.00 Wednesdays, 2.00–6.00 Sundays, April to October, plus Chelsea Flower Show openings. Largest olive tree in UK, also grapefruit and pomegranate.

Chesters Walled Garden and Nursery, Chollerford, Hexham, Northumberland, NE46 4BQ. Tel. 01434 681483. Open 10.00–5.00 daily, April to October. National collections *Origanum* and *Thymus*.

Claire Austin Hardy Plants, The Stone House, Cramp Pool, Shifnal, Shropshire, TF11 8PE. Tel. 01952 463700. 8 acres of plants including *Iris, Hemerocallis, Paeonia* and plant combinations.

Compton Acres Gardens, Poole, Dorset, BH13 7ES. Tel. 01202 70078. Open 9.00–6.00 daily, except Christmas Day. Italian garden, Spanish water garden.

Coleton Fishacre Garden, Dartmouth, Devon, TQ6 0EQ. Tel. 01803 752466. Open 11.00–5.00 Saturdays and Sundays, March; 10.30–5.30 or dusk, Wednesday to Sunday, bank holidays, April to October. Mimosa groves.

The Dower House, Morville Hall, Morville, Bridgnorth, Shropshire, WV16 5NB. Tel. 01746 714407. Open 2.00–6.00, Sundays, Wednesdays and bank holiday Mondays, April to September. Parterre, citrus pots, boarded beds, ornamental fruit and vegetable garden, Mediterranean climate region species.

Dudmaston, Quatt, Bridgnorth, Shropshire, WV15 6QN. Tel. 01746 780866. The National Trust. Open 12.00–6.00, Sunday to Wednesday, April to September.

Dunge Valley Hidden Gardens and Nursery, Windgather Rocks, Kettleshulme, High Peak, Cheshire, SK23 7RF. Tel. 01663 733787. Open 10.30–5.00 Thursday to Sunday, March and mid-June to end of August; daily except Mondays 1 April to mid-June, also bank holiday Mondays. Tender plants high in the Pennines.

Dunrobin Castle Gardens, Golspie, Sutherland, Highlands, KW10 6SF. Tel. 01408 633177. Open 10.30–4.30 April, May and October, 10.30–5.30 June to September. French style garden with ornate parterres including potagers.

Earlscliffe, Baily, Co. Dublin, Ireland. Tel. 00 353 1 8322556. Open by appointment only. Mediterranean climate region plants, world-wide.

East Ruston Old Vicarage, Norwich, NR12 9HN. Tel. 01692 650432. Open 2.00–5.30 Wednesdays, Fridays, weekends, bank holidays April to October. Mediterranean climate region plants, gravel beds, *Aeonium, Acacia,* palms, *Agave, Aloe.*

Exeter University Gardens, EX4 4PX. Tel. 01392 263059. Open dawn to dusk daily all year. Australasian plants including *Acacia, Callistemon* and *Eucalyptus.*

The Garden House, Yelverton, Devon, PL20 7LQ. Tel. 01822 854769. Open 10.30–5.00 daily, March to October. Cretan cottage garden, South African garden, Californian plants.

Glendurgan, Mawnan Smith, Falmouth, Cornwall, TR11 5JZ. Tel. 01326 250906. The National Trust. Open 10.30–5.30 Tuesday to Saturday, mid-February to October. Bank holiday Mondays. Closed Good Friday. Steep valley with Mediterranean climate species plants including *Agave americana, Eucriphia, Myrtus.*

Greenways, 40 Osler Road, Headington, Oxford, OX3 9BJ. Tel. 01865 767680. Check for opening times. Italianate garden, tender plants and bulbs.

Hampton Court Gardens, Hope Under Dinmore, Herefordshire, HR6 0PN. Tel. 01568 797676. Open 11.00–5.00 daily April to October. Large ornamental vegetable garden with parterres and potagers.

Hardwicke House, Fen Ditton, Cambridge, CB5 8TF. Tel. 01223 292246. Check for opening times. Special collections of Turkish plants and bulbs.

Headland, Polruan-by-Fowey, Cornwall, PL23 1PW. Tel. 01726 870243. Open 2.00–6.00 Thursdays, May to September. Cacti, succulents and salt tolerant plants.

Herterton House Gardens and Nursery, Hartington, Cambo, Northumberland, NE61 4BN. Tel. 01670 774278. Open 1.30–5.30 daily except Tuesdays and Thursdays, April to

September. Parterres, knot garden, tender plants, herbs.

Hidcote Manor Garden, Chipping Campden, Gloucestershire, GL55 6LR. Tel. 01386 438333. The National Trust. Open 10.30–6.00, 5.00 in October, Saturday to Wednesday, April to October. French and Italian influences, Mediterranean species.

Highdown, Littlehampton Road, Goring-by-Sea, West Sussex, BN12 6PE. Open 10.00–6.00 daily, April to September; 10.00–4.30 February, March, October, November; 10.00–4.00 January and December. No weekends October to March. Chalk garden, Mediterranean plants.

Hoghton Tower, Hoghton, Preston, Lancashire, PR5 0SH. Tel. 01254 852986. Open 11.00–4.00 Monday to Thursday, 1.00–5.00 Sundays, July to September. 11.00–5.00 bank holiday Mondays. Courtyards and walled gardens.

The Hundred House Hotel and Garden, Bridgnorth Road, Norton, near Shifnal, Telford, Shropshire, TF11 9EE. Tel. 01952 730353. Arbours, box parterres, ornamental fruit, vegetable and herb garden.

Ickworth, Horringer, Bury St Edmunds, Suffolk, IP29 5QE. The National Trust. Open 10.00–5.00 daily, except Christmas. Italian garden, Mediterranean plants, olive tree.

Inverewe, Poolewe, Ross and Cromarty, IV22 2LG. Tel. 01445 781200. The National Trust for Scotland. Open daily, all year, 9.30–9.00 March to October, 9.30–4.00 November to March. Mediterranean, Australasian and tender plants.

Jessamine Cottage, Kenley, Shrewsbury, Shropshire, SY5 6NS. Tel. 01694 771297. Open 2.00–6.00, Fridays, Sundays and bank holidays, June to August. Tender plants, parterre.

Kiftsgate Court, Chipping Campden, Gloucestershire, GL55 6LW. Tel. 01386 438777. Open 2.00–6.00 Wednesdays, Thursdays, Sundays and bank holiday Mondays, April, May, August and September; 12.00–6.00 Mondays, Wednesdays, Thursdays, Saturdays and Sundays, June and July. Themed borders, tender plants including *Abutilon*, *Echium* and tree peonies.

Knightshayes Garden, Tiverton, Devon, EX16 7RG. Tel. 01884 254665. The National Trust. Open 11.00–5.30 Saturdays and Sundays, March; daily April to end of October. Topiary, cyclamen, tender plants.

Lamorran House, St Mawes, Cornwall, TR2 5BZ. Tel. 01326 270800. Open 10.30–5.00 Wednesdays, Fridays and first Saturday of the month, April to September. Mediterranean garden, with collections of Mediterranean climate species.

Leeds Castle, Maidstone, Kent, ME17 1PL. Tel. 01622 765400. Open 10.00–5.00 March to October; 10.00–3.00 November to February. Closed 25 December and certain other days. National collection of *Monarda*, herbs and Mediterranean style plantings.

Long Cross Hotel and Victorian Gardens, Trelights, Port Isaac, Cornwall, PL29 3TF. Tel. 01208 880243. Tender plants within windbreaks on windswept coastline.

Lyme Park, Disley, Cheshire, SK12 2NX. Tel. 01663 762023. The National Trust. Open 11.00–5.00 daily, except 1.00–5.00 on Wednesdays and Thursdays, March to October; 12.00–3.00 weekends, November and early December. Magnificent-box and ivy parterre with extravagant bedding displays.

Mawley Hall, Cleobury Mortimer, Shropshire. Occasional openings. Parterres, courtyards and gardens.

Mount Edgcumbe, Torpoint, Cornwall, PL10 1HZ. Tel. 01752 822236. Open formal gardens and park, dawn to dusk all year; Earl's garden with house 11.00–4.30 Sunday to Thursday, April to September. Italian garden dating from the 1790s, French garden, modern American garden and New Zealand garden.

Mount Stewart, Grey Abbey, Newtownards, Co. Down, Northern Ireland, BT22 2AD. Tel. 028 4278 8387. Formal gardens open 10.00–8.00 daily, April to September, weekends only in March and October, closes at 6.00 in April and October. Sunken Spanish garden, Mediterranean climate region plants.

Mount Stuart, Isle of Bute, Strathclyde, PA20 9LR. Tel. 01700 503877. Open 10.00–6.00 daily except Tuesdays and Thursdays, May to August. Rare plant collections including tender Australian and New Zealand species.

Museum of Garden History, Lambeth Palace Road, London, SE1 7LB. Tel. 0207 401 8865. Open 10.30–5.00 daily, early February to mid-October. Fascinating museum and attractive small garden with knot garden.

The National Botanic Garden of Wales, Middleton Hall, Llanarthne, Carmarthern, Dyfed, SA32 8HG. Tel. 01558 668768. Open 10.00–6.00 or dusk daily, except Christmas Day. The largest single-span glasshouse in the world concentrating specifically on Mediterranean climate species.

Newby Hall, Ripon, North Yorkshire, HG4 5AE. Tel. 01423 322583. Open 11.00–5.30 Tuesday to Sunday, bank holiday Mondays, April to September. Mediterranean species.

Portmeirion, Penrhyndeudraeth, Gwynedd, LL48 6ET. Tel. 01766 770000. Open 9.30–5.30 daily, all year. Mediterranean and exotic plants.

Powis Castle Garden, Welshpool, Powys, SY21 8RF. Tel. 01938 551920. The National Trust. Open 11.00–6.00 Thursday to Monday, March to October. Italianate terraces, tender and Mediterranean species.

Preen Manor, Church Preen, Church Stretton, Shropshire, SY6 7LQ. Tel. 01694 771207. Open various dates. Chess garden, gravel garden, Mediterranean climate species.

RHS garden Harlow Carr, Crag Lane, Beckwithshaw, Harrogate, West Yorkshire, HG3 1QB. Tel. 01423 565418. Open 9.30–6.00 or dusk, daily, all year. Herbs, grasses, National Plant Collections, fruit, vegetables, herbaceous borders including Mediterranean species.

RHS garden Hyde Hall, Rettendon, Chelmsford, Essex, CM3 8ET. Tel. 01245 400256. Open 10.00–6.00 daily, April to September; 10.00–5.00 or dusk daily, October to March. Renowned dry garden with more than 4000 plants, themed borders, tender species.

RHS garden Rosemoor, Great Torrington, Devon, EX38 8PH. Tel. 01805 624067. Open 10.00–6.00 daily, April to September; 10.00–5.00 daily, October to March, except 25 December. Plant collections, Mediterranean climate species, herbs.

RHS garden Wisley, Woking, Surrey, GU23 6QB. Tel. 01483 224234. Open 10.00–6.00 daily, except 25 December. Important world-wide plants, special collections.

Royal Botanic Gardens Edinburgh, 20a Inverleith Row, Edinburgh, EH3 5LR. Tel. 0131 552 7171. Open 1.00–7.00 daily, April to September; 1.00–6.00, March and October; 10.00–4.00 November to February. Closed 25 December and 1 January. Tender, Mediterranean and sub-tropical plants.

Royal Botanic Gardens Kew, Richmond, Surrey, TW9 3AB. Tel. 0208 332 5655. Open 9.30–6.30 (7.30 at weekends) daily all year, except 24 and 25 December. Some variable winter opening, so check first. Mediterranean plants, herbs, grasses (more than 550 species), juniper collection, pinetum.

Sledmere House, Driffield, East Riding of Yorkshire, YO25 3XG. Tel. 01377 236637. Open 11.00–4.30 daily except Mondays and Saturdays, Easter weekends, then from May to September. Mediterranean plants.

Sleightholmedale Lodge, Fadmoor, Kirkbymoorside, North Yorkshire, YO62 7JG. Tel. 01751 431942. Open by appointment. Mexican and Mediterranean plants.

Snowshill Manor, Snowshill, Broadway, Worcestershire, WR12 7JU. Open 11.00–5.30 Wednesday to Sunday, April to October, plus bank holiday Mondays. Steps and terraces, clipped hedges and tender plants.

Stansfield, 49 High Street, Stanford-in-the-Vale, Oxfordshire, SN7 8NQ. Tel. 01367 710340. Open 10.00–4.00, first Tuesday of each month, April to September. Mediterranean plants.

Stockton Bury Gardens, Kimbolton, Leominster, Herefordshire, HR6 0HB. Tel. 01568 613432. Open 12.00–5.00 Wednesday to Sunday and bank holidays, April to mid-October. Immaculate and full of tender and exotic plants.

Tapley Park, Instow, Devon, EX39 4NT. Tel. 01271 342558. Open 10.00–5.00 daily except Saturdays, March to October. Italian formal garden around 1900.

Trebah Garden Trust, Mawnan Smith, Falmouth, Cornwall, TR11 5JZ. Tel. 01326 250448. Open 10.30–5.00 daily all year. Palms and succulents.

Tresco Abbey, Isles of Scilly, TR24 0QQ. Tel. 01720 424105. Open 10.00–4.00 daily, all year. South African, Australian and New Zealand plants, plus cacti, succulents and exotics.

Ugbrooke Park, Chudleigh, Devon, TQ13 0AD. Tel. 01626 852179. Open 1.30–5-30 Tuesdays, Thursdays and Sundays, July and August. Spanish garden.

University of Bristol Botanic Garden, Bristol, BS8 3PF. Tel. 0117 973 3682. Open 9.00–5.00 Monday to Friday, all year except public holidays. New Zealand and South African plants, *Aeonium, Cistus, Salvia* and *Sempervivum* etc.

University of Dundee Botanic Garden, Riverside Drive, Dundee, DD2 1QH. Tel. 01382 647190. Open 10.00–4.30 March to October, 10.00–3.30 November to February. Closed 1–2 January, 25–26 December. Mediterranean garden, South American and Australasian plants.

University of Oxford Botanic Garden, Rose Lane, Oxford, OX1 4AZ. Tel. 01865 286690. Open 9.00–5.00 daily, March to September, except Good Friday; 9.00–4.30 daily, October to February, except Christmas Day. The oldest botanic garden in England. Parterre, Mediterranean climate region collections.

Ventnor Botanic Garden, Isle of White, PO38 1UL. Tel. 01983 855397. Open dawn to dusk daily all year. Southern hemisphere plants; palms; olives and medicinal herbs.

Wrest Park, Silsoe, Bedfordshire, MK45 4HS. Tel. 01525 860152. Contact for opening times. An 'English Versailles'.

Wightwick Manor, Wightwick, Wolverhampton, West Midlands, WV6 8EE. Tel. 01902 761400. The National Trust. Open 11.00–6.00 Wednesdays, Thursdays, Saturdays and bank holidays, March to 24 December. Topiary, yew avenue.

Nurseries

United Kingdom

Abbey Brook Cactus Nursery, Matlock, Derbyshire, DE4

2QJ. Tel. 01629 580306. Open 1.00–4.00 Wednesday to Friday; 1.00–5.00 Saturdays, Sundays and Bank Holidays; closed 1 January and 25–26 December. Cacti, National collections of *Conophytum*, *Echinopsis* hybrids, *Gymnocalycium*, *Haworthia* and *Lithops*.

Arne Herbs, Limeburn Nurseries, Limeburn Hill, Chew Magna, Bristol, BS40 8GW. Tel. 01275 333399. Open generally 10.00–4.00 but telephone first. Herbs, wild flowers and authentic plants for the re-creation of historic gardens.

Bill White Nurseries, Lem Hill Plant Centre, Lemm Hill, Far Forest, Rock, Kidderminster, Worcestershire, DY14 9DU. Tel. 01299 266326. Lawn substitute plants.

Burncoose Gardens and Nursery, Redruth, Cornwall, TR16 6BJ. Tel. 01209 860316. Open 8.30–5.00 (11.00–5.00 Sundays), daily except 25 December. Tender and unusual plants.

Clifton Nurseries, Little Venice, London, W9 2PH. Tel. 0207 286 4215. Open 8.30–6.00 Monday to Saturday, 10.30–4.30 Sundays, March to September; 8.30–5.30 Monday to Saturday, 10.00–4.00 Sundays, October to February. Topiary trees, containers, statuary.

Cotswold Garden Flowers, Sands Lane, Badsey, Evesham, Worcestershire, WR11 5EZ. Tel. 01386 422829. Open 9.00–5.30 Monday to Friday, 10.00–5.30 Saturday and Sunday; closed weekends mid-October to March. Rare plants including Mediterranean species

County Park Nursery, Hornchurch, Essex, RM11 3BU. Tel. 01708 445205. Open 9.00–6.00 Monday to Saturday, 1.00–5.00, Sundays from March to October; closed Wednesdays. Australian and New Zealand plants.

David Austin Roses, Bowling Green Lane, Albrighton, Wolverhampton, West Midlands, WV7 3HB. Tel. 01902 376376. Open 9.00–5.00 daily. Roses, roses, roses.

Downderry Nursery, Tonbridge, Kent, TN11 9SW. Tel. 01732 810081. Open 10.00–5.00 daily, May to October; closed Mondays. *Lavandula* and *Rosemarinus*.

East Northdown Farm Nurseries, Margate, Kent, CT9 3TS. Tel. 01843 862060. Open 9.00–5.00 daily all year, except Easter Sunday and Christmas week; 10.00–5.00 Sundays and bank holidays. Mediterranean species, specializing in drought tolerant plants for chalk and seaside.

Elsworth Herbs, Elsworth, Cambridge, CB3 8HY. Tel. 01954 267414. Open by appointment. Herbs. National Collections of *Artemisia* and *Nerium oleander*.

Fibrex Nurseries Ltd., Honeybourne Road, Pebworth, Stratford-upon-Avon, Warwickshire, CV37 8XP. Tel. 01789 720788. Open 10.30–4.00 all year, except last two weeks December, first week January, Easter Sunday and bank holiday Monday. National collection of *Pelargonium* and *Hedera*.

Fulham Palace Garden Centre, London, SW5 6EE. Tel. 0207 736 2640. Open 9.30–5.30 Monday to Thursday; 9.30–6.00 Friday and Saturday, 10.00–5.00 Sunday. Earlier closing in winter. Topiary, containers, herbs, olives, figs and citrus.

Hales Hall Gardens and Reads Nursery, Loddon, Norfolk, NR14 6QW. Tel. 01508 548395. Open 10.00–5.00 (4.00 in winter) Monday to Saturday all year; 11.00–4.00 Sundays from April to October. Citrus trees, vines, figs, potager.

Hall Farm Nursery, Vicarage Lane, Kinnerley, Oswestry, Shropshire, SY10 8DH. Tel. 01691 682135. Open 10.00–5.00, Tuesday to Saturday, March to October. *Aeonium*, *Astrantia*, *Geranium*, *Sempervivum*, grasses and ornamentals.

Hillview Hardy Plants, Worfield, Bridgnorth, Shropshire, WV15 5NT. Tel. 01746 716454. Open 9.00–5.00 Monday to Saturday, March to October. South African plants, National Collection *Acanthus*.

Holly Gate Cactus Nursery, Billingshurst Road, Ashington, West Sussex, RH20 3BB. Tel. 01903 892930. Open 9.00–6.00 daily, except 25–26 December. Cactus garden, specializing in cacti and succulents, more than 50,000 plants.

Langley Boxwood Nursery, Rake, Liss, Hampshire, GU33 7JL. Tel. 01730 894467. Open 8.00–4.30 Monday to Friday, 10.00–4.00 Saturdays. Specialist growers of *Buxus* and *Taxus*.

The National Herb Centre, Banbury Road, Warmington, near Banbury, Oxfordshire, OX17 1DF. Tel. 01295 690999. Herbs and display gardens.

The Ornamental Plant Nursery, Church Farm, Westgate, Rillington, Malton, North Yorkshire, YO17 8LN. Tel. 07913 327886. Open 9.30–4.30 Tuesday to Sunday, Easter to September. Ornamental grasses.

The Palm Centre, Ham Street, Ham, Richmond, Surrey, TW10 7HA. Tel. 0208 255 6191. Open 9.00–5.00 or dusk, daily, all year. Hardy exotics, Mediterranean plants, palms, *Cycad*, *Yucca*, *Cordyline*.

Pine Lodge Gardens and Nursery, St Austell, Cornwall, PL25 3RQ. Tel. 01726 73500. Open 10.00–6.00 daily, March to October. Mediterranean and southern hemisphere plants.

Pleasant View Nursery and Garden, Two Mile Oak, Denbury, Newton Abbot, Devon, TQ12 6DG. Tel. 01803 813388. Open Garden 2.00–5.00 Wednesdays and Fridays, May to September. Nursery 10.00–5.00 Wednesday to Friday, mid-March to September. *Salvia*.

The Romantic Garden Nursery, Swannington, Norwich, Norfolk, NR9 5NW. Tel. 01603 261488. Open 10.00–5.00 Wednesdays, Fridays, Saturdays and bank holidays. Topiary and frames.

Seeds of Italy, 260 West Hendon Broadway, London, NW9 6BE. Tel. 0208 930 2516. Open 9.30–5.00 Monday to Friday, 10.00–4.00 Saturday. Family run, Franchi Sementi flower and vegetable seeds, including hard-to-find varieties.

Snowshill Lavender, Hill Barn Farm, Snowshill, Broadway, Worcestershire, WR12 7JY. Tel. 01386 854821. Open 10.00–5.00 Tuesdays and Sundays, April to Christmas; open daily mid-June to mid-August, and bank holidays. Lavender fields and sales.

Special Plants, Chippenham, Gloucestershire, SN14 8LA. Tel. 01225 891686. Nursery open 10.00–5.00 daily, March to September; Garden variable. Gravel garden and nursery, outstanding Mediterranean climate region plants.

Stone House Cottage Garden and Nursery, Stone, Kidderminster, Worcestershire DY10 4BG. Tel. 01562 69902. Open 1.00–5.30 Wednesday to Saturday, March to September, or by appointment. Rare and unusual plants.

Toobees Exotics, Blackhorse Road, Woking, Surrey, GU22 0QT. Tel. 01483 797534. Open 10.00–5.00, Thursday to Sunday and bank holidays, April to September. Succulents from South Africa and Madagascar.

The Vernon Geranium Nursery, Cuddington Way, Cheam, Sutton, Surrey, SM2 7JB. Tel. 0208 393 7616. Open 9.30–5.30, Monday to Saturday, Sundays March to June. Pelargonium specialist.

Westdale Nurseries, Hold Road, Bradford-on-Avon, Wiltshire, BA15 1TS. Tel. 01225 863258. Open 9.00–6.00 (10.00–5.00 October to March), 1.00–4.00 Sundays, all year except Christmas. *Bougainvillea*, tender plants.

France

Bulb'Argence, Mas d'Argence, 30300 Fourques. Tel. +33 (0)466 016 519. Specialist Mediterranean climate region bulbs. Mail order world-wide.

Germany

Flora Mediterranea, Königsgütler 5, 84072 Au/Hallertau. Tel. +49 (0)8752-1238.
Flora Toskana, Schillerstrasse 25, 89278 Nersingen OT Strass. Tel. 0 73 08/92 83 387.

Switzerland

Gartenwerke GmbH, Schlösslistrasse 25, CH-5408 Ennetbaden. Tel. 056 210 04 60.

Landscape Architects

Robin Williams and Associates, 32 Ferguson Road, Devizes, Wiltshire. Tel. 01380 728999.

Societies

The Australian Plant Society, Secretary Jeff Irons, Stonecourt, 74 Brimstage Road, Heswall, Wirral, Cheshire, L60 1XQ.

The Half Hardy and The Hardy Plant Society, Little Orchard, Great Comberton, Pershore, Worcestershire, WR10 3DP.

The Hedera Project, Miss A. Rutherford, 19 South King Street, Helensburgh, Dunbartonshire, G84 7DU. Tel. 01436 675603.

The Lavender Bag, Joan Head, 6 Church Gate, Clipston on the Wolds, Keyworth, Nottinghamshire, NG12 5PA. Tel. 0115 989 2718. Twice-yearly journal for lavender enthusiasts.

The Mediterranean Garden Society, Sparoza, PO Box 14, GR-190 02 Peania, Greece. Tel +30–210 664 3089. www.MediterraneanGardenSociety.org. For gardening enthusiasts in all Mediterranean climate regions and beyond. Quarterly journal *The Mediterranean Garden*.

The National Trust, Enquiries: PO Box 39, Bromley, Kent, BR1 3XL.

The National Trust for Scotland, Wemyss House, 28 Charlotte Square, Edinburgh, EH2 4ET. Tel. 0131 243 9300.

The Royal Horticultural Society, 80 Vincent Square, London, SW1P 2PE. Tel. 0207 834 4333. www.rhs.org.uk

The Royal Horticultural Society Lindley Library, 80 Vincent Square, London, SW1P 2PE. Tel. 0207 821 3050. Reference books, historical books and picture library.

Further Reading

Anderson, M., *The World Encyclopaedia of Cacti and Succulents* (Hermes House, 2003)

Berry, S., *The Small Garden: Designing and Planting Outdoor Living Space* (Salamander Books, 2001)

Boisset, C. (ed.), *The Garden Source Book: the Essential Guide to Planning, Planting and Garden Style* (Mitchell Beazley, 2001)

Brickell, C. (ed.), *The Royal Horticultural Society Gardeners' Encyclopaedia of Plants and Flowers* (Dorling Kindersley, 1990)

Chatto, B., *Beth Chatto's Gravel Garden* (Frances Lincoln, 2000)

—, *The Dry Garden* (J.M. Dent and Sons, 1978)

Cooke, I., *The Plantfinder's Guide to Tender Perennials* (David and Charles, 1998)

Elliott, R., *Australian Plants for Mediterranean Climate Gardens* (Rosenberg, 2003)

Gardner, C., and W. Musgrave, *The Plant Hunters: Two Hundred Years of Adventure and Discovery Around the World* (Seven Dials, 1998)

Gildemeister, H., *Gardening the Mediterranean Way* (Thames and Hudson, 2004)

—, *Mediterranean Gardening: a Waterwise Approach* (Editorial Moll, 1995)

Jones, L., *Gardens in Provence* (Flammarion, 2002)

McNaughton, V., *Lavender: the Grower's Guide* (Garden Art Press, 2000)

Noailles, Vicomte de, and R. Lancaster, *Mediterranean Plants and Gardens for Everyone* (Floraprint, 2001)

Nottle, T., *Plants for Mediterranean Climate Gardens* (Rosenberg, 2004)

Page, G., *Garden Plants for Mediterranean Climates* (The Crowood Press, 2002)

Pitt, M., *Gardening in Spain* (Santana Books, 1991)

Phillips, R., and M. Rix, *Annuals and Biennials* (Macmillan, 1999)

—, *Bulbs* (Pan Books, 1989)

—, *Conservatory and Indoor Plants*, 2 vols (Pan Books, 1998)

—, *Perennials*, 2 vols (Pan Books, 1991)

—, *Shrubs* (Pan Books, 1989)

—, *Vegetables* (Pan Books, 1993)

Rice, G., *Hardy Perennials* (Viking, 1995)

Russell, V., *Edith Wharton's Italian Gardens* (Frances Lincoln, 1997)

Segall, B., *Gardens of Spain and Portugal* (Mitchell Beazley, 1999)

Smithen, J., *Sun Drenched Gardens: the Mediterranean Style* (Harry Abrams Inc., 2002)

Squire, D., *Containers* (Chancellor Press, 1995)

Taylor, J., *Plants for Dry Gardens: Beating The Drought* (Frances Lincoln, 1993)

Tyrwhitt, J., *Making a Garden on a Greek Hillside* (Denise Harvey, 1998)

Waters, G., *The Pacific Horticulture Book of Western Gardening* (David R. Godine, 1990)

Index

Abutilon × *suntense* 175
 A. vitifolium 145
Acacia 17, 39, 130, 173, 181, 188
 A. dealbata 39, 130, 173
 A. retinodes 190
Acaena caesiiglauca 68
 A. microphylla 68
Acer griseum 142
Acanthus mollis 153
Achillea 19, 71, 145
 A. millefolium 71, 181
 A. 'Moonshine' 145
Aconitum 200
Aegopodium podagraria, 17
Aeonium 172
Africa, North, 22, 62, 65, 185, 213, 222, 224, 225
 South 17, 18, 22, 25, 44, 133, 134, 184, 186, 209, 211, 214, 218, 220
Agapanthus 17, 22, 62, 152, 184, 187, 192
 A. campanulatus 187
Agave 27, 130, 171, 172
 A. americana 130, 171, 172
Ajuga 71, 179, 189
 A. reptans 71
Akebia quinata 226
Alcea rosea 40
Alfabia, Mallorca 171
Algerian iris 185, 210
Alhambra, Spain 113, 169, 171
Allium 19, 71, 159, 181, 183
 A. cernuum 207
 A. flavum 207
 A. oleraceum 71
A. scorodoprasum, syn. *A. jajlae* 207
A. vineale 71
Almond tree 25, 28, 39, 44, 156, 163, 170, 173, 225
Aloe 130, 172, 177
Amarylis 17, 185, 200
Amelanchier 17, 189
America 17, 191
 California 18, 25, 29, 134, 188, 189, 190, 221, 222
 North 18, 22, 44, 190, 207, 212, 217, 218, 222
 South 190, 191
Anchusa azurea 212
Anemone 17, 39, 40, 62, 181, 183
 A. blanda 65, 176, 207
 A. coronaria 39, 208, 183
 A. pavonina 208
Angel Gardens, Shropshire, 58, 83, 86, 87, 92, 95, 105, 113, 126, 140, 200, 229
Anthemis tinctoria 212
Anthericum liliago 129
Apple tree 156, 157, 158, 162, 163
Arabis 105, 179
 A. alpina subs. *caucasica*
 A. caucasica see *A. alpina* 105
Araucaria araucana 130, 188
Arbours 43, 46, 53, 58, 59, 60, 62, 82, 89–91, 136, 139, 144, 154, 164, 181
 plants for 91
Arbutus 17, 133, 156, 157, 165

 A. unedo 165
Arches, 35, 38, 43, 45, 46, 61, 62, 82, 89–91, 151, 160, 162, 169, 200
 plants for 91
Architectural salvage 45, 85, 177
Arctosis 175
Arisaema candidissimum 208
Artemisia, 68, 136, 145
 A. abrotanum 145
A. 'Powis Castle' 145
 A. schmidtiana 'Nana' 68
Asia 22, 23, 212, 215, 221
Asphodeline lutea 145, 181, 212
Asphodelus 145, 181, 212
 A. albus 145
Aster 166, 188
Atriplex 127
Aubrieta deltoidea 106, 181, 212
 'Argenteo-variegata' 106
Auricula 20
Australia 17, 25, 133, 134, 188, 189, 190, 191, 196
Azulejos 172

Ballota pseudodictamnus 129
Balls, E.K. 18, 176
Bamboo 124, 141, 197
Banks, Sir Joseph 18
Banksia 17
Bark 102, 121, 122
Barry, Charles 158
Bay 39, 62, 138, 152, 153, 160, 224
Beds 30, 62, 73, 75, 88, 113, 138, 140, 141, 151, 159, 160, 162, 163, 172, 185
 design 72, 73, 88, 159, 160, 161
 herb 138
 island 72, 139, 140, 141
 raised 72, 88, 111, 113, 136, 141, 151, 159, 160, 172, 185
Bellis perennis 71, 180
Belsay, Northumberland 189
Beneficial insects 195–6
Benthall Hall, Shropshire, The National Trust, 13, 229
Berberis darwinii 124
Beth Chatto Garden, Essex, 52, 102, 109, 121, 129, 131, 143, 172, 174, 193, 194, 204, 229
Bide-a-Wee Cottage Garden, Northumberland 109, 130, 132, 152, 154, 229
Bill White Nursery, Worcestershire 69, 70, 71, 233
Biological control 195–9
Birds 194, 195, 197
Bladder Senna 175
Boboli Gardens, Italy 148
Bodnant Garden, Wales, The National Trust 90, 133, 229
Bolfracks Garden, Tayside 48, 156, 229
Bonded fibre fleece 123
Borago officinalis 15, 16
Borde Hill Garden, Sussex 130, 131, 176, 230
Boscastle, Cornwall 137
Bosco 148
Botanical Gardens
 Palmengarten, Germany 129

 Royal Botanic Garden, Kew 18, 232
 Tradescant's 18
 University of Cambridge 130, 230
 University of Dundee 21, 26, 132, 133, 232
 University of Oxford 79, 232
 University of Padua 148
 University of Pisa 16, 148
 Ventnor Botanic Garden, Isle of Wight 184, 232
Bougainvillea 25, 170
Box 39, 58, 62, 73, 74, 75, 78, 79, 134, 135, 138, 139, 144, 147, 148, 151, 152, 153, 156, 157, 159, 160, 164, 170, 197
Brachyscome iberidifolia 180
Brassica oleracea acephala 165
 'Cottager's' 165
 'Dwarf Green Curled' 165
 'Tall Green Curled' 165
 'Thousand Headed' 165
Bricks, designs and structures 31, 45, 47, 49, 57, 66, 73, 82–5, 88, 94, 96, 98–100, 104, 107, 110, 113, 144, 152, 169
Bridgnorth, Shropshire 136
Brook Cottage, Oxfordshire, 60, 92, 101, 135, 154, 172, 229
Brougham, Lord 28
Brown, 'Capability' 177
Brugmansia 58, 90, 188, 200
Bryan's Ground, Herefordshire 122, 230
Buckthorn 134
Buddleja 17, 200
Bulbs 37, 62, 63, 142, 163, 164, 170, 176, 177, 180, 184, 185
Burning Bush 214
Burton Agnes Hall, Yorkshire 130
Buscot Park, Oxfordshire, National Trust 134, 230
Buxus 39, 62, 134, 135, 138, 151, 153, 180, 181, 200, 203
 B. sempervirens 39, 62, 134, 135, 138, 153, 180, 181
 B. 'Suffruticosa' 151, 180

Cacti 130, 172, 177, 204
Calendula officinalis 13
Californian privet 124
 fuchsia 190, 221
Callistemon 130, 173
 C. citrinus, 173
Calycanthus occidentalis, 190
Camellia 27, 36, 179
Campanula 13, 44, 106, 166
 C. carpatica 106
 C. rapunculus 13
Campsis grandiflora, syn. *Bignonia grandi flora* 173, 177, 226
Canary Islands 22
Capitularo de villis 16
Caraway 16
Cardinal climber 22–7
Cardoon 159, 165, 213
Carex comans 189
Carnation 20, 185
Carol Valentine garden, California 189
Carpenteria californica 190, 222
Carpinus betulus 160

Carpobrotus edulis 177
Carum carvi 16
Castle Kennedy, Scotland 130
Castle and Gardens of Mey, Scotland 133, 230
Castle Ward, Northern Ireland 133
Caucasus 207, 212, 214, 215, 217, 218, 219, 223
Ceanothus 27, 188
Centaurea 13, 213
 C. cyanus 13
 C. montana 213
Ceramics 136, 172
Cercis 62, 64, 164, 174, 222
 C. canadensis 'Forest Pansy' 222
 C. siliquastrum 62, 174, 222
Cerinthe major 'Purpurascens' 213
Cestrum nocturnum 58
Chamomile 58, 68, 69, 71, 179, 181
Chamaecyparis lawsoniana 'Ellwoodii' 180
 C. pisifera 'Boulevard' 181
Chamaemelum nobile 68
 C. nobile 'Treneague' 69
Channel Islands 133
Charlemagne 16
Chasmanthe 185
Chateau de Versailles, France 113
Cheiranthus cheiri 181, 213
Chelsea Physic Garden, London 18, 133, 134, 230
Chenopodium bonus-henricus 12
Cherry tree 156, 163
Chesters Walled Garden, Northumberland 31, 43, 66, 72, 78, 130, 154, 230
Chestnut tree 156
Chile 17, 18, 25, 130, 133, 134, 175, 188, 189, 211
Chilean bellflower 180
 firebush, 64
China 20, 22, 64, 208, 220, 226, 227
Chinese trumpet vine 173, 226
Chionochloa conspicua 'Rubra' 142
Chives 159
Chocolate vine 226
Choisya ternata 127, 222
 C. 'Sundance' 222
Chrysanthemum coronarium 39
Chusan Palm 20
Cistus 17, 22, 62, 116, 129, 133, 173, 222
 C. ladanifer 145, 222
 C. parviflorus 222
 C. × *purpureus* 62, 116
Citrus 25, 27, 28, 39, 130, 133, 134, 139, 150, 152, 170, 176
Clary 16
Clematis 91, 153, 158, 200
 C. armandii 153
 C. cirrhosa 13
 C. flammula 91
 C. montana 200
Clianthus 133
Climate 43, 134, 169, 171, 172
 change 21
Clove pink 12
Clover, white 69
Cobbles 43, 57, 85, 88, 98, 100, 101, 104, 109

Cocoa shell 121
Colchicum 17, 22, 200
Colutea arborescens 175
Companion planting 159
Complete Herbal 19
Compost 32, 111, 118-120, 122, 142, 143, 144, 145, 159, 179, 199
   ericaceous 179
   mushroom 121
Compost heap 55, 56, 58, 67, 118, 119, 144
Compton Acres, Dorset 171, 230
Concrete 100, 101
Containers and pots 45, 46, 53, 59, 62, 63, 86, 88, 90, 107, 109, 120, 134, 136, 137, 139, 141, 144, 152, 156, 168, 172, 175, 177-9, 180, 183, 185, 187, 194, 195
   plants for 180-1
Convolvulus cneorum 213
   C. sabatius, syn. C. mauritanicus 112, 213
   C. mauritanicus, see C. sabatius 112
Cordyline 26, 130, 133, 188
   C. australis 20, 188
Coriander 16
Coriandrum sativum 16
Cornflower 13
   perennial 213
Cornus 188, 223
   C. kousa 223
Coronilla varia 21
Corsican curse 70
   pine 127
Cortaderia 141
Cotinus 197
Cotoneaster 69, 110
   C. 'Skogholm' 69
   C. 'Skogsholmen' 69
Cotton lavender 75, 153, 162, 226
Cotula coronopifolia 69
   C. dioica 69
   C. lineariloba 69
   C. squalida 69
Courtyard 42, 50, 60, 66, 144, 151, 172, 177, 185, 187
Cranesbill 216
Crassula 130, 177
Crinodendron 188, 223
   C. hookerianum syn. Tricuspidaria lanceolata 223
Crinum 17, 27, 62, 185, 186
   C. × powellii 186
Croatia 209, 213, 221, 224
Crocosmia 17, 22, 185, 187
Crocus 16, 17, 27, 180, 185, 208
   C. sativus 16, 17
   C. species 208
   C. tommasinianus 208
   C. 'Zwanenburg Bronze' 209
Crown daisy 39
   vetch 21
Crusaders 12
Cucurbita pepo 167
Culpepper, Nicholas 19
Cupressus 39, 60, 73, 127, 133, 136, 139, 144, 153, 160, 185
   C. arizonica 'Glauca' 153
   C. macrocarpa 127
   C. sempervirens 39, 133, 139, 153
      'Stricta', 60, 139
Cycad 184
Cyclamen 8, 11, 13, 17, 19, 27, 37, 62, 133, 209
   C. coum 8, 209
   C. hederifolium 11
Cydonia 181
Cymbalaria muralis 17, 18
Cynara cardunculus 165, 213
Cypress 39, 62, 148, 152, 153, 156, 170
Cyprus 222
Cyrus the Great 14

Daisy, common 71, 180
Daniel, Henry 16
Daphne mezereum 153
   D. sericea 223
Datura 177, 200
David Austin Roses 171, 172, 233
David, Douglas 18
Decking 45, 58, 85, 86, 92, 95, 101, 189
Decumaria barbara 91

Delosperma 174, 185
   D. sutherlandii 174, 185
Delphinium staphisagria 214
De materia medica 14
Dianthus caryophyllus 12
Diascia 184, 185
   D. cordata 214
Dictamnus albus var. 'Purpureus' 214
Digitalis ferruginea 189
Dioscorides 14, 20
Disease 159, 179, 193, 195-199
   Armillaria fungus 197
   botrytis 197
   fungicides 196
   fusarium wilt 197
   mildew 196, 198
   rust 198
   sooty mould 196, 199
Draba aizoides 112
Dracunculus 177, 181
   D. vulgaris 177, 181
Dragon arum 177, 181
Drainage 53, 68, 72, 75, 87, 88, 110-11, 113, 117, 120, 134, 143, 144, 147, 178, 193-4, 204
Drought tolerant plants 7, 11, 21, 22-3, 27, 28, 29, 30, 33, 34, 47, 54, 59, 61, 72, 78, 113, 116, 126, 129, 130, 132, 133, 138, 139, 140, 141, 143, 144, 145, 147, 174, 182, 189, 193, 194, 195, 204, 205, 206
Dry gardens 143-5, 174, 189
Dudmaston Hall, Shropshire, The National Trust 50
Dunge Valley Hidden Gardens, Pennines 125, 130, 230
Dunrobin Castle, Sutherland, 157, 158, 167, 230

Earlscliffe, Irish Republic 133, 230
East Ruston Old Vicarage, Norfolk 130, 230
Ebers Papyrus 14
Echeveria 36, 130, 172, 177
Echium 35, 130, 181
   E. pininana 35, 130
Elaeagnus × ebbingei 'Gilt Edge' 124
   E. pungens 'Maculata' 142
El Huerto del Cura, Spain 170
El Jardin de Monforte, Spain 170
Embothrium 64, 130, 133, 188
   E. coccineum 64, 130
Emperor Marcus Aurelius 12
English Nature 34
Epimedium 180
Eranthis hyemalis 180, 209
Erica 179, 184
Erigeron alpinus 106
   E. karvinskianus 106
Eryngium 129, 145, 214
   E. amethystinum 145
   E. giganteum 'Miss Wilmott's Ghost', 142
   E. × oliverianum 214
Erysimum cheiri 13
Escallonia 'Apple Blossom' 127
Eschscholzia 17, 22, 188
Eucalyptus 27, 126, 188, 189
   E. gunnii 189
Eucomis 185, 186
   E. comosa, 186
Eucryphia glutinosa 'Plena' 155
   E. × intermedia 'Rostrevor' 153
Euonymus 24, 127, 165, 181, 200
   E. europaeus 165
   E. fortunei 181
      E. japonicus 127
Euphorbia 27, 135, 142, 145, 189, 200, 214
   E. acanthothamnos 135
   E. amygdaloides 214
   E. characias 142, 145
   E. characias subs. wulfenii 214
      'Purple and Gold' 189
   E. griffithii 'Dixter' 189
      'Fireglow' 215
Evelyn, John 19
Evergreens 29, 62, 75, 124, 127, 134, 135, 136, 138, 142, 148, 152,154, 165, 177, 178, 180-1, 185, 203

Fascicularia 37

Feat of Gardening 19
Fences 49, 53, 55, 5, 82, 138, 189, 199
Fennel 15, 16
Fenugreek 16
Fertiliser 178, 199
Ficus carica 223
Fig tree 44, 92, 156, 185, 223
Firethorn 127
Fish 114, 115, 204
Flame creeper 227
Flax 16
Flora Graeca 19, 20
Florists' Societies 20
Foeniculum vulgare 15, 16
Forficula auricularia 197
Fountains 43, 49, 50, 88, 113, 114, 136, 148, 152, 156, 158, 163, 164, 169, 171, 185, 204
Fragaria × ananassa 165
Francoa sonchifolia 112
Freesia 17, 185, 209
Fremontodendron 200
French style gardens
   Dunrobin Castle, Sutherland 157, 158, 167, 230
   elements for 166-7
   'English Versailles' 157
   Hampton Court Gardens, Herefordshire 157
   Mount Edgcumbe Garden, Devon 157
   Oxburgh Hall, Norfolk 157
      plants for 165
      potager 157, 159
      'Renaissance-style' chateau 157
   Royal Gardens of Herrenhausen, Hanover 157
   Sanssouci Palace, Potsdam 157
   UNESCO World Heritage, Augustusburg, Brühl 157
   Waddesdon Manor, Bedfordshire 157
   West Park, Bedfordshire 157
Frescoes 16
Fritillaria 12, 13, 177, 181, 209
   F. graeca 177
   F. meleagris 12, 13, 209
Fuchsia 172, 188
Fungicides 196, 197, 198
Furniture 23, 45, 58-60, 92, 136, 141, 144, 164, 167, 172, 185, 200

Galanthus nivalis 142, 180
Galega officinalis 215
Galen, Greek surgeon 12
Galtonia 185, 187, 209
   G. candicans 187, 209
Gardener, Master John 19
Garrigue 156
Gartenwerke Nursery, Switzerland 129
Gates 55, 141, 151, 185, 199, 200
Gazania 17, 173, 175
   G. 'Orange Beauty' 173
Genista 27
   G. sagittalis 112
Geranium clarkei 'Kashmir White', syn. G. pratense 112, 215
   G. endressii 215
   G. macrorrhizum 215
   G. × magnificum 216
   G. × oxonianum 'Thurstonianum' 215
   G. phaeum 216
   G. pratense, see G. clarkei 112
   G. psilostemon syn. G. armenum 216
Gerard, John 13, 19
Giardini Botanica Hanbury, Italy 148
Giusti Gardens, Italy 148
Gladiolus 17, 181, 189, 210
   G. papilio 189
   G. tristis 210
Glaucium flavum 216
Glendurgan, Cornwall, The National Trust 130, 230
Global Warming 33-5, 44
Goat's rue 215
Golden hop 160
Grapefruit tree 134
Grape hyacinth 39, 210
Grasses 132, 139, 140, 145, 172, 189
Gravel 35, 43, 45, 57, 58, 59, 71, 72, 73, 75, 78, 85, 86, 87, 88, 89, 94, 98, 102, 108, 109, 111, 120, 122,

123, 129, 138, 139, 143, 144, 145, 147, 152, 172, 174, 179, 189
   gardens 143-5
   plants for 145
   mulch 111, 122, 123, 129
   retaining 97-8, 102, 144
Greece 11, 13, 14, 28, 32, 39, 40, 41, 42, 43, 65, 176, 181, 208, 212, 213, 215, 217, 222
   Aegean 13, 181
   Ancient 14, 201
   Crete 223
   islands 176
Greek style gardens 14, 32, 42, 130, 183
   Borde Hill, Sussex 130, 176
   elements for 182-3
   Nottingham 176-7
   Stowe, Buckinghamshire 177
Grigson, Geoffrey 12
Good King Henry 12
Grevillea 17
Griselinia littoralis 127
Grotto 151, 152
Gulf Stream 26, 130, 132

Hampton Court Gardens, Herefordshire 160, 230
Hanbury, Daniel 148
Hanbury, Sir Thomas 148
Hanging baskets 47, 136, 137, 177
Hanmer, Sir Thomas 19
Hardscaping 43, 53, 85, 97-115
Harlow Carr, Yorkshire, The Royal Horticultural Society, 130, 140, 178, 181, 183, 206, 232
Hazel tree 159, 162, 163
Headland Garden, Cornwall 130, 230
Hebe 181, 197
   H. × andersonii 'Variegata' 181
   H. × franciscana 'Variegata' 181
Hedera 'Buttercup' 69
   H. canariensis 'Gloire de Marengo' 70
   H. colchica 91
   H. 'Dentata' 91
   H. 'Dentata Variegata' 91
   H. 'Glacier' 69
   H. 'Goldheart' 70
   H. helix 172
   H. helix ssp. helix 69
   H. hibernica 70
   H. maderensis 70
   H. maroccana 70, 185
   H. 'Nigra' 69
   H. 'Nigra Aurea' 69
Hedges 43, 55, 56, 62, 73, 75, 123, 125, 138, 140, 141, 143, 148, 149, 151, 152, 154, 156, 157, 159, 160, 163, 164, 185, 199
Helianthemum 17, 106, 110, 145
   H. 'Ben Ledi' 106
   H. 'Ben Phada' 106
   H. nummularium 'Amy Baring' 145
Helianthus annuus 165
   H. salicifolius 165
   H. decapetalus 217
Helichrysum 79, 180, 188
   H. bracteatum 79
   H. petiolare 180
Heliotrope 159
Helleborus 44, 200, 201, 217
   H. foetidus 217
   H. orientalis 201
Hemlock 16
Henbane 16
Henry I 14
Henry III 14
Herb gardens 14, 15, 141, 151
   planters 181
   parterre 151, 157
Herterton House Garden, Northumberland 10, 49, 57, 130, 138, 151, 230
Heterocentron elegans 70
Heuchera sanguinea 217
   H. 'Palace Purple' 165
Hibiscus syriacus 175, 177
   'Blue Bird' 173
Hidcote Manor Garden, Gloucestershire, The National Trust 56, 231
Highdown Garden, Sussex 18, 115, 176, 231
Himalayas 20, 214

Hippocrates 14
Hippophaë rhamnoides 127
Hoghton Tower, Lancashire 67, 95
Holly 62, 124, 152, 153
Hollyhock 44, 195
Honeysuckle 65, 89, 90, 136, 153, 154, 185
Hop, Golden 91, 160, 180
Hornbeam 160
Horticultural Societies 20
Houseleek 16, 70, 112
Houses of Parliament 158
Humulus lupulus 'Aurea' 91, 160, 180
Huntington Gardens, San Marino, California 189
Hyacinth 20
Hyacinthoides hispanica 173, 175
Hyde Hall, Essex, The Royal Horticultural Society 46, 48, 54, 94, 103, 129, 131, 135, 138, 140, 143, 146, 168, 203, 232
Hydrangea, climbing 91
Hydrated lime 120
Hypericum 110, 217
  H. calycinum 217
  H. olympicum 'Citrinum' 217

Iberis saxatilis 106
Ickworth, Suffolk, The National Trust, 133, 134, 231
Ilex aquifolium 62, 124, 153
  I. 'Aureamarginata' 153
  I. 'Fructu Luteo' 153
Industrial Revolution 33
Insecticides 196, 197, 198
Inverewe, Scotland, The National Trust 130, 132, 231
Ipomoea 91, 136, 180, 200, 226–7
  I. × *multifidia* syn. *I.* × *sloteri* 226
  I. purpurea 91
  I. tricolor 180
Iran 207, 211, 212, 218
Iraq 14, 211
Iris 13, 14, 16, 17, 27, 37, 44, 62, 113, 115, 164, 180, 181, 185
  I. cretensis 37
  I. danfordiae 180
  I. germanica 13
  I. reticulata 180
  I. unguicularis 185, 210
Iron oxide 134
Irrigation 14, 170, 204
Italian cypress 139, 153
Italianate gardens 148
  Borde Hill, Sussex 130
  Bridgnorth 50, 114, 150, 151
  Ludlow 79, 82, 104, 114, 149, 151
    Shrewsbury 149
  Mawley Hall 63, 74, 78, 80, 103
  Mount Edgcumbe Garden, Devon 157
  plan 139
  plants for 153
  Powis Castle 148
  Tapeley Park 99, 149
Italy 19, 40, 43, 113, 130, 148, 212, 213, 214, 221, 222, 223, 224, 225
  Capri 148
  Ischia 148
  Sardinia 148
  Sicily 148
Ivy 79, 152, 172
  Common 172
  Italian 70
  Madeira 70
  Moroccan 70, 185
  Persian 91
Ivy-leaved toadflax 17, 18

Japan 20, 226, 227
Jardin del Parterre, Spain 170
Jasmine 39, 58, 62, 65, 90, 91, 136, 148, 152, 153, 185
  star 227
  summer 91
  white 39
Jasminum grandiflorum 65
  J. officinale 39, 91
  J. polyanthum 153
Jerusalem sage 225
Jessamine Cottage, Shropshire 33, 78, 83, 85, 86, 231
Johnson Hall, Staffordshire 138

Johnson, Major Lawrence 156
Judas tree 62, 64, 164, 174, 222
Juniper 110, 165
Juniperus communis 165

Kaffir lily 211
Kalanchoe 177
Kale 159, 165
  'Cottager's' 165
  'Dwarf Green Curled' 165
  'Tall Green Curled' 165
  'Thousand Headed' 165
Kempton 14
Kent, William 18, 177
Kiftsgate Court, Gloucestershire 115, 128, 152, 180, 231
Kirstenbosch Gardens, South Africa 184
Kitchen garden 141
Kniphofia 17, 23, 129, 184, 186
  K. rooperi 186
Knot gardens 73, 75, 78–9, 138, 147, 151

Laburnum 90, 200
La Chevre d'Or, France 157
Lady of the night 58
Lagerstroemia indica 130
Lamium galeobdolon syns. *Galeobdolon luteum, Lamiastrum galeobdolon* 217
  L. maculatum 218
  L. orvala 218
Lamorran House, Cornwall 130
La Mortella, Ischia 148
La Mortola, Italian Riviera 130, 148
Lampranthus 130, 172, 185, 218
  L. spectabilis 218
Lance Hattatt Design Garden 50
La Landriana, Italy 148
Lantana 200, 224
  L. camara 'Arlequin' 224
Lantern tree 223
Lapageria 180, 188
  L. rosea 180
Lathyrus cyaneus 218
Laurus nobilis 39, 153, 224
Laurustinus 124, 156
Lavandula 12, 13, 27, 37, 39, 44, 75, 90, 96, 104, 129, 136, 138, 139, 141, 152, 156, 157, 159, 160, 161, 163, 165, 166, 195, 224, 225
  L. angustifolia 'Hidcote' 224
    'Munstead' 225
  L. × *intermedia* 12
  L. latifolia syn. *L. spica* 224
  L. multifidia 224
  L. 'Munstead' syn. *L. angustifolia* 'Munstead' 225
  L. stoechas 165, 225
Lavatera olbia 129, 225
Lavender, *see* Lavandula
Lawn 28, 30, 35, 45, 56, 57, 67–79, 81, 98, 110, 113, 140, 141, 163
  edible 71
  naturalised 73, 141
  preparation and maintenance 56, 68, 73, 75–7, 97, 98, 136, 141
  reducing 67, 76, 97, 141
  replacing 45, 67, 75, 81–90, 136, 138, 139, 147
  substitute plants 58, 68–71, 138
Lebanon 65, 215
Le Clos du Peyronnet, France 157
Leeds Castle, Kent 35, 63, 77, 83, 95, 100, 108, 139, 177, 188, 231
Lemon tree 133–4
Leptinella squalida 69
Leptospermum 188
Liatris spicata 191
Ligustrum ovalifolium 124
  L. vulgare 134
Lilium candidum 12, 165
  L. 'Harmony' 65
  L. martagon 12, 13
Lily 12, 16, 17, 27, 39, 59, 62, 65, 90, 92, 165, 166, 180, 185
Limonaia 133
Limonium sinuatum 218
Lobb, William 18
Lobularia maritima 180
Long Cross Victorian Garden, Cornwall, 35, 105, 125, 182, 126, 231
Lonicera caprifolium 153
  L. etrusca 91

L. periclymenum 65
Love-in-a-mist 44, 219
Ludlow, Shropshire 31, 79, 82, 104, 114
Lyme Park, Cheshire, The National Trust 78, 231

Maintenance 199–204
Mallorcan peony 173, 210
Mandragora 16, 181, 200, 202, 218
  M. officinarum 202, 218
Mandrake 16, 181, 200, 202, 218
Manure 121
Maquis 156
Marble 45, 143, 177
Maritime pine 127
Marjoram 16, 156
Masson, Francis 18
Matthiola 188
Mawley Hall, Shropshire 63, 74, 78, 80, 103, 204, 231
Medicago arborea 177
Mediterranean climate regions 20, 25, 29
Melon 159
Metalwork 141, 151, 152, 159, 163, 164, 170, 172, 177
Mexican orange 124, 222
Middle East 14, 23, 223
Mimosa 39, 133, 156, 173
Mind Your Own Business 70
Mint 16
Mirrors 45, 93, 138
Monarda didyma 'Cambridge Scarlet' 219
Monastic gardens 15, 15, 16, 17
Monkey puzzle tree 130, 188
Monterey cypress 127
Moors 65, 169
Moorish architecture 169, 170
  culture 172
  Empire 17
  influence 39, 41, 136, 171
Morecombe Bay, Lancashire 111
Morisia hypogaea, see *M. monanthos* 106
  M. monanthos, syn. *M. hypogaea* 106
Morning glory 91, 180
Mosaic 85, 100, 101, 105, 171, 185
Mountain ash 62
Mount Edgcumbe Garden, Cornwall 157, 231
Mount Stewart, Northern Ireland 133, 231
Mourning widow 216
Mulberry tree 151
Mulch 32, 67, 102, 111, 120, 143, 185, 194, 197
  application 120
  types 111, 120–3, 143, 185
Mural 152
Muscari 39, 180, 185, 210
  M. armeniacum 210
  M. commutatum 39
  M. latifolium 210
Museum of Garden History, London 59, 231
Mushroom compost 121
Myrtle, *see* Myrtus
Myrtus 39, 136, 153, 156, 170
  M. communis 153

Narcissus 12, 17, 27, 37, 62, 180, 185
Nasturtium 159, 172
National Herb Centre, Oxfordshire 34, 86, 134, 179, 234
Nectarine 92
Nemesia 17
Neolithic 11, 12, 14
Nepeta 112, 136, 219
  N. grandiflora 112, 219
Nerine 17, 187
  N. bowdenii 187
Nerium oleander 180, 200
Newby Hall, Yorkshire 94, 231
New Zealand 25, 26, 64, 226
New Zealand style gardens
  Mount Edgcumbe, Cornwall 157
Nicandra physaloides 'Violacea' 219
Nicotiana 188
Nigella damascena 219
Normans 12

Oak tree 156
  bog 189
  cork 185
Oenothera 17, 23

Olea europaea 130, 133, 177
Olearia 129, 188, 191
  O. × *haastii* 129
  O. 'Waikariensis' 191
Olive tree 25, 41, 44, 130, 133, 134, 156, 160, 163, 170, 176, 185
Opium poppy 16
Opuntia 177
Orange tree 133–4
Orangeries 133
Origanum 'Kent Beauty' 112
  O. *vulgare* 166
  O. *vulgare* 'Aureum' 165, 166
Ornithogalum 200
Osteospermum 183, 184, 219
  O. 'Cannington Roy' 219
Oxburgh Hall, Norfolk 157
Oxford Physic Garden 18

Paeonia 6, 17, 21, 44, 65, 154, 166, 171, 173, 174, 181, 210
  'Bowl of Beauty' 166
  P. cambessedesii 6, 171, 173, 210
  P. 'Just dessert' 65
  P. mascula 17, 210
Palm tree 27, 130, 133, 136, 169, 171, 172, 185
Pampas grass 141
Pancratium maritimum 177
Pansy, 'Universal Mixed' 180
Papaver rhoeas 12
Paradisus Terrestris 19
Parkinson, John 19
Parsley 16, 159
Passiflora caerulea 227
Passion flower 227
Parterres 50, 62, 73, 74–5, 78–9, 138, 139, 141, 147, 148, 151, 152, 157, 158, 163, 170, 172
Parterres de broderie 156
Parthenocissus tricuspidata 164, 165
Path design 45, 77, 97, 98, 102, 103, 110, 141
  grass 30, 31, 54, 77, 97
  materials for 31, 43, 45, 49, 54, 57, 73, 77, 86, 96–8, 100–2, 104, 105, 152, 159, 171
  planning 55, 58, 61
Patio 45, 57, 61, 62, 81–95, 139, 141, 171
  construction and design 82, 87, 88, 94, 95
  heaters 141
Paving 43, 58, 59, 71, 73, 85, 86, 88, 98, 99, 136, 139, 147, 152, 163, 177
  construction and design 98, 99
  materials 45, 84, 85, 98–105, 103
  plants in 102, 103, 106
  terraces 147
Peach tree 90
Pearlwort 70
Pear tree 151, 156, 163
Peat 120
Pebbles 43, 45, 58, 84, 98, 100, 101, 113, 120, 122, 144
  mosaics 100, 101
  mulch 120, 122
  water feature 113, 114, 144
Pelargonium 17, 23, 39, 44, 136, 139, 152, 172, 180, 184, 185, 186, 220
  ivy-leaved 180
  P. grossularioides 185
  P. 'Lord Bute' 186
  P. 'Royal Oak' 220
  P. zonale 39, 180
  scented 180
Peony 6, 17, 21, 44, 65, 154, 166, 171, 173, 174, 181, 210
Peppers 92, 163, 176
Pergolas 35, 43, 45, 46, 47, 53, 57, 61, 62, 82, 83, 89–91, 141, 146, 152, 154, 164, 170, 172, 181, 185, 200
  plants for 91
Perlite 179
Permeable membrane 123, 144
Persian gardens 14
Pests 159, 179, 193, 195–9
  ants 179
  aphids 195, 196
  biological control 195
  caterpillars 196, 197

cranefly 197
earwigs 179, 197
Forficula auricularia 197
froghoppers 197
fungicides 196
insecticides 196
leaf miners 197
Lilioceris lilii 197–8
lily beetle 197–8
mealy bug 196, 198
mice 198
moths 196
Oniscus asellus 199
Otiorhynchus sulcatus 199
pesticides 196
pollen beetle 198
rats 198
red spider mite 198
scale insect 196, 198
slugs 179, 195, 196, 198
snails 195, 196, 198
thrips 196
vine weevil 196, 198
whitefly 196, 199
woodlice 179, 195
Petroselinum crispum 16
Petunia 172
Phaseolus vulgaris 165
Philaenus spumaris 197
Phlomis 27, 64, 225, 156
  P. fruticosa 64, 225
Phlox 17, 23, 188, 189, 190
  P. paniculata 190
Phoenicians 170
Phoenix canariensis 20
  P. dactylifera 170
Phormium 27, 133, 188
  P. tenax 188
Photosynthesis 27, 204
Phuopsis stylosa 145, 182
Phyllostachys aurea 142
Physic gardens 14, 15, 16, 151
Pine tree 39, 127, 156
Pinks 20
Pinus nigra maritima 127
  P. pinaster 127
Pistacia lentiscus 129, 130
Pittosporum 64, 130, 133
  P. tenuifolium 64, 130
  'Purpureum' 64
Plane tree 156, 160
Plant adaptations 36, 136
  grouping 32
  supports 200, 201
Plantago lanceolata 71
  P. major 71
  P. media 71
Platanus × acerifolia 160
Platycledus orientalis 'Aurea Nana' 181
Plectranthus 188
Plum tree 163
Poinsettia 170
Poisons 200
Polyanthus 20
Polygonum amplexicaule, syn. *Bistorta amplexicaulis* 220
Polypropylene 123, 144
Polythene sheeting 122
Pomegranate 133, 134, 176, 182, 185
Poncirus trifoliate 134
Pools 14, 49, 88, 113, 114-115, 136, 138, 139, 140, 141, 148, 152, 156, 160, 161, 163, 164, 169, 172, 185, 200, 204
  fish 113
  plants 113
Poplar tree 156
Poppy 16, 44, 189
  horned 216
Portmeirion, Wales 133, 232
Portugal 172, 213, 218, 222, 224, 225
Portuguese laurel 124
Potager 139, 157, 159, 160, 161, 162, 163
Pot marigold 13, 14, 44, 185
Powis Castle, Wales, The National Trust 148, 231
Preen Manor, Shropshire 31, 33, 34, 38, 43, 59, 62, 79, 90, 93, 94, 98, 104, 107, 108, 115, 228, 231
Privet, common 134
Protea 184
Prunella vulgaris 71

Pruning 200, 202
Prunus 39, 124, 142, 173, 202, 225
  P. dulcis 39, 173, 225
  P. laurocerasus 200
  P. lusitanica 124
  P. serrula 142
Punica granatum 130, 133, 134, 176, 181, 182, 185
Puya alpestris 175
Pyracantha rogersiana 164
  P. × 'Watereri' 127
Pyrus salicifolia 'Pendula Bostock' 151

Railway sleepers 45, 47, 48, 73, 85, 88, 98, 107, 110, 111, 152
Ranunculus 17, 20
Raoulia australis 70
  R. hookeri 70
  R. tenuicaulis 70
Raxa, Mallorca 171
Rea, John 19
Rhamnus alaternus 134
Rhodochiton atrosanguineum 191
Rhododendron ponticum 124
Ricinus 200
Robinia 200
Rollison, William 18
Roman gardens 14
Romania 212, 215
Romans 12, 13, 14, 16
Romneya 188, 197
Rosa × alba 13
  R. 'Albertine' 91
  R. arvensis 13
  R. banksiae banksiae 165
  R. banksiae lutea 91, 165
  R. 'Blanc double de Coubert' 165
  R. 'Blush Noisette' 91
  R. 'Bouquet d'Or' 165
  R. × centifolia 165
  R. 'Château de Clos Vougeot' 165
  R. 'Climbing Étoile de Hollande' 91
  R. damascena 13, 165
  R. gallica 13, 165
  R. 'L'Aimant' 165
  R. 'Lawrence Johnston' 165
  R. 'Madame Alfred Carrière' 91
  R. 'Madame Louise Laperriére' 165
  R. 'Mme Sancy de Parabère' 165
  R. 'Mermaid' 91
  R. 'Michèle Meilland' 165
  R. 'Paul's Himalayan Musk' 91
  R. 'Paul's Lemon Pillar' 91
  R. 'Rambling Rector' 91
  R. 'René André' 165
  R. 'Roseraie de l'Hay' 165
  R. 'Souvenir de la Malmaison' 165
  R. 'The Garland' 91
  R. 'Zépherine Drouhin' 165
Rose of Sharon 217
Rosemoor, Devon, The Royal Horticultural Society 46, 47, 48, 64, 78, 88, 95, 96, 97, 100, 107, 109, 113, 114, 123, 135, 159, 162, 164, 167, 177, 232
Rosmarinus 15, 16, 27, 37, 44, 136, 138, 139, 141, 153, 156
  R. officinalis 15, 16, 27, 37, 44, 138, 153, 226
  'Albus' 153
  'Majorca pink' 153
  ' Roseus' 153
Rosemary 15, 16, 27, 37, 44, 136, 139, 141, 152, 153, 156, 226
Royal Gardens of Herrenhausen, Germany, 157
Royal Horticultural Society, *see* Hyde Hall, Essex; Rosemoor, Devon; Harlow Carr, Yorkshire
Lindley Library, London 19
Rubus cockburnianus 142
  R. tricolor 142
Rue 16
Rules of water-wise gardening 29
Rumex acetosa 71

Saffron 16, 17
Saffron Walden Essex, 17
Sage 16, 156
Sagina sublate 70
Salix caprea 124
Salvia 27, 129, 136, 145, 181, 188, 220
  S. involucrata 188

S. greggii 220
S. guaranitica syn. *S. ambigens* 220
S. patens 220
S. × superba 221
S. 'Trebah' 145
S. 'Van Houttei' 221
Sand leek 207
Sanssouci Palace, Germany 157
Santolina 75, 134, 136, 153, 157, 162, 226
  S. chamaecyparissus 75, 153, 162, 226
  'Lambrook Silver' 153
  'Little Ness' 153
  S. pinnata 134
Saponaria × oliviana 106
Schizostylis coccinea 187, 211
Scilla 17, 211
  S. bifolia 211
Scilly Islands 133
Scoria 120, 172
Scotland 26, 27, 129, 130, 132, 133, 134, 157, 158, 182, 216
Scree 42, 43
Screens 49, 58, 82, 141
Sculpture 49, 88, 137, 151, 172
Sea buckthorn 127
Sea holly 214
Seating 46, 57, 58, 59, 83, 87, 89, 92, 110, 136, 138, 152, 177, 179, 228
Seaweed 121
Sedum 27, 68, 70, 111, 130, 172, 177, 189
  S. lydium 70
  S. obtusatum 70
Self heal 71
Sempervivum 27, 70, 111, 112, 172, 177
  S. arachnoideum 70, 112
  S. tectorum 70
Senecio greyi = *Brachyglottis greyi* 226
Serre de la Madone, France 156
Sesleria heufleriana 142
Sets 99, 100
Sheds 45, 53, 57
Sheep's sorrel 71
Shoo fly 219
Shrubs 23, 28, 35, 53, 58, 62, 73, 82, 133, 135, 139, 142, 152, 156, 175, 177, 185, 190
  containers 177
  golden 152
  winter flowering 142
Sibthorp, John 19, 20
Sicily 212, 213, 223, 224, 225
Silver leaved pear tree 151
Silver wattle 190
Sisyrinchium striatum 190, 211
Skimmia japonica 'Rubella' 180
Slabs 45, 84, 85, 86, 87, 88, 94, 95, 98, 99, 102, 104, 105, 108, 141
Slate 45, 98, 143
Sledmere House, Yorkshire 130, 232
Sleightholmedale Lodge, Yorkshire 130, 232
Smyrnium olustratum 12
Snake's head fritillary 12, 209
Snowdrops 12
Snowshill Lavender, Worcestershire 13, 156, 234
Snowshill Manor, Worcestershire, The National Trust 181, 232
Soil 32, 117-18, 134, 176, 185
Soleirolia soleirolii 70
Sorbus aria 62
  S. aucuparia 62
South African gardens 184–5
  Kirstenbosch, Cape Town 184
  The African Garden, Plymouth, 184–5
  Ventnor Botanic Garden, Isle of Wight 184, 233
Southernwood 145
Spain 14, 16, 17, 39, 41, 43, 65, 82, 113,169, 208, 214, 215, 217, 222, 224, 225
  Arunjuez 170
  Balearic islands 171
  climate 169
  Granada 169
  Mallorca 29, 67, 72, 171
  Muslim conquest of 169
  Seville 169

Valencia 170
Spanish bluebell 173, 175
  broom 173
  garlic 207
  jasmine 65
  pottery 172
Spanish style gardens 171–2
  Compton Acres, Dorset 171
  elements for 174–5
  plants for 173
  Ugbrook Park, Devon 171
Sparoza, Greece 42, 176
Spartium junceum 173, 200
Spindle berry 24, 165
St. Bernard's Lily 129
Stachys 27, 36
Stansfield, Oxfordshire 42, 232
Statuary 43, 45, 62, 73, 107, 136, 141, 148, 151, 152, 154, 160, 170, 172, 177, 183
Steps 48, 49, 58, 87, 88, 107, 108–9, 141, 152, 157, 177
Stern, Sir Frederick and Lady 18, 176
Sternbergia lutea 177, 211
Stockton Bury Garden, Herefordshire 20, 54, 57, 59, 64, 88, 92, 95, 98, 102, 108, 114, 130, 132, 154, 155, 183, 232
Stonecrop 111
Stone House Cottage Garden, Worcestershire 44, 47, 62, 83, 89, 94, 234
Straw 121
Strawberry 159, 165, 181
  tree 165
Succulents 36, 68, 70, 130, 172, 174, 177, 179, 184, 189
Sunflower 156, 159, 165, 195, 217
Sweet alyssum 180
  pea 44, 159
  violet 165
Sweet, Robert 19
Syria 212, 223, 225

Tamarind 36
Tamarix gallica 127
  T. ramosissima 'Rosea' 127
  T. tetrandra 127
Tanacetum densum, subsp. *amani* 112
  T. vulgare 112
Tapeley Park, Devon 77, 99, 104, 155, 166, 232
Taxus baccata 62, 124, 126, 134, 153, 160, 203
Terrace 43, 45, 58, 61, 106, 110, 111, 141, 148, 149, 151, 152, 154, 156, 157, 169, 176, 184, 189
Teucrium pyrenaicum 70, 71
Thalictrum flavum ssp. *glaucum* 129
Thamnocalamus spathaceus 124
The African Garden 184–5, 229
The Dower House, Morville Hall, Shropshire 150, 230
The Englishman's Flora 12
The Herball or Generall Historie of Plants 19
The Hundred House Garden, Shropshire 57, 60, 75, 79, 162, 183
The Mediterranean Garden Society 176, 235
The National Trust, *see* individual gardens
Thuja 160, 181
  T. orientalis 'Aurea Nana' 181
Thyme 16, 58, 68, 71, 72, 106, 112, 156, 161, 163, 179
Thymus × citriodorus 'Aureus' 112
  T. 'Bertram Anderson' 71
  T. druce, see *T. praecox* 71,
  T. herba-barona 71
  T. lanuginosus 71
  T. praecox arcticus, syn. *T. druce* 71
  T. pseudolanuginosus 71
  T. pulegioides 71
  T. serpyllum 106
  T. 'Silver Queen' 112
  T. vulgaris 16
Tiles 45, 82, 84, 85, 88, 94, 98, 100, 109, 138, 141, 170, 171, 172, 185
  Azulejos 172
Topiary 49, 73, 141, 148, 151, 152, 172, 203
  clipping shapes 203
Tournefort, Joseph Pitton 18, 19